D0909474

Three Tragedies of Seneca

Three Tragedies
of
Seneca

Hercules Furens
Troades
Medea

WITH AN INTRODUCTION

AND NOTES BY

Hugh MacMaster Kingery

•

UNIVERSITY OF OKLAHOMA PRESS
NORMAN

872
S475

Library of Congress Catalog Card Number: 65-24194

Reprinted 1966 by the University of Oklahoma Press, Publishing Division of the University, Norman, from the edition originally published 1908 by the Macmillan Company.

PREFACE

THE last decade has seen a revival of interest in the Latin Tragedy, which had long been neglected. In many colleges and universities the plays are studied now either in independent courses or as supplementary to work in the Comedy. The neglect, no doubt, was due in part to the want of available editions with English notes. On the Continent of Europe, especially in Germany, much labor has been devoted to the constitution of the text, and many monographs on various phases of the subject have been published. In England and America, on the other hand, little has been done for many years.

It has been the fashion to dismiss the Senecan tragedies airily as unworthy of serious attention; but such criticism seems to have been based in most cases on slight first-hand acquaintance with them. Undeniably they have their faults, yet have withal a real interest and value, first as the sole remains of an important branch of Roman literature, second for their own content and style, and third for their direct and powerful influence upon the English drama of the Elizabethan age. Most of them, furthermore, may be compared directly with their Greek originals, an advantage we do not enjoy in studying the Latin Comedy.

In this edition no attempt at a critical treatment of the text has been made, but the aim throughout has been to give such aid as will enable an intelligent student of average preparation to understand and appreciate the plays themselves. The mythological lore in which they are so

rich is explained or illustrated in the notes by frequent
citation of Latin (and occasionally of Greek) authors. Such
original authorities as Apollodorus for Hercules and Apol-
lonius Rhodius for Medea and the Argonauts have been
consulted, but, being outside the range of works usually
studied by undergraduates, are quoted very sparingly. Seneca's indebtedness to Ovid and Vergil is illustrated by numerous quotations from those poets.

It is assumed that the student of these tragedies has a
good reading knowledge of the Latin of Vergil, Horace and
Ovid; hence little notice is taken of ordinary questions of
form or syntax, and no direct reference to the grammars is
given. Particular reference to the dictionary is made for a
few extraordinary word-meanings, but in general all necessary explanation is given in the notes, which are very
full.

The treatment of versification in the introduction has
been governed by a desire to present the essentials in
simple and practical form with a minimum of technical
terminology. Especially may the discussion of iambic verse
appear to some unduly elementary ; but in view of the un-
satisfactory handling of the subject in our school grammars
it has seemed wise to err on the side of too great rather
than too little fullness. For the same reason, in the interest of simplicity, the glyconic and asclepiadean measures
are presented as choriambic instead of logaoedic. As a
guide to the reading of the verse the principal ictus of
each measure is indicated in the text by printed accents,
as is common in editions of Plautus and Terence.

The text in the main follows Leo (Berlin, 1879), modified in a few instances by reference to Richter's edition of
1902. In most cases any departure from Leo's text is mentioned in the notes; but for the purpose of this series it has

not been thought desirable either to print the variants or to devote much space to discussion of textual questions.

Acknowledgment is due to Professor James C. Egbert, the general editor of the series, for his courtesy and helpful suggestions, and to my colleague, Professor Daniel D. Hains, for assistance in the difficult work of reading proof on the Latin text.

WABASH COLLEGE.

CONTENTS

INTRODUCTION   PAGE

Tragic Literature at Rome 1

The Senecan Tragedies 3

Greek Models 6

Stage Setting 8

The Question of Authorship 9

Seneca's Life 11

The Language and Style 14

Seneca's Works 15

Versification 16

     Iambic Measures 16

     Trochaic Measures 19

     The Sapphic 19

     Choriambic Measures 20

     Dactylic Verse 21

     Anapestic Verse 21

Manuscripts 23

Editions 23

TEXT

Hercules Furens 27

Troades 73

Medea 115

NOTES

On the Hercules Furens 153

On the Troades 211

On the Medea 265

ABBREVIATIONS USED IN THE INTRODUCTION AND NOTES

A., Aen. Aeneid.
Ach. Achilleis (Statius).
Ag. Agamemnon (Seneca).
Am. Amores (Ovid).
Ann. Annales (Tacitus).
A.P. Ars Poetica.
Brev. Vit. De Brevitate Vitae (Seneca).
C., Carm. The Odes of Horace or Catullus.
C.S. Carmen Saeculare.
De Prov. De Providentia (Seneca).
E. Eclogues of Vergil.
Epig. Epigrams (Seneca).
Epist. Epistles (Cicero, Seneca, Pliny).
Eur. Euripides.
F. Fasti (Ovid).
Fab. Fabulae (Hyginus).
frag. Fragments of Latin tragedy.
G. Georgics of Vergil.
Germ. Germania (Tacitus).
Hec. Hecuba (Euripides).
H.F. Hercules Furens (Euripides, Seneca).
H.O. Hercules Oetaeus (Seneca).
Il. Iliad.
I.O. Institutio Oratoria (Quintilian).
M., Met. Metamorphoses.
Med. Medea (Seneca).

N.D. De Natura Deorum (Cicero).
N.H. Naturalis Historia (Pliny).
N.Q. Naturales Quaestiones (Seneca).
Oct. Octavia (Seneca).
Od. Odyssey.
Oed: Oedipus (Seneca).
Phaed. Phaedra (Seneca).
Phars. Pharsalia (Lucan).
Phil. Philippics (Cicero).
Rem.Am. Remedium Amoris (Ovid).
R.N. De Rerum Natura (Lucretius).
S., Sat. Satires (Horace, Juvenal).
Tac. Tacitus.
Theb. Thebais (Statius).
Thy. Thyestes (Seneca).
Tr., Trist. Tristia (Ovid).
Tro. Troades (Euripides, Seneca).

art., artt. article, articles.
cf. *confer*, compare.
Cl. Dict. Classical Dictionary.
f., ff. following.
fin. at or near the end.
init. at or near the beginning.
lit. literally.
n. note.
p., pp. page, pages.
sc. *scilicet*, understand, supply.
tr. translate.
v., vv. verse, verses.

Three Tragedies of Seneca

INTRODUCTION

Tragic Literature at Rome

For the first five centuries of her history Rome was too busily engaged in maintaining her existence against the perils of dissension within and the attacks of hostile neighbors to give much attention to the gentler arts. By the end of that time she had extended her control over the whole of Italy (except the valley of the Po), and had come into contact with the Greek colonies that fringed the southern coasts. Educated Greeks were brought to Rome as captives, and to some of them was given the duty of teaching the young. This led to the development of the first formal literature of Rome.

One of the prisoners so employed was L. Livius Andronicus, who in the year of the city 514 (B.C. 240) produced the first formal play ever given at Rome. Probably it was little more than a translation of some Greek play, but it was a revelation to the uncultured Romans, and so appealed to their fancy that other works soon were produced by Livius and his imitators.

Gradually practice and rivalry brought about an improvement in form and workmanship, and presently one and another ventured to introduce new features. In place of mere translation, whether bald or free, came the interpolation of incidents and dialogue not in the original, the welding together of two plots (*contaminatio*) and the

1

introduction of bits of local color to render the scenes more intelligible to the untraveled Roman. Especially was this done in the Comedy, as is seen in the extant plays of Plautus and Terence.

In Tragedy the earliest names after Livius are those of Naevius, Ennius and Pacuvius. All these borrowed freely from the Greek; but presently the Roman's national pride suggested an attempt at a national drama, and the result is seen in the *fabulae praetextae* of Naevius and his successors. In these, while the form of the Greek play was preserved, both plot and characters were purely Roman. We meet such titles as the *Romulus* of Naevius, the *Paullus* of Pacuvius, and the *Brutus* and the *Aeneadae* of Accius.

Unfortunately we have of these earliest products of the Roman tragic muse nothing more than a list of titles and a few of the merest fragments — too meager data for the formation of any independent judgment of their merits. For this we must rely on the opinions of ancient critics who had access to the plays in their entirety. Cicero constantly professed a great admiration for Ennius, though rather as an epic than as a tragic poet. Varro is quoted as having declared Pacuvius a model of richness in diction. To Pacuvius and Accius Quintilian assigns the foremost place among the early tragic writers in vigor of thought and expression and in the dignity of the characters they had created. The popularity still enjoyed by these old productions in the time of Augustus provoked the sarcastic protest of Horace (see especially Epist. 2. 1. 18–75). In general, the Roman critics of later times admitted the courage and vigor of these pioneers in literature, while at the same time they deplored the rudeness of their style; but this, as Quintilian observes, was due less to themselves than to their time.

Interest in Tragedy soon was overshadowed by the growing popularity of the Comedy, which appealed more powerfully to the Roman taste; and, while the comedies of Plautus and Terence were still popular in the Augustan Age, the custom of presenting tragedies on the stage seems soon to have died out. A natural result was the diversion of literary effort into other channels, and in the half century following the death of Accius there was but one tragic writer of any note — L. Julius Caesar Strabo. After Accius, indeed, it is probable that works of this sort were composed rather as literary experiments and for private reading or at most for declamation than for exhibition on the stage. Many of the later poets tried their skill in tragic composition, among them Q. Cicero, Varro, Varius, Asinius Pollio, Ovid, Pomponius Secundus and Seneca — some of them with considerable success, if we may accept the judgment of Quintilian (I.O. 10. 1. 98). In all we meet the names of thirty-six Roman poets who wrought or dabbled in this field, and the number of their works amounts to about one hundred and fifty.

THE SENECAN TRAGEDIES

Of all this mass of tragic literature we have to-day, aside from inconsiderable fragments, only the plays which bear the name of Seneca. Nine of the ten are adaptations from the Greek, while one, the *Octavia*, is a *praetexta*. Fortunately most of the Greek originals are extant, so that comparison with them is possible — an advantage we do not enjoy in studying the Latin Comedy. Thus we find that Seneca's *Agamemnon* was borrowed

from Aeschylus, the *Oedipus* from Sophocles, and no less
than five of the others — the *Medea*, the *Hippolytus* or
Phaedra, the *Hercules Furens*, the *Troades* or *Hecuba*,
and the *Phoenissae* — from Euripides. In fact, it is
worthy of note that from the first it was not the solemn,
stately idealism of Aeschylus and Sophocles but the human
realism of Euripides that most attracted the Romans.
From the time of Ennius down it was Euripides who was
copied most often.

In most cases the Senecan characters bear the same
names as in the Greek originals, and in essential features
are the same; though they differ in matters of detail
and often are inferior in distinctness of conception and
consistency of development. In plot the Roman author
has not ventured to vary far from his models, though
here and there he has altered the arrangement as well as
the relative importance of certain scenes. For instance,
the *Hercules Furens* opens with a scene, not in Euripides,
in which Juno foreshadows the catastrophe; and the
Troades is a contamination of two plays of Euripides.
As a rule the Latin plays are considerably shorter than
their Greek prototypes. New characters are not introduced, but frequently one or another is omitted.

The chorus is retained as in the Greek, though (since
the orchestral pit in the Roman theater was occupied by
seats for the senators) there was no space provided for
the choral dance. In early times the chorus may have
had a place on the stage, and its retention in tragic composition after public representation ceased was due probably to tradition and to the opportunity thus afforded for
experiment in lyric passages. Horace's precept, *Actoris
partes chorus . . . defendat*, can hardly be said to have

been observed in these plays. There is little of that direct participation in the development of the plot which is assigned the chorus by the Greeks and especially by Aeschylus. Its part here is more formal and artificial — it is rather a set passage on some lyric theme suggested more or less directly by the context than an integral part of the whole. In this as in his handling of the characters our author carries to an extreme an innovation of Euripides.

The *Octavia* is constructed on the same general plan as the other nine tragedies, having its dialogue and choruses, but differing of course in plot and scene and presenting also some peculiarities of versification. Scholars are pretty generally agreed now that it is later than the age of Nero, though its author evidently was a close student of Seneca's thought and style.

While the Senecan tragedies are not arranged in trilogies, there are some pairs in which both plays contain the same principal characters. These are (1) the *Oedipus* and the *Phoenissae* or *Thebais*, in which the downfall and exile of the hapless Theban king are portrayed; (2) the *Thyestes* and the *Agamemnon*, whose theme is the house of Pelops and its dark destiny; and (3) the two tragedies in which the hero Hercules overshadows all the other characters — the *Hercules Furens* and the *Hercules Oetaeus*. The remaining plays are unconnected — the *Hippolytus* or *Phaedra*, whose double title suggests its plot; the *Troades* or *Hecuba*, dealing with the fortunes of the royal house after the fall of Troy; and the *Medea*. The three presented in this edition are the best, though others, notably *Thyestes*, *Agamemnon*, *Phaedra* and *Octavia*, are well worthy of study.

Greek Models

The three plays contained in this volume conform closely to corresponding plays of Euripides. The title *Hercules Furens* is the Latin translation of the Greek Ἡρακλῆς Μαινόμενος, and the content of the two tragedies is practically identical. The action of each begins with a scene in which Amphitryon and Megara are standing near the altar and the usurper Lycus enters to them. In each Lycus threatens the others with death. In each Hercules returns opportunely and kills the tyrant. In each the hero becomes violently insane, kills his wife and children, and then wakens to remorse and despair. There is some difference in the machinery of the plot, however. Euripides represents the frenzy of Hercules as caused by the actual apparition of Lyssa, the spirit of madness, led in by Juno's messenger, Iris. This is omitted by the Latin author, who instead introduces Juno in the first scene, declaring her purpose to use Hercules' power against himself as the only possible means of subduing him. This is less repellent to our modern taste, and by foreshadowing the hero's madness makes that the natural climax of the plot and gives it unity. Seneca also introduces a new element in making Lycus propose marriage to Megara, whose spirited refusal adds a new motive for his attempt to take her life. Again, Euripides makes Theseus come to Thebes after the madness of his friend. Seneca represents him as coming with Hercules in the first place, and so opens the way naturally for the description of the infernal world which he gives to Amphitryon and Megara during Hercules' absence in search of Lycus.

Though there is little doubt that Seneca drew upon

other sources and may have originated portions of the plot himself, it is fair to say that the *Troades* is a contamination of two plays of Euripides. In the *Hecuba* of the Greek poet the scene is laid in the Thracian Chersonesus and the catastrophe is the death of Polyxena; in his *Troades* the scene is Troy and the climax the death of Astyanax. Seneca in his *Troades* skillfully weaves the two plots together, laying the scene at Troy immediately after its capture and working up naturally to the double tragedy, which is reported to the Trojan women by a messenger in the closing scene. Many differences of detail may be pointed out: *e.g.* that in the Greek play it is Ulysses who prevails on the Grecian leaders to sacrifice Polyxena and who himself comes to lead her away; that in the Greek she speaks at length and with spirit, but in the Latin utters not a word; that Euripides makes the herald announce the result of the lot to the captive women, while Seneca lays this duty upon Helen, and so on.

In the *Medea* of Euripides as well as that of Seneca time and scene are the same; in both she protests against the injustice of her banishment and gains a respite of a single day; in both she seeks a final interview with Jason and upbraids him with his faithlessness, listening with scorn to his excuses; in both she tries at first to recall her recreant husband to his duty, and, failing in that, dissembles her wrath but begins to plot her revenge. Of the Euripidean characters Seneca omits the *paedagogos* and Aegeus, king of Athens, and makes the two boys purely *mutae personae*. He omits Medea's long address to the chorus and the latter's promise of silence. On the other hand, the entire fourth act of the Latin play is new. In both versions the heroine is by far the strongest character, but she overshadows the rest more completely in the Latin than in the Greek. Jason in the one play affirms that his purpose in wedding the Corinthian princess is to gain means of protection and support for Medea and her children; in the other he frankly confesses that fear is his motive. In the one case he is a smooth-tongued egoist, in the other a self-confessed coward.

These are but typical points at which the Latin author has departed from his Greek models; it will be an interesting and valuable exercise for the student to make the comparison exhaustive for one or more of the tragedies. One matter should not be forgotten: that while Seneca undoubtedly had these plays of Euripides before him as his ultimate models, he certainly was familiar with later Greek versions and with some of them in Latin. He was a great reader and imitator of Ovid, and Ovid was the author of a *Medea*, now lost, of which Roman critics (*e.g.* Quintilian and Tacitus) speak in the highest terms. There were Latin tragedies also which dealt with the scenes attending the fall of Troy (*e.g.* the *Troades* and the *Astyanax* of Accius), and it is likely that so alert and omnivorous a reader as Seneca was acquainted with them all.

Stage Setting

Permanent theaters were long unknown at Rome. Of those that finally were built the general plan was the same. The stage was very long and narrow, with a permanent background representing the street front of one or more houses which might stand for whatever scene the particular play required. Immediately before the stage and somewhat lower was a large space exactly semicircular, filled with seats for the magistrates and those of senatorial rank; and back of these rose the *cavea*, or general seating, in semicircular tiers. The *cavea* often would accommodate many thousands of spectators. There was no roof, though sometimes an awning was stretched overhead to keep off the heat of the sun.

In the *Hercules Furens* the background would represent the temple of Jupiter — possibly also the royal house — with an altar in the foreground. For the *Troades* it is possible we must think of the scene as changing. Certainly in Act III the action must take place before the tomb of Hector, while the interview of Pyrrhus with Agamemnon and the later scenes of the play would find a fitter place within the burning city or in the Grecian camp. For the *Medea* the background would represent the royal palace and the home of Medea, and the final appearance of the latter would be on the flat roof of her house.

Two elements are recognized in the text of each play — the *diverbium* or dialogue proper, and the *cantica* or passages which were chanted to musical accompaniment. In general the iambic verse represents dialogue and the other meters *cantica*, though exceptions may be pointed out.

The Question of Authorship

While all the manuscripts ascribe these tragedies to "Seneca," there are circumstances which open the way for the raising of a "Senecan question," and critics have not been slow to embrace it. The several theories advanced are (1) that the plays are the work of the well-known philosopher; (2) that some of them are his and the remainder from another hand, or other hands; (3) that all are the product of collaboration by Marcus and Lucius Seneca, the latter's brother Mela and the young poet Lucan; and (4) that all are the work of an entirely different person, whose real or assumed name was Seneca.

It is impossible here to discuss these theories at length. The opinion now prevails that the *Octavia* is not Lucius Seneca's, and that the other nine are his, with the possible exception of the *Agamemnon* and the *Hercules Oetaeus*. Of external evidence in support of this conclusion we have the mention of Seneca as a poet by Quintilian, Pliny and Tacitus, the citation of the *Medea* as his by Quintilian (see Med. 453 n.), the ascription of four other tragedies in this collection to him by well-known writers in the early centuries of our era (*Oedipus*, *Phaedra*, *Thyestes* and *Troades*), and the negative fact that we have no proof of the existence of a separate Seneca *tragicus*. Of internal evidence we have the occasional reference to contemporary events in which Seneca was deeply interested; the close parallel in philosophical principles and general tone of thought between the tragedies and the prose works which are indisputably his; and the identity of literary style.

The case of the *Octavia* is different. Its omission from the oldest and best manuscript, the fact that the philosopher himself is one of the *dramatis personae*, the remarkable forecasting (629–631) of the fate that befell Nero three years after Seneca's death, and certain peculiarities of style and meter, all have been cited as going to prove a later origin; and, while none of these arguments is conclusive in itself, their cumulative force is consider-

able. Various dates have been assigned for its composition, as early as the reign of Domitian and as late as that
of Hadrian or even later, but no definite conclusion has
been reached. Historically the *Octavia* agrees almost
perfectly with Tacitus. It is of especial interest as the
only example extant of the *fabula praetexta*.

SENECA'S LIFE

Like so many other literary men of the Silver Age —
e.g. M. Seneca, Lucan, Martial, Quintilian — L. Annaeus
Seneca was a native of Spain.   Born at Corduba (modern
Cordova) about the beginning of the Christian era, he
was brought to Rome at an early age and received a
liberal education.   His natural taste led him in the direction of philosophy, and he seems to have studied the
theories of all the schools.   Sotion the Alexandrian inspired in him a great admiration of Pythagoras and his
doctrines, and at one time he actually began to abstain
from the eating of flesh in accordance with the rules of
that sect; but later he received a deeper and more lasting
impression from association with his instructor Attalus
the Stoic, and his own philosophy, so far as it can be
assigned to any school, is Stoic.

Under the advice of his father, the distinguished rhetori-
cian M. Annaeus Seneca, he entered public life as an advocate.   Here his pleadings were so successful as to arouse
the jealousy of the emperor Caligula, and he prudently
went into retirement.   But other perils awaited him.
Claudius mounted the throne in A.D. 41, and almost
immediately was persuaded by his wife Messalina to
order Seneca's banishment to Corsica.   There he solaced

his grief and discontent by study and literary work. It was at this time that he composed his epigrams, two treatises "on consolation" (*ad Polybium* and *ad Helviam*), and probably the tragedy *Medea*.

On Messalina's death in 49 her successor Agrippina procured Seneca's recall and made him tutor to her son, L. Domitius, afterward the emperor Nero. The next five years were comparatively uneventful for Seneca, but were marked by the gradual development of Agrippina's ambitious plans. She secured her son's adoption by the emperor and his marriage with Claudius' daughter Octavia; and on the emperor's death (A.D. 54) her prompt action caused the recognition of Nero as his successor instead of his own son Britannicus.

From this time on the life of Seneca is linked inseparably with the history of Nero and his reign. As secretary of the young monarch he composed the eulogy on Claudius which Nero delivered in the senate, and shortly after produced the *Apocolocyntosis*, a bitter satire on the dead emperor. He is thought also to have prepared most of the state papers during the early years of Nero's reign.

During his first five years of power the young prince was almost wholly under the influence of his counselors Burrus and Seneca, and governed with such wisdom and moderation that the *quinquennium Neronis* was long remembered for its peace and happiness. Agrippina, however, whose courage and determination had advanced her son to his high station, felt she was entitled to a controlling voice in affairs, and soon came into conflict with his more politic advisers. Enraged at being thwarted in her plans, she began to utter threats of displacing Nero with the true heir, Britannicus; and this led to the first act in the career of bloodshed that has rendered the name of Nero forever infamous. Feeling that he could not be safe while Britannicus lived, Nero had him taken off by poison (A.D. 55). Then he began to treat his young wife Octavia with coldness and cruelty. In time his mistress Acte was displaced by Poppaea Sabina, who soon aspired to be his lawful wife. Agrippina stood in the way of this design, and she in turn was assassinated (A.D. 59); but it was not till three years later that Nero finally dared to divorce Octavia and marry Poppaea. In June of A.D. 62 Octavia was banished to the island Pandataria, and shortly after was murdered.

Meantime Seneca had maintained his position amid increasing difficulties. He saw but dared not vigorously oppose the growing depravity of his ward. He opposed Agrippina's ambitious schemes, yet it can scarcely be believed that he advocated her death; though he probably wrote the dispatches in which Nero reported that event to the senate, and Tacitus (Ann. 14. 11) says that he incurred the hatred of the people by his attempt to gloss over a deed so unnatural.

In A.D. 62 Seneca's friend and fellow-counselor Burrus died, and thenceforth his own influence rapidly waned. Soon he begged permission to go into retirement. For three years more he lived, a mere spectator of events, employing his enforced leisure in writing, as he had done in Corsica. At last the blow fell. He was accused of complicity in the plot of Piso (A.D. 65), and without a trial was commanded to die. The story of his calm fortitude in the closing scene is too familiar to require repetition.

Seneca has been criticised severely both as man and as

author. He has been accused of insincerity and inconsistency in his life and of empty verbosity in his writings.
It certainly is unfortunate for his fame that he lived under
such conditions. Inheriting wealth and rising early into
prominence, he could know the sweets of poverty, of which
he wrote so glibly, only in theory and not by experience.
His learning and ability cannot be questioned, and the
range and variety of his works prove his industry as an
author. In spite of some inconsistencies his philosophy
is pure and elevated, and his ethics so nearly Christian
as to have caused the belief in early times that he had
known and been influenced by the Apostle Paul, whose
first imprisonment in Rome occurred in Seneca's lifetime.
It was his misfortune that his relations with Nero were
such as to render his practice of these principles so
difficult.

The Language and Style

In regard to word forms and syntax the Latin of Seneca
is essentially that of the Golden Age. Occasionally he
uses in his prose constructions which earlier were admissi-
ble only in verse, and gives this word and that a slightly
different shade of meaning, but in the main the mastery
of Cicero, Ovid and Vergil gives one the key to Seneca's
grammar. It was in his rhetoric that he founded a new
school. Ovid had made a beginning, but Seneca went
much further. Form became the essential thing. An
affectation of brevity, a straining after antithesis and epi-
gram, came to be the characteristics of his work and that
of his imitators (see Quintilian's criticism, I.O. 10. 1. 129).
In spite, however, of undeniable faults of style, there is
much that is good and more that is pleasing, and both for

his own works and on account of his great influence no
study of Roman literature can afford to leave Seneca out
of account.

SENECA'S WORKS

Seneca was a prolific and versatile writer.   Of his prose
works the best known are some of the twelve books classed
as *dialogi :* (1) *De Providentia,* (2) *De Constantia Sapientis,* (3–5) *De Ira,* (6) *De Consolatione ad Marciam,*
(7) *De Vita Beata,* (8) *De Otio,* (9) *De Tranquillitate
Animi,* (10) *De Brevitate Vitae,* (11) *De Consolatione ad
Polybium,* (12) *Ad Helviam Matrem de Consolatione.*

His other prose works still extant are: (*a*) two books
de Clementia ; (*b*) seven books *de Beneficiis ;* (*c*) *Naturales
Quaestiones,* a compilation of contemporary science in
seven books; (*d*) *Epistulae Morales,* a collection of 124
letters or moral essays in the form of letters, addressed
to Lucilius; and (*e*) fourteen short letters, indorsed as
genuine by St. Jerome but usually regarded as spurious,
purporting to have passed between Seneca and the Apostle
Paul (eight written by Seneca, six by Paul).

All together the prose works of Seneca now extant,
counting only those admitted to be authentic, cover more
than a thousand closely printed duodecimo pages.   From
fragments, and citations in later writers, moreover, we
know that he wrote much in the fields of science, philosophy and history that has been lost.   Mention has been
made also of letters addressed to Novatus, and it is well
known that he composed many speeches and state papers
for Nero.   His literary activity therefore must have been
very great.

The *Apocolocyntosis,* partly in prose, partly in verse,

is the only complete example known to be extant of the *Satura Menippea*. Its theme is the search of the lately deceased emperor Claudius for his proper place in the other world, and while it displays a good deal of ingenuity and talent of a certain order, its flippancy and irreverence make it distasteful to the modern reader.

The purely poetical works ascribed to Seneca are the epigrams and the ten tragedies already discussed. All display skill in the use of metrical forms, without, however, any high endowment of poetic genius.

The approximate order of composition has been placed as follows: Before A.D. 41 the consolation *ad Marciam*; during the period of exile (41–49) some of the tragedies, including possibly the *Medea*, the epigrams, and two treatises on consolation, *ad Polybium* and *ad Helviam*; within the next five years dialogues 3, 4, 5, 9, 10; within the eight years following Nero's succession (54–62) *De Clementia*, *De Beneficiis*, dialogues 2 and 7, and the *Apocolocyntosis*; and in the last three years of his life dialogues 1 and 8, the *Naturales Quaestiones*, and the *Epistulae*. The remaining tragedies were composed at uncertain intervals. The *Octavia* must, of course, have been written after 62 A.D.

VERSIFICATION

Iambic

The standard verse for dramatic dialogue in both Greek and Latin was the iambic trimeter. The characteristic foot is the iambus ($\cup$ _), arranged in pairs or dipodies ($\cup \angle \cup$ _), three of which constitute a line. In the dipody the ictus or metrical stress was stronger on the first than on the second member, and it is usual in printing to represent only this heavier ictus. The theoretical form of the trimeter, therefore, is ∪⁀∪—∪⁀∪—∪⁀∪—, as seen in Horace's *Beátus ille quí procul negótiis*, Epod. 2. 1, and throughout Catullus 4.

This theoretical form, however, is rarely met in practice, and if used constantly would have proved extremely monotonous. To secure variety, or, as Horace put it (A.P. 251), "that it might come to the ears more slowly and with greater weight," the iambus came to be replaced by the equivalent tribrach (∪ ∪̆ ∪), or, in the first foot of each measure (the first, third and fifth feet of the line), by the spondee (—⁀), and the typical form of the dipody became —⁀∪—. From this it was but a short step to the substitution of any equivalent of the spondee, and so we meet its various resolutions — the anapest (∪∪⁀) or the dactyl (—∪̆∪) as the first member of any dipody, and rarely the proceleusmatic (∪∪∪̆∪) only in the first foot of the verse. The sixth foot always is dissyllabic, either iambic or pyrrhic (∪∪̆). The subjoined tables show the variations found in each foot, and in each dipody.

THE VARIOUS FEET

1	2	3	4	5	6
∪ —	∪ —	∪ —	∪ —	∪ —	∪ ⌣
∪ ∪ ∪	∪ ∪ ∪	∪ ∪ ∪	∪ ∪ ∪		
— —		— —		— —	
∪ ∪ —		— ∪ ∪		∪ ∪ —	
— ∪ ∪		— ∪ ∪		— ∪ ∪	
∪ ∪ ∪ ∪					

c

The Various Measures

1	2	3
∪— ∪—	∪— ∪—	∪— ∪∪̱
∪— ∪∪∪	∪— ∪∪∪	
∪∪∪ ∪—		
∪∪∪ ∪∪∪		
—— ∪—	—— ∪—	—— ∪∪̱
—— ∪∪∪	—— ∪∪∪	
∪∪— ∪—	∪∪— ∪—	∪∪— ∪∪̱
∪∪— ∪∪∪	∪∪— ∪∪∪	
—∪∪ ∪—	—∪∪ ∪—	—∪∪ ∪∪̱
—∪∪ ∪∪∪	—∪∪ ∪∪∪	
∪∪∪∪ ∪—		

It will be observed that the iambus may occur in any of the six places, though it is rare in the fifth, which as a rule is either spondee or anapest. In theory the tribrach might appear in any foot except the last, but actually it is found only in the first four. The remaining feet, the spondee and its equivalents, each of four *morae*, can occur, of course, only in the odd-numbered places, that is in the first half of each dipody (see, however, notes on Tro. 264 and 932); and the proceleusmatic only in the first place. The sixth foot is always dissyllabic, either iambus (∪ —) or pyrrhic (∪ ∪), the final syllable being *anceps*.

It is an interesting fact that the ictus of the third foot (the second printed accent) almost invariably coincides with the prose accent. Sometimes the word is an unimportant monosyllable, but the only exceptions to the rule are found in a few polysyllables, usually containing several short syllables, whose original accent is supposed to have

been recessive. If we regard this original accent as sur-
viving here the apparent exceptions become no exceptions at all. Examples are *Dánaides*, H. F. 757; *cíneribus*,
Tro. 195; *míserias*, Med. 253; *scéleribus*, 499; *fácinorum*,
561. *Máchinatrix*, Med. 266, and *cóniugi* (for *cóniugii*),
481, can be explained on the same principle. *Sígeon*,
Tro. 932, is discussed in the note on that line.

In Med. 771–786 the trimeter alternates with the iambic
dimeter, in which the same principles of quantity are
observed. The only other iambic verse met in these three
plays is in the short chorus, Med. 849–878, in anacreontics
(iambic dimeter catalectic), each stanza or strophe closing with a line one syllable shorter (iambic dimeter
brachycatalectic).

Trochaic

The only simple trochaic verses found in these three
tragedies are in Med. 740–751; these are in the trochaic
tetrameter catalectic, often called the trochaic septenarius.
This consists in theory of seven trochees plus one long
syllable, the thesis of an incomplete foot; or, to state it
differently, of four trochaic dipodies ($\angle \cup \_ \smile$), lacking
the arsis or final short syllable of the last. In practice
the first member of a dipody often is a tribrach (a trochee
resolved), and the second member either a spondee or
one of its resolutions, anapest or dactyl.

The Sapphic

Seneca uses the lesser sapphic in several of his choruses.
In H.F. 830–874 is a series of sapphics uninterrupted.
In Tro. 814–860 the series is broken up into stanzas of

irregular length by the insertion of three adonics, and the chorus in Tro. 1009–1055 contains one adonic. In Med. 579–669 by supplying one hemistich (half verse) in 660 we have fourteen sapphic stanzas or strophes, seven of four lines each (as in Horace's odes) and seven of nine lines each, the last of each strophe being an adonic.

The lesser sapphic may be regarded as composed of two trochaic dipodies ($\angle \cup$ _ _) separated by a (cyclic) dactyl, the normal scheme of the whole line being $\angle \cup$ _ _ $\angle \cup \cup \angle \cup$ _ $\smile$, from which there are few variations. In Tro. 836, 1051, and in Med. 636 the arsis of the second foot is resolved, bringing two dactyls in succession. In Tro. 824 and 853 the dactyl in the third foot is replaced by a spondee, and the same is true of 852 unless we regard *cui* in *cuicumque* as having two short syllables instead of one long one. The caesura, always masculine, occurs regularly in the third foot.

Choriambic

The lesser asclepiadean and the glyconic may be regarded as variations of trochaic verse, but more simply as choriambic. Each line opens with a spondee and closes with an iambus (or pyrrhic); between these the glyconic has one choriambus and the lesser asclepiadean two. Their schemes, therefore, which are invariable, are: For the glyconic $\angle$ _ | $\angle \cup \cup \angle$ | $\cup \smile$, and for the lesser asclepiadean $\angle$ _ | $\angle \cup \cup \angle$ | $\angle \cup \cup \angle$ | $\cup \smile$. The latter is met in H.F. 524–591, Tro. 371–407 (408 being incomplete with the scheme $\angle$ _ $\angle \cup \cup \angle$), Med. 56–74, 93–109. The glyconic occurs in H.F. 875–894, Med. 75–92.

Dactylic

Seneca makes little use of the dactylic hexameter, the six verses at the close of the first chorus in the *Medea* (110-115) being the only examples in the plays here treated. Of these v. 113 is spondaic.

Anapestic

The favorite choral measure in all the tragedies (occurring twice in each of our three plays) is the anapestic dimeter, consisting of four anapests or their equivalent. In spite of its name there is no one of the four places in which some substitute does not occur oftener than the anapest itself. Thus the spondee is the favorite in the first, second and fourth positions, and the dactyl in the third. The dactyl does not occur at all in the second or fourth place. Occasionally a short syllable is allowed to stand at the end of the line, making a trochee instead of a spondee or a tribrach instead of an anapest; but this is relatively rare, being met but five times in *Hercules Furens*, eight times in *Troades*, and twice in *Medea;* and nearly all of these examples come at a distinct pause in the sense. In order to preserve the quantity at the end of a verse it often is necessary to count its final consonant with the initial consonant of the following verse to "make position." Hiatus between verses, which the Greeks did not allow in this measure, is admitted by Seneca; there are five instances in the *Medea* and six each in *Hercules Furens* and *Troades*. Seneca does not use the paroemiac, with which the Greeks regularly concluded an anapestic passage.

At irregular intervals throughout the anapestic pas sages appear monometers, or half-lines. In parts of the first chorus in the *Troades* these may have been intro duced to assist in producing the effect of strophe and anti strophe, but in most cases there is no apparent law governing their appearance.

In the following tables it is shown what feet occur in each place, and also what combinations are found in each dipody.

THE VARIOUS FEET

1	2	3	4
∪ ∪ —	∪ ∪ —	∪ ∪ —	∪ ∪ —
— —	— —	— —	— —
— ∪ ∪		— ∪ ∪	
	∪ ∪ ∪¹		∪ ∪ ∪
	— ∪¹		— ∪

THE VARIOUS MEASURES

Arranged according to their frequency of occurrence

1		2	
— —	∪ ∪ —	— ∪ ∪	— —
— ∪ ∪	— —	— —	∪ ∪ —
— —	— —	— —	— —
∪ ∪ —	— —	∪ ∪ —	∪ ∪ —
∪ ∪ —	∪ ∪ —	∪ ∪ —	— —
— ∪ ∪	∪ ∪ —	— ∪ ∪	— ∪
∪ ∪ —	∪ ∪ ∪¹	— —	∪ ∪ ∪
— ∪ ∪	— ∪¹		

¹ Only in monometers.

Manuscripts

The manuscripts of the Senecan tragedies are grouped in two general classes. The first of these includes the *Codex Etruscus* (*Laurentianus* 37, 6), the oldest complete copy (which, however, does not contain the *Octavia*), dating from the eleventh or twelfth century; the *Ambrosianus* (D 276) and the *Vaticanus* (lat. 1769), both of the fourteenth century and derived from a lost copy of the *Codex Etruscus*, but containing the *Octavia;* and fragments of a much older manuscript (*fragmenta Ambrosiana*) containing detached portions of the *Oedipus* and the *Medea* (of the latter vv. 196–274, 694–708 and 722–744). The remains of the *Codex Thyaneus*, of the ninth or tenth century, have only fragmentary passages from three plays (Tro. 64–164, Med. 579–594, and a few scattered lines from the *Oedipus*).

To the second class are referred a considerable number of copies, more or less corrupt, derived from a common archetype of unknown date. This is supposed to have been the work of a man of some learning, who did not hesitate to modify the text when it suited his convenience.

Of all the manuscripts the Etruscan has been accepted since the days of Gronovius as most authoritative.

Editions

The literature now accessible to the student of the tragedies is relatively scanty. The most recent and authoritative editions of the text are those of F. Leo, Berlin, 1879, and G. Richter, Leipzig, 1902.

The old annotations in Latin by Delrius, Lipsius,

Gruter, Scriverius, Gronovius and Schroeder have become very rare. Two plays were edited with brief English notes two generations ago by Professor Charles Beck of Harvard College — *Medea*, 1834; *Hercules Furens*, 1845 — but these little volumes are long out of print and hard to find.

In the latter part of the sixteenth century a considerable interest was taken in the tragedies of Seneca, and there can be no question that they, with Ovid's poems, exercised a marked influence upon the English literature of that period. A collection of English translations by different hands was published in London in 1581 under the title "The Tenne Tragedies," and this was reprinted some years ago by the Spenser Society of Great Britain. There is a German translation and commentary in three volumes (two volumes of translation and one of notes) by W. A. Swoboda, published at Prague, 1828–1830. Quite recently an English metrical version was published by Ella Isabel Harris, Ph.D. (The Clarendon Press, 1904). An English translation in verse has just appeared from the pen of Professor Frank J. Miller, Ph.D., of the University of Chicago.

HERCULES

DRAMATIS PERSONAE

Iuno
Amphitryon
Megara
Lycus
Hercules
Theseus
Chorus

Scaena Thebis

THE PARTS TAKEN BY EACH ACTOR

I Hercules
   Lycus
II Amphitryon
   Iuno
III Theseus
   Megara

HERCULES

Iuno

Sorór Tonantis (hóc enim solúm mihi
nomén relictum est) sémper alienúm Iovem
ac témpla summi vídua deserui aétheris
locúmque caelo púlsa paelicibús dedi;
tellús colenda est: paélices caelúm tenent.   5
hinc Árctos alta párte glacialís poli
sublíme classes sídus Argolicás agit;
hinc, quá recenti vére laxatúr dies,
Tyriaé per undas véctor Europaé nitet;
illínc timendum rátibus ac pontó gregem   10
passím vagantes éxerunt Atlántides.
ferró minax hinc térret Orión deos
suásque Perseus aúreus stellás habet;
hinc clára gemini sígna Tyndaridaé micant
quibúsque natis móbilis tellús stetit.   15
nec ípse tantum Bácchus aut Bacchí parens
adiére superos: né qua pars probró vacet,
mundús puellae sérta Cnosiacaé gerit.
   Sed vétera querimur — úna me dira ác fera
Thebána tellus spársa nuribus ímpiis   20
quotiéns novercam fécit! escendát licet
meúmque victrix téneat Alcmené locum,
paritérque natus ástra promissa óccupet,
in cúius ortus múndus impendít diem
27

tardúsque Eoo Phoébus effulsít mari   25
retinére mersum iússus Oceanó iubar —
non síc abibunt ódia; vivacés aget
violéntus iras ánimus et saevús dolor
aetérna bella páce sublatá geret.
   Quae bélla?   quidquid hórridum tellús creat   30
inimíca, quidquid póntus aut aér tulit
terríbile dirum péstilens atróx ferum,
fractum átque domitum est.   súperat et crescít malis
iráque nostra frúitur; in laudés suas
mea vértit odia: dúm nimis saeva ímpero,   35
patrém probavi, glóriae fecí locum.
qua Sól reducens quáque deponéns diem
binós propinqua tínguit Aethiopás face,
indómita virtus cólitur et totó deus
narrátur orbe.   mónstra iam desúnt mihi   40
minórque labor est Hérculi iussa éxequi,
quam míhi iubere: laétus imperia éxcipit.
quae féra tyranni iúra violentó queant
nocére iuveni?   némpe pro telís gerit
quae tímuit et quae fúdit: armatús venit   45
leóne et hydra.   néc satis terraé patent:
effrégit ecce límen infermí Iovis
et opíma victi régis ad superós refert.   48
vidi ípsa, vidi nócte discussa ínferum   50
et Díte domito spólia iactantém patri
fratérna.   cur non vínctum et oppressúm trahit
ipsúm catenis pária sortitúm Iovi
Erebóque capto pótitur et retegít Styga?
parum ést reverti, foédus umbrarúm perit: 49
patefácta ab imis mánibus retró via est   55
et sácra dirae mórtis in apertó iacent.

at ílle, rupto cárcere umbrarúm ferox,
de mé triumphat ét superbificá manu
atrúm per urbes dúcit Argolicás canem.
visó labantem Cérbero vidí diem 60
pavidúmque Solem; mé quoque invasít tremor,
et térna monstri cólla devicti íntuens
timui ímperasse. lévia sed nimiúm queror;
caeló timendum est, régna ne summa óccupet
qui vícit ima: scéptra praeripiét patri. 65
nec in ástra lenta véniet ut Bacchús via:
itér ruina quaéret et vacuó volet
regnáre mundo. róbore expertó tumet,
et pósse caelum víribus vincí suis
didicít ferendo; súbdidit mundó caput 70
nec fléxit umeros mólis immensaé labor
meliúsque collo sédit Herculeó polus.
immóta cervix sídera et caelúm tulit
et mé prementem: quaérit ad superós viam.

Perge íra, perge et mágna meditantem ópprime, 75
congrédere, manibus ípsa dilacerá tuis:
quid tánta mandas ódia? discedánt ferae,
ipse ímperando féssus Eurystheús vacet.
Titánas ausos rúmpere imperiúm Iovis
emítte, Siculi vérticis laxá specum, 80
tellús gigante Dóris excussó tremens
suppósita monstri cólla terrificí levet — 82
sed vícit ista. quaéris Alcidaé parem?
nemo ést nisi ipse: bélla iam secúm gerat. 85
adsínt ab imo Tártari fundo éxcitae
Euménides, ignem flámmeae spargánt comae,
vipérea saevae vérbera incutiánt manus.
i núnc, superbe, caélitum sedés pete,

humána temne.   iám Styga et manés feros   90
fugísse credis?   híc tibi ostendam ínferos.
revocábo in alta cónditam calígine,
ultrá nocentum exília, discordém deam
quam múnit ingens móntis opposití specus;
edúcam et imo Dítis e regno éxtraham   95
quidquíd relictum est: véniet invisúm Scelus
suúmque lambens sánguinem Impietás ferox
Errórque et in se sémper armatús Furor —
hoc hóc ministro nóster utatúr dolor.

Incípite, famulae Dítis, ardentém citae   100
concútite pinum et ágmen horrendum ánguibus
Megaéra ducat átque luctificá manu
vastám rogo flagránte corripiát trabem.
hoc ágite, poenas pétite vitiataé Stygis.
concútite pectus, ácrior mentem éxcoquat   105
quam quí caminis ígnis Aetnaeís furit:
ut póssit animo cáptus Alcidés agi,
magnó furore pércitus, vobís prius
insániendum est — Iúno, cur nondúm furis?
me mé, sorores, ménte deiectám mea   110
versáte primam, fácere si quicquam ápparo
dignúm noverca; vóta mutentúr mea:
natós reversus vídeat incolumés precor
manúque fortis rédeat.   invení diem,
invísa quo nos Hérculis virtús iuvet.   115
me vícit; et se víncat et cupiát mori
ab ínferis revérsus.   hic prosít mihi
Iove ésse genitum.   stábo et, ut certo éxeant
emíssa nervo téla, librabó manu,
regám furentis árma, pugnanti Hérculi   120
tandém favebo — scélere perfectó licet

admíttat illas génitor in caelúm manus.
 Movénda iam sunt bélla: clarescít dies
ortúque Titan lúcidus croceó subit.

CHORUS

Iam rára micant sidéra prono   125
languída mundo; nox vícta vagos
contráhit ignes lucé renata,
cogít nitidum Phosphóros agmen;
signúm celsi glaciále poli   129
lucém verso temóne vocat.   131
iam caéruleis evéctus equis
Titán summa prospícit Oeta;
iam Cádmeis inclúta Bacchis
aspérsa die duméta rubent   135
Phoebíque fugit reditúra soror.
labor éxoritur durús et omnes
agitát curas aperítque domos.
 Pastór gelida caná pruina
grege dímisso pabúla carpit;   140
ludít prato libér aperto
nondúm rupta fronté iuvencus,
vacuaé reparant ubéra matres;
errát cursu levis íncerto
mollí petulans haedús in herba;   145
pendét summo stridúla ramo
pennásque novo tradére soli
gestít querulos intér nidos
Thracía paelex, turbáque circa
confúsa sonat murmúre mixto   150
testáta diem.

carbása ventis credít dubius
navíta vitae, laxós aura
complénte sinus.   hic éxesis
pendéns scopulis aut déceptos   155
instrúit hamos aut súspensus
spectát pressa praemía dextra:
sentít tremulum linéa piscem.
   Haec, ínnocuae quibus ést vitae
tranquílla quies et laéta suo   160
parvóque domus; spes ímmanes
urbíbus errant trepidíque metus: 163
illé superbos aditús regum
durásque fores expérs somni   165
colit, híc nullo finé beatas
compónit opes gazís inhians
et cóngesto paupér in auro;
illúm populi favor áttonitum
fluctúque magis mobíle vulgus   170
aurá tumidum tollít inani;
hic clámosi rabiósa fori
iurgía vendens impróbus iras
et vérba locat.   novít paucos
secúra quies, qui vélocis   175
memorés aevi tempóra numquam
reditúra tenent.   Dum fáta sinunt
vivíte laeti: properát cursu
vitá citato volucríque die
rota praécipitis vertítur anni;   180
duraé peragunt pensá sorores
nec súa retro filá revolvunt.
at géns hominum flatúr rapidis
obvía fatis incérta sui:

Stygiás ultro quaerímus undas.   185
nimium, Álcide, pectóre forti
properás maestos visére manes:
certó veniunt tempóre Parcae,
nullí iusso cessáre licet,
nullí scriptum proférre diem: 190
recipít populos urná citatos.
  Aliúm multis gloría terris
tradát et omnes famá per urbes
garrúla laudet caelóque parem
tollát et astris; aliús curru   195
sublímis eat: me méa tellus
lare sécreto tutóque tegat.
venit ád pigros caná senectus,
humilíque loco sed cérta sedet
sordída parvae fortúna domus: 200
alté virtus animósa cadit. —
Sed maésta venit criné soluto
  Megará parvum comitáta gregem,
tardúsque senio gráditur Alcidaé parens.

Amphitryon

O mágne Olympi réctor et mundi árbiter,   205
iam státue tandem grávibus aerumnís modum
finémque cladi.   núlla lux umquám mihi
secúra fulsit . . .
      . . . fínis alteriús mali
gradus ést futuri: prótinus reducí novus
parátur hostis; ántequam laetám domum   210
contíngat, aliud iússus ad bellúm meat;
nec úlla requies témpus aut ullúm vacat,

nisi dúm iubetur. séquitur a primó statim
infésta Iuno: númquid immunís fuit
infántis aetas? mónstra superavít prius   215
quam nósse posset. gémina cristatí caput
angués ferebant óra, quos contra óbvius
reptábat infans ígneos serpéntium
oculós remisso lúmine ac placido íntuens;
artós serenis vúltibus nodós tulit,   220
et túmida tenera gúttura elidéns manu
prolúsit hydrae. Maénali perníx fera,
multó decorum praéferens auró caput,
deprénsa cursu est; máximus Nemeaé timor
pressús lacertis gémuit Herculeís leo.   225
quid stábula memorem díra Bistonií gregis
suísque regem pábulum armentís datum,
solitúmque densis híspidum Erymanthí iugis
Arcádia quatere némora Maenaliúm suem,
taurúmque centum nón levem populís metum?   230
intér remotos géntis Hesperiaé greges
pastór triformis lítoris Tartésii
perémptus, acta est praéda ab occasu último;
notúm Cithaeron pávit Oceanó pecus.
penetráre iussus sólis aestiví plagas   235
et adústa medius régna quae torrét dies
utrímque montes sólvit ac rupto óbice
latám ruenti fécit Oceanó viam.
post haéc adortus némoris opulentí domos
aurífera vigilis spólia serpentís tulit;   240
quid? saéva Lernae mónstra, numerosúm malum,
non ígne demum vícit et docuít mori,
solitásque pennis cóndere obductís diem
petít ab ipsis núbibus Stymphálidas?

non vícit illum caélibis sempér tori   245
regína gentis vídua Thermodóntiae,
nec ad ómne clarum fácinus audacés manus
stabulí fugavit túrpis Augeí labor.
   Quid ísta prosunt?   órbe defensó caret.
sensére terrae pácis auctorém suae   250
abésse: rursus prósperum ac felíx scelus
virtús vocatur; sóntibus parént boni,
ius ést in armis, ópprimit legés timor.
ante óra vidi nóstra truculentá manu
natós paterni cádere regni víndices   255
ipsúmque, Cadmi nóbilis stirpem últimam,
occídere, vidi régium capití decus
cum cápite raptum — quís satis Thebás fleat?
feráx deorum térra, quem dominúm tremis?
e cúius arvis éque fecundó sinu   260
strictó iuventus órta cum ferró stetit
cuiúsque muros nátus Amphión Iove
struxít canoro sáxa modulatú trahens,
in cúius urbem nón semel divúm parens
caeló relicto vénit, haec quae caélites   265
recépit et quae fécit et (fas sít loqui)
fortásse faciet, sórdido premitúr iugo.
Cadméa proles átque Ophioniúm genus
quo réccidistis?   trémitis ignavum éxulem.
suís carentem fínibus, nostrís gravem.   270
qui scélera terra quíque persequitúr mari
ac saéva iusta scéptra confringít manu
nunc sérvit absens fértque quae fierí vetat,
tenétque Thebas éxul Herculeás Lycus.
sed nón tenebit.   áderit et poenás petet   275
subitúsque ad astra emérget; inveniét viam

aut fáciet. adsis sóspes et remeés precor
tandémque venias víctor ad victám domum.

Megara

Emérge, coniunx, átque dispulsás manu
abrúmpe tenebras; núlla si retró via   280
itérque clusum est, órbe diductó redi
et quídquid atra nócte possessúm latet
emítte tecum. dírutis qualís iugis
praecéps citato flúmini quaeréns iter
quondám stetisti, scíssa cum vasto ímpetu   285
patuére Tempe; péctore impulsús tuo
huc móns et illuc céssit et rupto ággere
nová cucurrit Théssalus torréns via:
talís, parentes líberos patriám petens,
erúmpe rerum términos tecum éfferens,   290
et quídquid avida tót per annorúm gradus
abscóndit aetas rédde et oblitós sui
lucísque pavidos ánte te populós age.
indígna te sunt spólia, si tantúm refers
quantum ímperatum est. mágna sed nimiúm loquor   295
ignára nostrae sórtis. unde illúm mihi
quo té tuamque déxteram amplectár diem
reditúsque lentos néc mei memorés querar?
tibi, ó deorum dúctor, indomití ferent
centéna tauri cólla; tibi, frugúm potens,   300
secréta reddam sácra: tibi mutá fide
longás Eleusin tácita iactabít faces.
tum réstitutas frátribus rebór meis
animás et ipsum régna moderantém sua
florére patrem. sí qua te maiór tenet   305

clausúm potestas, séquimur: aut omnés tuo
defénde reditu sóspes aut omnés trahe —
trahés nec ullus ériget fractós deus.
AMPH. O sócia nostri sánguinis, castá fide
serváns torum natósque magnanimi Hérculis, 310
melióra mente cóncipe atque animum éxcita.
aderít profecto, quális ex omní solet
labóre, maior. MEG. Quód nimis miserí volunt
hoc fácile credunt. AMPH. Ímmo quod metuúnt nimis
numquám moveri pósse nec tollí putant: 315
prona ést timoris sémper in peiús fides.
MEG. Demérsus ac defóssus et toto ínsuper
oppréssus orbe quám viam ad superós habet?
AMPH. Quam túnc habebat cúm per arentém plagam
et flúctuantes móre turbatí maris 320
adít harenas bísque discedéns fretum
et bís recurrens, cúmque desertá rate
deprénsus haesit Sýrtium brevibús vadis
et púppe fixa mária superavít pedes.
    MEG. Iníqua raro máximis virtútibus 325
fortúna parcit; némo se tutó diu
perículis offérre tam crebrís potest:
quem saépe transit cásus, aliquando ínvenit.
    Sed écce saevus ác minas vultú gerens
et quális animo est tális incessú venit 330
aliéna dextra scéptra concutiéns Lycus.

LYCUS

Urbís regens opulénta Thebanaé loca
et ómne quidquid úberi cingít solo
oblíqua Phocis, quídquid Ismenós rigat,

quidquíd Cithaeron vértice excelsó videt,   335
et bína findens Ísthmos exilís freta
non vétera patriae iúra possideó domus
ignávus heres; nóbiles non súnt mihi
aví nec altis ínclitum titulís genus,
sed clára virtus: quí genus iactát suum,   340
aliéna laudat.   rápta sed trepidá manu
sceptra óbtinentur; ómnis in ferro ést salus:
quod cívibus tenére te invitís scias
strictús tuetur énsis.   alieno ín loco
haut stábile regnum est; úna sed nostrás potest   345
fundáre vires iúncta regalí face
thalamísque Megara: dúcet e genere ínclito
novitás colorem nóstra.   non equidém reor
fore út recuset ác meos spernát toros;
quod si ímpotenti pértinax animo ábnuet,   350
stat tóllere omnem pénitus Herculeám domum.
invídia factum ac sérmo popularís premet?
ars príma regni est pósse † invidiám pati.
temptémus igitur, fórs dedit nobís locum.
namque ípsa, tristi véstis obtentú caput   355
veláta, iuxta praésides astát deos
lateríque adhaeret vérus Alcidaé sator.
MEG. Quidnam íste, nostri géneris exitium ác lues,
noví parat? quid témptat? LYC. O clarúm trahens
a stírpe nomen régia, facilís mea   360
parúmper aure vérba patienti éxcipe.
si aetérna semper ódia mortalés gerant
nec coéptus umquam cédat ex animís furor,
sed árma felix téneat infelíx paret,
nihíl relinquent bélla; tum vastís ager   365
squalébit arvis, súbdita tectís face

altús sepultas óbruet gentés cinis.
pacém reduci vélle victori éxpedit,
victó necesse est — párticeps regnó veni;
sociémur animis, pígnus hoc fideí cape: 370
contínge dextram. quíd truci vultú siles?
MEG. Egone út parentis sánguine aspersám manum
fratrúmque gemina caéde contingám? prius
extínguet ortus, réferet occasús diem,
pax ánte fida nívibus et flammís erit   375
et Scýlla Siculum iúnget Ausonió latus,
priúsque multo vícibus alternís fugax
Eurípus unda stábit Euboicá piger.
patrem ábstulisti, régna, germanós, larem
patriúm — quid ultra est? úna res superést mihi   380
fratre ác parente cárior, regno ác lare:
odiúm tui, quod ésse cum populó mihi
commúne doleo: párs quota ex illó mea est?
domináre tumidus, spíritus altós gere:
sequitúr superbos últor a tergó deus.   385
Thebána novi régna: quid matrés loquar
passás et ausas scélera? quid geminúm nefas
mixtúmque nomen cóniugis natí patris?
quid bína fratrum cástra? quid totidém rogos?
rigót superba Tántalis luctú parens   390
maestúsque Phrygio mánat in Sipyló lapis.
quin ípse torvum súbrigens cristá caput
Illýrica Cadmus régna permensús fuga
longás reliquit córporis tractí notas.
haec té manent exémpla: dominare út libet,   395
dum sólita regni fáta te nostrí vocent.
LYC. Agedum éfferatas rábida voces ámove
et dísce regum impéria ab Alcidé pati.

ego rápta quamvis scéptra victricí geram
dextrá regamque cúncta sine legúm metu   400
quas árma vincunt, paúca pro causá loquar
nostrá. cruento cécidit in belló pater?
cecidére fratres? árma non servánt modum;
nec témperari fácile nec reprimí potest
stricti énsis ira, bélla delectát cruor.   405
sed ílle regno pró suo, nos ímproba
cupídine acti? quaéritur belli éxitus,
non caúsa. sed nunc péreat omnis mémoria:
cum víctor arma pósuit, et victúm decet
depónere odia. nón ut inflexó genu   410
regnántem adores pétimus: hoc ipsúm placet
animó ruinas quód capis magnó tuas;
es rége coniunx dígna: sociemús toros.
MEG. Gelidús per artus vádit exangués tremor.
quod fácinus aures pépulit? haut equidem hórrui,   415
cum páce rupta béllicus murós fragor
circúmsonaret, pértuli intrepide ómnia:
thalamós tremesco; cápta nunc videór mihi.
gravént catenae córpus et longá fame
mors prótrahatur lénta: non vincét fidem   420
vis úlla nostram; móriar, Alcidé, tua.
LYC. Animósne mersus ínferis coniúnx facit?
MEG. Inférna tetigit, pósset ut supera ássequi.
LYC. Tellúris illum póndus immensaé premit.
MEG. Nulló premetur ónere, qui caelúm tulit.   425
LYC. Cogére. MEG. Cogi quí potest nescít mori.
LYC. Effáre potius, quód novis thalamís parem
Regále munus. MEG. Aút tuam mortem aút meam.
LYC. Moriére demens. MEG. Cóniugi occurrám meo.
LYC. Sceptróne nostro fámulus est potiór tibi?   430

MEG. Quot íste famulus trádidit regés neci.
LYC. Cur érgo regi sérvit et patitúr iugum?
MEG. Impéria dura tólle: quid virtús erit?
LYC. Obicí feris monstrísque virtutém putas?
MEG. Virtútis est domáre quae cunctí pavent. 43⁴
LYC. Tenebráe loquentem mágna Tartareaé premunt.
MEG. Non ést ad astra móllis e terrís via.
LYC. Quo pátre genitus caélitum sperát domos?
AMPH. Miseránda coniunx Hérculis magní, sile:
partés meae sunt réddere Alcidaé patrem 44⁰
genúsque verum. póst tot ingentís viri
memoránda facta póstque pacatúm manu
quodcúmque Titan órtus et labéns videt,
post mónstra tot perdómita, post Phlegram ímpio
sparsám cruore póstque defensós deos 445
nondúm liquet de pátre? mentimúr Iovem?
Iunónis odio créde. LYC. Quid violás Iovem?
mortále caelo nón potest iungí genus.
AMPH. Commúnis ista plúribus causa ést deis.
LYC. Famulíne fuerant ánte quam fierént dei? 45⁰
AMPH. Pastór Pheraeos Délius pavít greges —
LYC. Sed nón per omnes éxul erravít plagas.
AMPH. Quem prófuga terra máter errante édidit.
LYC. Num mónstra saeva Phoébus aut timuít feras?
AMPH. Primús sagittas ímbuit Phoebí draco. 455
LYC. Quam grávia parvus túlerit ignorás mala?
AMPH. E mátris utero fúlmine eiectús puer
mox fúlminanti próximus patrí stetit.
quid? quí gubernat ástra, qui nubés quatit,
non látuit infans rúpis Idaeaé specu? 46⁰
sollícita tanti prétia natalés habent
sempérque magno cónstitit nascí deum.

Lyc. Quemcúmque miserum víderis, hominém scias.
Amph. Quemcúmque fortem víderis, miserúm neges.
Lyc. Fortém vocemus cúius ex umerís leo,   465
donúm puellae fáctus, et clava éxcidit
fulsítque pictum véste Sidoniá latus?
fortém vocemus cúius horrentés comae
maduére nardo, laúde qui notás manus
ad nón virilem týmpani movít sonum,   470
mitrá ferocem bárbara frontém premens?
Amph. Non érubescit Bácchus effusós tener
sparsísse crines néc manu mollí levem
vibráre thyrsum, cúm parum fortí gradu
auró decorum sýrma barbaricó trahit: 475
post múlta virtus ópera laxarí solet.
Lyc. Hoc Eúryti fatétur eversí domus
pecorúmque ritu vírginum oppressí greges;
hoc núlla Iuno, núllus Eurystheús iubet:
ipsíus haec sunt ópera. Amph. Non nosti ómnia: 480
ipsíus opus est cáestibus fractús suis
Erýx et Eryci iúnctus Antaeús Libys,
et qui hóspitali cáede manantés foci
bibére iustum sánguinem Busíridis;
ipsíus opus est vúlneri et ferro ínvius   485
mortém coactus ínteger Cycnús pati
nec únus una Géryon victús manu.
eris ínter istos — quí tamen nulló stupro
laesére thalamos. Lyc. Quód Iovi hoc regí licet:
Ioví dedisti cóniugem, regí dabit;   490
et té magistro nón novum hoc discét nurus,
etiám viro probánte meliorém sequi.
sin cópulari pértinax taedís negat,
vel éx coacta nóbilem partúm feram.

Meg. Umbráe Creontis ét penates Lábdaci 495
et núptiales ímpii Oedipodáe faces,
nunc sólita nostro fáta coniugió date.
nunc, núnc, cruentae régis Aegyptí nurus,
adéste multo sánguine infectáe manus.
dest úna numero Dánais: explebó nefas. 500
Lyc. Coniúgia quoniam pérvicax nostra ábnuis
regémque terres, scéptra quid possínt scies.
compléctere aras: núllus eripiét deus
te míhi, nec orbe sí remolitó queat
ad súpera victor númina Alcidés vehi. 505
congérite silvas: témpla supplicibús suis
iniécta flagrent, cóniugem et totúm gregem
consúmat unus ígne subiectó rogus.
Amph. Hoc múnus a te génitor Alcidáe peto,
rogáre quod me déceat, ut primús cadam. 510
Lyc. Qui mórte cunctos lúere suppliciúm iubet
nescít tyrannus ésse: diversa ínroga;
miserúm veta períre, felicém iube.
ego, dúm cremandis trábibus accrescít rogus,
sacró regentem mária votivó colam. 515
Amph. Pro núminum vis súmma, pro caeléstium
rectór parensque, cúius excussís tremunt
humána telis, ímpiam regís feri
compésce dextram — quíd deos frustrá precor?
ubicúmque es, audi, náte. cur subitó labant 520
agitáta motu témpla? cur mugít solum?
audímur, est est sónitus Herculeí gradus. 523

Chorus

Ó Fortúna virís ínvida fórtibus,
quám non aéqua bonís praémia dívidis.   523
'Eúrystheús facilí régnet in ótio;
Álcmená genitús bélla per ómnia
mónstris éxagitét caéliferám manum:
sérpentís resecét cólla ferácia,
déceptís referát mála soróribus,   530
cúm somnó dederít pérvigilés genas
pómis dívitibús praépositús draco.'
Íntravít Scythiaé múltivagás domos
ét gentés patriís sédibus hóspitas,
cálcavítque fretí térga rigéntia   535
ét mutís tacitúm lítoribús mare.
íllic dúra carént aéquora flúctibus,
ét qua pléna ratés cárbasa ténderant,
íntonsís teritúr sémita Sármatis.
stát pontús, vicibús móbilis ánnuis,   540
návem núnc facilís núnc equitém pati.
íllic quaé viduís géntibus ímperat,
aúrató religáns ília bálteo,
détraxít spoliúm nóbile córpori
ét peltam ét niveí víncula péctoris,   545
víctorém positó súspiciéns genu.
Quá spe praécipités áctus ad ínferos,
aúdax íre viás ínremeábiles,
vídistí Siculaé régna Prosérpinae?
íllic núlla Notó núlla Favónio   550
cónsurgúnt tumidís flúctibus aéquora;
nón illíc geminúm Týndaridaé genus
súccurrúnt timidís sídera návibus:

stát nigró pelagús gúrgite lánguidum,
ét cum Mórs avidís pállida déntibus 555
géntes ínnumerás mánibus íntulit,
úno tót populí rémige tránseunt.
   Évincás utinám iúra feraé Stygis
Párcarúmque colós nón revocábiles.
híc qui réx populís plúribus ímperat, 560
béllo cúm peterés Néstoreám Pylon,
técum cónseruít péstiferás manus
télum térgeminá cúspide praéferens:
éffugít tenuí vúlnere saúcius
ét mortís dominús pértimuít mori. 565
fátum rúmpe manú, trístibus ínferis
próspectús pateát lúcis et ínvius
límes dét facilés ád superós vias.
   Ímmités potuít fléctere cántibus
úmbrarúm dominós ét prece súpplici 570
Órpheus, Eúrydicén dúm repetít suam.
quaé silvás et avés sáxaquc tráxerat
árs, quae praébuerát flúminibús moras,
ád cuiús sonitúm cónstiteránt ferae,
múlcet nón solitís vócibus ínferos 575
ét surdís resonát clárius ín locis.
déflent Eúrydicén Thréiciaé nurus,
déflent ét lacrimís dífficilés dei,
ét qui frónte nimís crímina tétrica
quaérunt ác veterés éxcutiúnt reos 580
fléntes Eúrydicén iúridicí sedent.
tándem mórtis aít 'víncimur' árbiter,
'évade ád superós, lége tamén data:
tú post térga tuí pérge virí comes,
tú non ánte tuám réspice cóniugem, 585

quám cum clára deós óbtulerít dies
Spártaníque aderít iánua Taénari.'
ódit vérus amór néc patitúr moras:
múnus dúm properát cérnere, pérdidit.
    Quaé vincí potuít régia cármine,   590
haéc vincí poterít régia víribus.

HERCULES

O lúcis almae réctor et caelí decus,
qui altérna curru spátia flammifero ámbiens
inlústre latis éxeris terrís caput,
da, Phoébe, veniam, sí quid inlicitúm tui   595
vidére vultus: iússus in lucem éxtuli
arcána mundi.   túque, caelestum árbiter
parénsque, visus fúlmine oppositó tege;
et tú, secundo mária qui sceptró regis,
imás pete undas.   quísquis ex alto áspicit   600
terréna, facie póllui metuéns nova,
aciém reflectat óraque in caelum érigat
porténta fugiens: hóc nefas cernánt duo,
qui advéxit et quae iússit.   in poenás meas
atque ín labores nón satis terráe patent   605
Iunónis odio: vídi inaccessa ómnibus,
ignóta Phoebo quáeque deteriór polus
obscúra diro spátia concessít Iovi;
et, sí placerent tértiae sortís loca,
regnáre potui: nóctis aeternáe chaos   610
et nócte quiddam grávius et tristés deos
et fáta vidi, mórte contemptá redi —
quid réstat aliud?   vídi et ostendi ínferos.
da sí quid ultra est, iám diu paterís manus

cessáre nostras, Iúno; quae vincí iubes?   615
   Sed témpla quare míles infestús tenet
liménque sacrum térror armorum óbsidet?

AMPHITRYON

   Utrúmne visus vóta decipiúnt meos,
an ílle domitor órbis et Graiúm decus
tristí silentem núbilo liquít domum?   620
estne ílle natus?   mémbra laetitiá stupent.
o náte, certa at séra Thebarúm salus,
teneóne in auras éditum an vaná fruor
decéptus umbra?   túne es?   agnoscó toros
umerósque et alto nóbilem truncó manum.   625
HERC. Unde íste, genitor, squálor et lugúbribus
amícta coniunx?   únde tam foedo óbsiti
paedóre nati?   quáe domum cladés gravat?
AMPH. Socer ést peremptus, régna possedít Lycus,
natós parentem cóniugem letó petit.   630
HERC. Ingráta tellus, némo ad Herculeáe domus
auxília venit?   vídit hoc tantúm nefas
defénsus orbis? — cúr diem questú tero?
mactétur hostia, hánc ferat virtús notam
fiátque summus hóstis Alcidáe Lycus.   635
ad haúriendum sánguinem inimicúm feror,
Theséu; resiste, né qua vis subita íngruat.
me bélla poscunt, díffer amplexús, parens,
coniúnxque differ.   núntiet Dití Lycus
me iám redisse.

Theseus

Flébilem ex oculís fuga,   640
regína, vultum, túque nato sóspite
lacrimás cadentes réprime: si novi Hérculem,
Lycús Creonti débitas poenás dabit.
lentum ést dabit: dat; hóc quoque est lentúm: dedit.
Amph. Votúm secundet quí potest nostrúm deus   645
rebúsque lapsis ádsit. O magní comes
magnánime nati, pánde virtutum órdinem,
quam lónga maestos dúcat ad manés via,
ut víncla tulerit dúra Tartareús canis.
Thes. Memoráre cogis ácta securáe quoque   650
horrénda menti.   víx adhuc certa ést fides
vitális aurae, tórpet acies lúminum
hebetésque visus víx diem insuetúm ferunt.
Amph. Pervínce, Theseu, quídquid alto in péctore
remanét pavoris néve te fructu óptimo   655
fraudá laborum: quáe fuit durúm pati,
meminísse dulce est.   fáre casus hórridos.
Thes. Fas ómne mundi téque dominantém precor
regnó capaci téque quam amotam ínrita
quaesívit Enna máter, ut iura ábdita   66c
et opérta terris líceat impune éloqui.
   Spartána tellus nóbile attollít iugum,
densís ubi aequor Taénarus silvís premit,
hic óra solvit Dítis invisí domus
hiátque rupes álta et immensó specu   ω
ingéns vorago faúcibus vastís patet
latúmque pandit ómnibus populís iter.
non caéca tenebris íncipit primó via;
tenuís relictae lúcis a tergó nitor

fulgórque dubius sólis adflictí cadit 670
et lúdit aciem : nócte sic mixtá solet
praebére lumen prímus aut serús dies.
hinc ámpla vacuis spátia laxantúr locis,
in quae ómne versum próperat humanúm genus.
nec íre labor est ; ípsa deducít via : 675
ut saépe puppes aéstus invitás rapit,
sic prónus aer úrguet atque avidúm chaos,
gradúmque retro fléctere haut umquám sinunt
umbraé tenaces. íntus immensí sinus
placidó quieta lábitur Lethé vado 680
demítque curas, néve remeandi ámplius
pateát facultas, fléxibus multís gravem
invólvit amnem : quális incertís vagus
Maeánder undis lúdit et cedít sibi
ínstátque dubius lítus an fontém petat. 685
palús inertis foéda Cocytí iacet ;
hic vúltur, illic lúctifer bubó gemit
oménque triste résonat infaustaé strigis.
horrént opaca frónde nigrantés comae,
taxum ímminentem quá tenet segnís Sopor 690
Famésque maesta tábido rictú iacet
Pudórque serus cónscios vultús tegit.
'Metús Pavorque fúrvus et frendéns Dolor
atérque Luctus séquitur et Morbús tremens
et cíncta ferro Bélla ; in extremo ábdita 695
inérs Senectus ádiuvat baculó gradum.
AMPH. Estne áliqua tellus Céreris aut Bacchí ferax ?
THES. Non práta viridi laéta facie gérminant
nec adúlta leni flúctuat Zephyró seges ;
non úlla ramos sílva pomiferós habet : 700
sterilís profundi vástitas squalét soli

et foéda tellus tórpet aeternó situ.   702
immótus aer haéret et pigró sedet
nox átra mundo: cúncta maerore hórrida   705
ipsáque morte péior est mortís locus.
AMPH. Quid ílle opaca quí regit sceptró loca,
qua séde positus témperat populós leves?
THES. Est ín recessu Tártari obscuró locus,
quem grávibus umbris spíssa caligo álligat.   710
a fónte discors mánat hinc unó latex,
altér quieto símilis (hunc iuránt dei)
tacénte sacram dévehens fluvió Styga;
at híc tumultu rápitur ingentí ferox
et sáxa fluctu vólvit Acheron ínvius   715
renávigari. cíngitur duplicí vado
advérsa Ditis régia, atque ingéns domus
umbránte luco tégitur. hic vastó specu
pendént tyranni límina, hoc umbrís iter,
haec pórta regni. cámpus hanc circá iacet,   720
in quó superbo dígerit vultú sedens
animás recentes díra maiestás dei.
frons tórva, fratrum quaé tamen speciém gerat
gentísque tantae, vúltus est illí Iovis,
sed fúlminantis: mágna pars regní trucis   725
est ípse dominus, cúius aspectús timet
quidquíd timetur. AMPH. Vérane est fama ínferis
tam séra reddi iúra et oblitós sui
scelerís nocentes débitas poenás dare?
quis íste veri réctor atque aequi árbiter?   730
THES. Non únus alta séde quaesitór sedens
iudícia trepidis séra sortitúr reis.
adítur illo Cnósius Minós foro,
Rhadamánthus illo, Thétidis hoc audít socer.

quod quísque fecit, pátitur; auctorém scelus   735
repetít suoque prémitur exempló nocens:
vidí cruentos cárcere includí duces
et ímpotentis térga plebeiá manu
scindí tyranni.   quísquis est placidé potens
dominúsque vitae sérvat innocuás manus   740
et íncruentum mítis imperiúm regit
animóque parcit, lónga permensús diu
felícis aevi spátia vel caelúm petit
vel laéta felix némoris Elysií loca,
iudéx futurus.   sánguine humano ábstine   745
quicúmque regnas: scélera taxantúr modo
maióre vestra.   AMPH. Cértus inclusós tenet
ıocús nocentes?   útque fert fama, ímpios
supplícia vinclis saéva perpetuís domant?
THES. Rapitúr volucri tórtus Ixión rota;   750
cervíce saxum gránde Sisyphiá sedet;
in ámne medio faúcibus siccís senex
sectátur undas, álluit mentúm latex,
fidémque cum iam saépe deceptó dedit,
perit únda in ore; póma destituúnt famem.   755
praebét volucri Títyos aeternás dapes
urnásque frustra Dánaides plenás gerunt;
erránt furentes ímpiae Cadméides
terrétque mensas ávida Phineás avis.
AMPH. Nunc éde nati nóbilem pugnám mei.   760
patruí volentis múnus an spoliúm refert?
THES. Ferále tardis ímminet saxúm vadis,
stupént ubi undae, ségne torpescít fretum.
hunc sérvat amnem cúltu et aspectu hórridus
pavidósque manes squálidus vectát senex.   765
inpéxa pendet bárba, deformém sinum

nodús coercet, cóncavae squalént genae;
regit ípse longo pórtitor contó ratem.
hic ónere vacuam lítori puppem ápplicans
repetébat umbras; póscit Alcidés viam   770
cedénte turba; dírus exclamát Charon:
' quo pérgis, audax?   síste properantém gradum.'
non pássus ullas nátus Alcmená moras
ipsó coactum návitam contó domat
scandítque puppem.   cúmba populorúm capax   775
succúbuit uni: sídit et graviór ratis
utrímque Lethen látere titubantí bibit.
tum vícta trepidant mónstra, Centaurí truces
Lapithaéque multo in bélla succensí mero;
Stygiaé paludis últimos quaeréns sinus   780
fecúnda mergit cápita Lernaeús labor.
post haéc avari Dítis apparét domus:
hic saévus umbras térritat Stygiús canis,
qui térna vasto cápita concutiéns sono
regnúm tuetur.   sórdidum tabó caput   785
lambúnt colubrae, víperis horrént iubae
longúsque torta síbilat caudá draco.
par íra formae: sénsit ut motús pedum,
attóllit hirtas ángue vibrató comas
missúmque captat aúre subrectá sonum,   790
sentíre et umbras sólitus.   ut propiór stetit
Iove nátus, antro sédit incertús canis
levitérque timuit — écce latratú gravi
loca múta terret; síbilat totós minax
serpéns per armos.   vócis horrendaé fragor   795
per óra missus térna felicés quoque
extérret umbras.   sólvit a laevá feros
tunc ípse rictus ét Cleonaeúm caput

oppónit ac se tégmine ingentí tegit,
victríce magnum déxtera robúr gerens.   800
huc núnc et illuc vérbere assiduó rotat,
ingéminat ictus. dómitus infregít minas
et cúncta lassus cápita summisít canis
antróque toto céssit. extimuít sedens
utérque solio dóminus et ducí iubet;   805
me quóque petenti múnus Alcidaé dedit.
  Tum grávia monstri cólla permulcéns manu
adamánte texto víncit; oblitús sui
custós opaci pérvigil regní canis
compónit aures tímidus et patiéns trahi   810
erúmque fassus, óre summisso óbsequens,
utrúmque cauda púlsat anguiferá latus.
postquam ést ad oras Taénari ventum ét nitor
percússit oculos lúcis ignotaé novus,
resúmit animos víctus et vastás furens   815
quassát catenas; paéne victorem ábstulit
pronúmque retro véxit et movít gradu.
tunc ét meas respéxit Alcidés manus;
geminís uterque víribus tractúm canem
irá furentem et bélla temptantem ínrita   820
intúlimus orbi. vídit ut clarúm diem
et púra nitidi spátia conspexít poli,   822
compréssit oculos ét diem invisum éxpulit
faciémque retro fléxit atque omní petit   825
cervíce terram; túm sub Herculeás caput
abscóndit umbras.—dénsa sed laetó venit
clamóre turba fróntibus laurúm gerens
magníque meritas Hérculis laudés canit.

Chorus

Nátus Eurystheús properánte partu   830
iússerat mundí penetráre fundum:
dérat hoc solúm numeró laborum,
tértiae regém spoliáre sortis.
aúsus es caecós aditús inire,
dúcit ad manés via quá remotos   835
trístis et nigrá metuénda silva,
séd frequens magná comitánte turba.
  Quántus incedít populús per urbes
ád novi ludós avidús theatri,
quántus Eleúm ruit ád Tonantem,   840
quínta cum sacrúm revocávit aestas;
quánta, cum longaé redit hóra nocti
créscere et somnós cupiéns quietos
líbra Phoebeós tenet aéqua currus,
túrba secretám Cererém frequentat   845
ét citi tectís properánt relictis
Áttici noctém celebráre mystae:
tánta per campós agitúr silentes
túrba; pars tardá graditúr senecta,
trístis et longá satiáta vita;   850
párs adhuc currít melióris aevi:
vírgines nondúm thalamís iugatae
ét comis nondúm positís ephebi
mátris et nomén modo dóctus infans.
hís datum solís, minus út timerent,   855
ígne praelató releváre noctem;
céteri vadúnt per opáca tristes.
quális est vobís animús, remota
lúce cum maestús sibi quísque sensit

óbrutum totá caput ésse terra?   860
stát chaos densúm tenebraéque turpes
ét color noctís malus ác silentis
ótium mundí vacuaéque nubes.
  Séra nos illó referát senectus:
némo ad id seró venit, únde numquam,   865
cúm semel venít, potuít reverti;
quíd iuvat durúm properáre fatum?
ómnis haec magnís vaga túrba terris
íbit ad manés faciétque inerti
véla Cocytó: tibi créscit omne,   870
ét quod occasús videt ét quod ortus
— párce venturís — tibi, mórs, paramur.
sís licet segnís, properámus ipsi:
príma quae vitám dedit hóra, carpit.
  Thébis laéta diés adest.   875
  áras tángite súpplices,
  píngues caédite víctimas;
  pérmixtaé maribús nurus
  sóllemnés agitént choros;
  céssent dépositó iugo   880
  árvi fértilis íncolae.
    Páx est Hérculeá manu
  Aúroram ínter et Hésperum,
  ét qua sól mediúm tenens
  úmbras córporibús negat;   885
  quódcumque álluitúr solum
  lóngo Téthyos ámbitu,
  Álcidaé domuít labor.
  tránsvectús vada Tártari
  pácatís redit ínferis;   890
  iám nullús superést timor:

níl ultrá iacet ínferos.
Stántes sácrificús comas
dílectá tege pópulo.

HERCULES

Victríce dextra fúsus adversó Lycus   895
terrám cecidit óre; tum quisquís comes
fuerát tyranni iácuit et poenaé comes.
nunc sácra patri víctor et superís feram
caesísque meritas víctimis arás colam.

Te té laborum sócia et adiutríx precor,   900
bellígera Pallas, cúius in laevá ciet
aegís feroces óre saxificó minas;
adsít Lycurgi dómitor et rubrí maris,
tectám virente cúspidem thyrsó gerens,
geminúmque numen Phoébus et Phoebí soror: 905
sorór sagittis áptior, Phoebús lyrae;
fratérque quisquis íncolit caelúm meus
non éx noverca fráter. huc appéllite
gregés opimos; quídquid Indorúm seges
Arabésque odoris quídquid arboribús legunt   91c
conférte in aras, pínguis exundét vapor.
popúlea nostras árbor exornét comas,
te rámus oleae frónde gentilí tegat,
Theseú; Tonantem nóstra adorabít manus,
tu cónditores úrbis et silvéstria   915
trucis ántra Zethi, nóbilis Dircén aquae
larémque regis ádvenae Tyriúm coles.
date túra flammis. AMPH. Náte, manantés prius
manús cruenta caéde et hostili éxpia.
HERC. Utinám cruore cápitis invisí deis   920
libáre possem: grátior nullús liquor

tinxísset aras; víctima haut ulla ámplior
potést magisque opíma mactarí Iovi,
quam réx iniquus. AMPH. Fíniat genitór *tuos*
optá labores, détur aliquando ótium   925
quiésque fessis. HERC. Ípse concipiám preces
Iove méque dignas.   stét suo caelúm loco
tellúsque et aequor; ástra inoffensós agant
aetérna cursus.   álta pax gentés alat;
ferrum ómne teneat rúris innocuí labor   930
ensésque lateant.   núlla tempestás fretum
violénta turbet, núllus irató Iove
exíliat ignis, núllus hiberná nive
nutrítus agros ámnis eversós trahat.
venéna cessent, núlla nocituró gravis   935
sucó tumescat hérba.   non saevi ác truces
regnént tyranni; sí quod etiamnum ést scelus
latúra tellus, próperet, et si quód parat
monstrúm, meum sit.   séd quid hoc?   mediúm diem
cinxére tenebrae.   Phoébus obscuró meat   940
sine núbe vultu.   quís diem retró fugat
agítque in ortus?   únde nox atrúm caput
ignóta profert?   únde tot stellaé polum
implént diurnae?   prímus en nostér labor
caelí refulget párte non minimá leo   945
iráque totus férvet et morsús parat.
iam rápiet aliquod sídus: ingentí minax
stat óre et ignes éfflat et rutilá iubam
cervíce iactans quídquid autumnús gravis
hiémsque gelido frígida spatió refert   950
uno ímpetu transíliet et verní petet
frangétque tauri cólla. AMPH. Quod subitum hóc malum
     est?

quo, náte, vultus húc et huc acrés refers
aciéque falsum túrbida caelúm vides?
HERC. Perdómita tellus, túmida cesserúnt freta,   955
inférna nostros régna sensere ímpetus:
immúne caelum est, dígnus Alcidé labor.
in álta mundi spátia sublimís ferar,
petátur aether — ástra promittít pater.
quid, sí negaret?   nón capit terra Hérculem   960
tandémque superis réddit.   en ultró vocat
omnís deorum coétus et laxát fores,
uná vetante.   récipis et reserás polum?
an cóntumacis iánuam mundí traho?
dubitátur etiam?   víncla Saturno éxuam   965
contráque patris ímpii regnum ímpotens
avúm resolvam; bélla Titanés parent,
me dúce furentes; sáxa cum silvís feram
rapiámque dextra pléna Centaurís iuga.
iam mónte gemino límitem ad superós agam: 970
videát sub Ossa Pélion Chirón suum,
in caélum Olympus tértio positús gradu
pervéniet aut mittétur.   AMPH. Infandós procul
avérte sensus; péctoris saní parum
magní tamen compésce dementem ímpetum.   975
HERC. Quid hóc?   Gigantes árma pestiferí movent.
profúgit umbras Títyos ac lacerúm gerens
et ináne pectus quám prope a caeló stetit.
labát Cithaeron, álta Pellené tremit
Macetúmque Tempe.   rápuit hic Pindí iuga,   980
hic rápuit Oeten, saévit horrendúm Mimans.
flammífera Erinys vérbere excussó sonat
rogísque adustas própius ac propiús sudes
in óra tendit; saéva Tisiphoné, caput

serpéntibus valláta, post raptúm canem 985
portám vacantem claúsit oppositá face —
sed écce proles régis inimicí latet.
Lycí nefandum sémen: invisó patri
haec déxtra iam vos réddet. excutiát leves
nervús sagittas — téla sic mittí decet 990
Hercúlea. AMPH. Quo se caécus impegít furor?
vastúm coactis fléxit arcum córnibus
pharetrámque solvit, strídet emissa ímpetu
harúndo — medio spículum colló fugit
vulnére relicto. HERC. Céteram prolem éruam 995
omnésque latebras. quíd moror? maiús mihi
bellúm Mycenis réstat, ut Cyclópia
evérsa manibus sáxa nostris cóncidant.
huc éat et illuc válva deiecto óbice
rumpátque postes; cúlmen impulsúm labet. 1000
perlúcet omnis régia: hic video ábditum
natúm scelesti pátris. AMPH. En blandás manus
ad génua tendens vóce miserandá rogat —
scelús nefandum, tríste et aspectu hórridum!
dextrá precantem rápuit et circá furens 1005
bis tér rotatum mísit; ast illí caput
sonuít, cerebro técta dispersó madent.
at mísera, parvum prótegens natúm sinu,
Megará furenti símilis e latebrís fugit.
HERC. Licét Tonantis prófuga condarís sinu, 1010
petet úndecumque témet haec dextra ét feret.
AMPH. Quo mísera pergis? quám fugam aut latebrám
    petis?
nullús salutis Hércule infesto ést locus.
ampléctere ipsum pótius et blandá prece
leníre tempta. MEG. Párce iam, coniúnx, precor, 1015

agnósce Megaram. nátus hic vultús tuos
habitúsque reddit; cérnis, ut tendát manus?
HERC. Teneó novercam. séquere, da poenás mihi
iugóque pressum líbera turpí Iovem;
sed ánte matrem párvulum hoc monstrum óccidat.   1020
MEG. Quo téndis amens? sánguinem fundés tuum?
AMPH. Pavefáctus infans ígneo vultú patris
perit ánte vulnus, spíritum eripuít timor.
in cóniugem nunc cláva libratúr gravis —
perfrégit ossa, córpori truncó caput   1025
abést nec usquam est. cérnere hoc audés, nimis
viváx senectus? sí piget luctús, habes
mortém paratam: péctus in tela índue,
vel stípitem istuc caéde nostrorum ínlitum
convérte. falsum ac nómini turpém tuo   1030
remové parentem, né tuae laudi óbstrepat.
CHOR. Quo te ípse, senior, óbvium morti íngeris?
quo pérgis amens? prófuge et obtectús late
unúmque manibus aúfer Herculeís scelus.
HERC. Bene habét, pudendi régis excisa ést domus.   1035
tibi húnc dicatum, máximi coniúnx Iovis,
gregém cecidi; vóta persolví libens
te dígna, et Argos víctimas aliás dabit.
AMPH. Nondúm litasti, náte: consummá sacrum.
stat écce ad aras hóstia, expectát manum   1040
cervíce prona; praébeo occurro ínsequor:
mactá — quid hoc est? érrat acies lúminum
visúsque marcor hébetat; an video Hérculis
manús trementes? vúltus in somnúm cadit
et féssa cervix cápite summissó labat;   1045
flexó genu iam tótus ad terrám ruit,
ut caésa silvis órnus aut portúm mari

datúra moles.   vívis an letó dedit
idém tuos qui mísit ad mortém furor?
sopor ést: reciprocos spíritus motús agit.   1050
detúr quieti témpus, ut somnó gravi
vis vícta morbi péctus oppressúm levet.
removéte, famuli, téla, ne repetát furens.

CHORUS

Lugeát aether magnúsque parens
aethéris alti tellúsque ferax   1055
et vága ponti mobílis unda,
tuque ánte omnes qui pér terras
tractúsque maris fundís radios
noctémque fugas oré decoro,
fervíde Titan: obitús pariter   1060
tecum Álcides vidít et ortus
novítque tuas utrásque domos.
Solvíte tantis animúm monstris,
solvíte superi, caecam ín melius
flectíte mentem.   tuque, ó, domitor   1065
Somné malorum, requiés animi,
pars húmanae meliór vitae,
volucre ó matris genus Ástraeae,
fratér durae languíde Mortis,
verís miscens falsá, futuri   1070
certús et idem pessímus auctor,
pax érrorum, portús vitae,
lucís requies noctísque comes,
qui pár regi famulóque venis,
pavidúm leti genus húmanum   1075
cogís longam discére noctem:

placidús fessum lenísque fove,
preme dévinctum torpóre gravi;
sopor índomitos allíget artus
nec tórva prius pectóra linquat,   1080
quam méns repetat pristína cursum.

  En fúsus humi saevá feroci
cordé volutat somnía: nondum est
tantí pestis superáta mali;
clavaéque gravi lassúm solitus   1085
mandáre caput quaerít vacua
pondéra dextra, motú iactans
bracchía vano. nec adhúc omnes
expúlit aestus, sed ut íngenti
vexáta Noto servát longos   1090
undá tumultus et iám vento
cessánte tumet . . . pelle ínsanos
fluctús animi, redeát pietas
virtúsque viro. vel sít potius
mens vésano concíta motu: 1095
errór caecus qua coépit eat;
solús te iam praestáre potest
furor ínsontem: proxíma puris
sors ést manibus nescíre nefas.

  Nunc Hérculeis percússa sonent   1100
pectóra palmis, mundúm solitos
ferré lacertos verbéra pulsent
victríce manu; gemitús vastos
audíat aether, audíat atri
regína poli vastísque ferox   1105
qui cólla gerit vinctá catenis
imó latitans Cerbérus antro;
resonét maesto clamóre chaos

latíque patens undá profundi: 1109
pectóra tantis obséssa malis   1112
non súnt ictu feriénda levi,
unó planctu tria régna sonent.
et tú collo decus ác telum   1115
suspénsa diu, fortís harundo,
pharetraéque graves, date saéva fero
verbéra tergo; caedánt umeros
robóra fortes stipésque potens
durís oneret pectóra nodis: 1120
plangánt tantos armá dolores.

    Ite ínfaustum genus, ó pueri,   1135
notí per iter tristé laboris,   1136
non vós patriae laudís comites   1122
ultí saevos vulnére reges,
non Árgiva membrá palaestra
flectére docti fortés caestu   1125
fortésque manu (1130) nondúmque ferae
tergá iubatae . . . iam támen ausi   1126
telúm Scythicis leve córytis
missúm certa libráre manu
tutósque fuga figére cervos: 1129
ite ád Stygios, umbraé, portus   1131
ite, ínnocuae, quas ín primo
limíne vitae scelus óppressit
patriúsque furor: 1134
ite, íratos visíte reges.   1137

HERCULES

    Quis híc locus, quae régio, quae mundí plaga?
ubi súm? sub ortu sólis, an sub cárdine
glaciális ursae? númquid Hesperií maris   1140

extréma tellus húnc dat Oceanó modum?
quas tráhimus auras? quód solum fessó subest?
certé redimus — únde prostrata ád domum
videó cruenta córpora? an nondum éxuit
simulácra mens inférna? post reditús quoque   1145
obérrat oculis túrba feralís meis?
pudét fateri: páveo; nescio quód mihi,
nesció quod animus gránde praesagít malum.
ubi és, parens? ubi ílla natorúm grege
animósa coniunx? cúr latus laevúm vacat   1150
spolió leonis? quónam abit tegimén meum
idémque somno móllis Herculeó torus?
ubi téla? ubi arcus? árma quis vivó mihi
detráhere potuit? spólia quis tanta ábstulit
ipsúmque quis non Hérculis somnum hórruit?   1155
libét meum vidére victorém, libet.
exúrge, virtus, quém novum caeló pater
genuít relicto, cúius in fetú stetit
nox lóngior quam nóstra — quod cernó nefas?
natí cruenta caéde confectí iacent,   1160
perémpta coniunx. quís Lycus regnum óbtinet
quis tánta Thebis scélera moliri aúsus est
Hercúle reverso? quísquis Ismení loca,
Actaéa quisquis árva, qui geminó mari
pulsáta Pelopis régna Dardanií colis,   1165
succúrre, saevae cládis auctorem índica.
ruat íra in omnes: hóstis est quisquís mihi
non mónstrat hostem. víctor Alcidaé, lates?
procéde, seu tu víndicas currús truces
Thracís cruenti síve Geryonaé pecus   1170
Libyaéve dominos, núlla pugnandí mora est.
en núdus asto; vél meis armís licet

petás inermem.   cúr meos Theseús fugit
patérque vultus?   óra cur condúnt sua?
différte fletus; quís meos dederít neci   1175
omnés simul, profáre — quid, genitór, siles?
at tu éde, Theseu, séd tua, Theseú, fide.
utérque tacitus óra pudibunda óbtegit
furtímque lacrimas fúndit.   in tantís malis
quid ést pudendum?   númquid Argivae ímpotens   1180
dominátor urbis, númquid infestúm Lyci
pereúntis agmen cláde nos tanta óbruit?
per té meorum fácinorum laudém precor,
genitór, tuique nóminis sempér mihi
numén secundum, fáre.   quis fudít domum?   1185
cui praéda iacui?   Amph.   Tácita sic abeánt mala.
Herc.   Ut inúltus ego sim?   Amph.   Saépe vindicta óbfuit.
Herc.   Quisquámne segnis tánta toleravít mala?
Amph.   Maióra quisquis tímuit.   Herc.   His etiám, pater,
quicquám timeri máius aut graviús potest?   1190
Amph.   Cladís tuae pars ísta quam ností quota est?
Herc.   Miserére, genitor, súpplices tendó manus.
quid hóc?   manus refúgit — hic errát scelus.
unde híc cruor?   quid ílla puerilí madens
harúndo leto?   tíncta Lernaea ést nece —   1195
iam téla video nóstra.   non quaeró manum.
quis pótuit arcum fléctere aut quae déxtera
sinuáre nervum víx recedentém mihi?
ad vós revertor; génitor, hoc nostrum ést scelus?
tacuére — nostrum est.   Amph.   Lúctus est istíc tuus, 1200
crimén novercae: cásus hic culpá caret.
Herc.   Nunc párte ab omni, génitor, iratús tona,
oblíte nostri víndica será manu
saltém nepotes.   stélliger mundús sonet

flammásque et hic et ílle iaculetúr polus;   1205
rupés ligatum Cáspiae corpús trahant
atque áles avida — cúr Prometheí vacant
scopulí?   vacat cur vértice immensó feras
volucrésque pascens Caúcasi abruptúm latus
nudúmque silvis?   ílla quae pontúm Scythen   1210
Symplégas artat hínc et hinc vinctás manus
disténdat alto, cúmque revocatá vice
in sé coibunt sáxaque in caelum éxpriment
actís utrimque rúpibus mediúm mare,
ego ínquieta móntium iaceám mora.   1215
quin strúctum acervans némore congesto ággerem
cruóre corpus ímpio sparsúm cremo?
sic, síc agendum est: ínferis reddam Hérculem.
AMPH.   Nondúm tumultu péctus attonitó carens
mutávit iras quódque habet propriúm furor,   1220
in se ípse saevit.   HERC.   Díra Furiarúm loca
et ínferorum cárcer et sontí plaga
decréta turbae — sí quod exiliúm latet
ultérius Erebo, Cérbero ignotum ét mihi:
hoc me ábde, tellus; Tártari ad finem últimum   1225
mansúrus ibo.   péctus o nimiúm ferum!
quis vós per omnem, líberi, sparsós domum
deflére digne póterit?   hic durús malis
lacrimáre vultus néscit.   huc arcúm date,
date húc sagittas, stípitem huc vastúm date.   1230
tibi téla frangam nóstra, tibi nostrós, puer,
rumpémus arcus; át tuis stipés gravis
ardébit umbris; ípsa Lernaeís frequens
pharétra telis ín tuos ibít rogos:
dent árma poenas.   vós quoque infaustás meis   1235
cremábo telis, ó novercalés manus.

Amph. Quis nómen usquam scéleris errori áddidit?

Herc. Saepe érror ingens scéleris obtinuít locum.

Amph. Nunc Hércule opus est: pérfer hanc molém mali.

Herc. Non síc furore céssit extinctús pudor,   1240
populós ut omnes ímpio aspectú fugem.
arma, árma, Theseu, flágito properé mihi
subtrácta reddi — sána si mens ést mihi,
reférte manibus téla; si remanét furor,
patér, recede: mórtis inveniám viam.   1245

Amph. Per sáncta generis sácra, per ius nóminis
utrúmque nostri, síve me altorém vocas
seu tú parentem, pérque venerandós piis
canós, senectae párce desertaé, precor,
annísque fessis; únicum lapsaé domus   1250
firmámen, unum lúmen afflictó malis
temét reserva.   núllus ex te cóntigit
fructús laborum; sémper aut dubiúm mare
aut mónstra timui; quísquis in totó furit
rex saévus orbe, mánibus aut arís nocens,   1255
a mé timetur; sémper absentís pater
fructúm tui tactúmque et aspectúm peto.

Herc. Cur ánimam in ista lúce detineam ámplius
morérque nil est: cúncta iam amisí bona,
mentem árma famam cóniugem natós manus,   1260
etiám furorem.   némo pollutó queat
animó mederi: mórte sanandum ést scelus.

Amph. Perimés parentem.   Herc. Fácere ne possim,
   óccidam.

Amph. Genitóre coram?   Herc. Cérnere hunc docuí
   nefas.

Amph. Memoránda potius ómnibus facta íntuens   1265
uníus a te críminis veniám pete.

HERC. Veniám dabit sibi ípse, qui nullí dedit?
laudánda feci iússus: hoc unúm meum est.
succúrre, genitor; síve te pietás movet
seu tríste fatum síve violatúm decus   1270
virtútis: effer árma; vincatúr mea
fortúna dextra. THES. Súnt quidem patriaé preces
satis éfficaces, séd tamen nostró quoque
movére fletu. súrge et adversa ímpetu
perfrínge solito. núnc tuum nulli ímparem   1275
animúm malo resúme, nunc magná tibi
virtúte agendum est: Hérculem irascí veta.
HERC. Si vívo, feci scélera; si moriór, tuli.
purgáre terras próperc — iamdudúm mihi
monstrum ímpium saevúmque et immite ác ferum   1280
obérrat: agedum déxtra, conare ággredi
ingéns opus, labóre bis seno ámplius.
ignáva cessas, fórtis in puerós modo
pavidásque matres? árma nisi dantúr mihi,
aut ómne Pindi Thrácis excidám nemus   1285
Bacchíque lucos ét Cithaeronís iuga
mecúm cremabo, aut tóta cum domibús suis
domonísque tecta, cúm deis templa ómnibus
Thebána supra córpus excipiám meum
atque úrbe versa cóndar, et, si fórtibus   1290
leve póndus umeris moénia immissa íncident
septémque opertus nón satis portís premar,
onus ómne media párte quod mundí sedet
dirimítque superos, ín meum vertám caput.
AMPH. Reddo árma — HERC. Vox est dígna genitore
    Hérculis.   1295
hoc én peremptus spículo cecidít puer —
AMPH. Hoc Iúno telum mánibus immisít tuis.

HERC. Hoc núnc ego utar. AMPH. Écce quam miserúm
  metu
cor pálpitat pectúsque sollicitúm ferit.
HERC. Aptáta harundo est. AMPH. Écce iam faciés
  scelus   1300
voléns sciensque. HERC. Pánde, quid fierí iubes?
AMPH. Nihíl rogamus: nóster in tuto ést dolor,
natúm potes serváre tu solús mihi,
erípere nec tu; máximum evasí metum:
miserum haút potes me fácere, felicém potes.   1305
sic státue, quidquid státuis, ut causám tuam
famámque in arto stáre et ancipití scias:
aut vívis aut occídis — hanc animám levem
fessámque senio néc minus fessám malis
in óre primo téneo. tam tardé patri   1310
vitám dat aliquis? nón feram ulteriús moram,
letále ferro péctus impresso índuam:
hic, híc iacebit Hérculis saní scelus.
HERC. Iam párce, genitor, párce, iam revocá manum.
succúmbe, virtus, pérfer imperiúm patris.   1315
eat ád labores híc quoque Herculeós labor:
vivámus. artus álleva afflictós solo,
Theseú, parentis. déxtra contactús pios
sceleráta refugit. AMPH. Hánc manum amplectór libens,
hac nísus ibo, péctori hanc aegro ádmovens   1320
pellám dolores. HERC. Quém locum profugús petam?
ubi mé recondam quáve tellure óbruar?
quis Tánais aut quis Nílus aut quis Pérsica
violéntus unda Tígris aut Rhenús ferox
Tagúsve Hibera túrbidus gazá fluens   1325
ablúere dextram póterit? arctoúm licet
Maeótis in me gélida transfundát mare

et tóta Tethys pér meas currát manus,
haerébit altum fácinus. in quas ímpius
terrás recedes? órtum an occasúm petes?   1330
ubíque notus pérdidi exilió locum.
me réfugit orbis, ástra transversós agunt
oblíqua cursus, ípse Titan Cérberum
melióre vultu vídit. o fidúm caput,
Theseú, latebram quaére longinquam ábditam;   1335
quoniámque semper scéleris alieni árbiter
amás nocentes, grátiam meritís refer
vicémque nostris: rédde me infernís precor
umbrís reductum, méque subiectúm tuis
substítue vinclis: ílle me abscondét locus —   1340
sed ét ílle novit. THES. Nóstra te tellús manet.
illíc solutam caéde Gradivús manum
restítuit armis: ílla te, Alcidé, vocat,
facere ínnocentes térra quae superós solet.

TROADES

DRAMATIS PERSONAE

Hecuba
Talthybius
Pyrrhus
Agamemno
Calchas
Andromacha
Senex
Astyanax
Ulixes
Helena
Nuntius
Polyxena TACITA
Chorus

Scaena Troiae

THE PARTS TAKEN BY EACH ACTOR

I Andromacha
Pyrrhus

II Hecuba
Agamemno
Ulixes

III Talthybius
Calchas
Senex
Helena
Nuntius

TROADES

HECUBA

Quicúmque regno fídit et magná potens
dominátur aula néc leves metuít deos
animúmque rebus crédulum laetís dedit,
me vídeat et te, Tróia: non umquám tulit
documénta fors maióra, quam fragilí loco   5
starént superbi.   cólumen eversum óccidit
polléntis Asiae, caélitum egregiús labor;
ad cúius arma vénit et qui frígidum
septéna Tanain óra pandentém bibit
et quí renatum prímus excipiéns diem   10
tepidúm rubenti Tígrin immiscét freto,
et quaé vagos vicína prospiciéns Scythas
ripám catervis Pónticam viduís ferit.
excísa ferro est, Pérgamum incubuít sibi.
en álta muri décora congestís iacent   15
tectís adusti; régiam flammae ámbiunt
omnísque late fúmat Assarací domus.
non próhibet avidas flámma victorís manus:
dirípitur ardens Tróia.   nec caelúm patet
undánte fumo: núbe ceu densa óbsitus   20
atér favilla squálet Iliacá dies.
stat ávidus irae víctor et lentum Ílium
metítur oculis ác decem tandém ferus
ignóscit annis; hórret afflictám quoque,

73

victámque quamvis vídeat, haut credít sibi   25
potuísse vinci. spólia populatór rapit
Dardánia; praedam mílle non capiúnt rates.
  Testór deorum númen adversúm mihi,
patriaéque cineres téque rectorém Phrygum
quem Tróia toto cónditum regnó tegit,   30
tuósque manes quó stetit stante Ílium,
et vós meorum líberum magní greges,
umbraé minores: quídquid adversi áccidit,
quaecúmque Phoebas óre lympható furens
credí deo vetánte praedixít mala,   35
prior Hécuba vidi grávida nec tacuí metus
et vána vates ánte Cassandrám fui.
non caútus ignes Íthacus aut Ithací comes
noctúrnus in vos spársit aut falláx Sinon:
meus ígnis iste est, fácibus ardetís meis.   40
sed quíd ruinas úrbis eversaé gemis,
viváx senectus? réspice infelíx ad hos
luctús recentes: Tróia iam vetus ést malum.
vidi éxecrandum régiae caedís nefas
ipsásque ad aras máius admissúm scelus   45
Aeácidis armis, cúm ferox, scaevá manu
comá reflectens régium tortá caput,
altó nefandum vúlneri ferrum ábdidit;
quod pénitus actum cúm recepissét libens,
ensís senili síccus e iuguló redit.   50
placáre quem non pótuit a caede éffera
mortális aevi cárdinem extremúm premens
superíque testes scéleris et quoddám sacrum
regní iacentis? ílle tot regúm parens
carét sepulcro Príamus et flamma índiget   55
ardénte Troia. nón tamen superís sat est:

dominum écce Priami núribus et natís legens
sortítur urna praédaque en vilís sequar.
hic Héctoris coniúgia despondét sibi,
hic óptat Heleni cóniugem, hic Anténoris;   60
nec dést tuos, Cassándra, qui thalamós petat —
mea sórs timetur, sóla sum Danaís metus.
   Laménta cessant? túrba captivaé mea,
feríte palmis péctora et planctús date
et iústa Troiae fácite — iamdudúm sonet   65
fatális Ide, iúdicis dirí domus.

CHORUS

   Non rúde vulgus lacrimísque novum
lugére iubes: hoc cóntinuis
egímus annis, ex quó tetigit
Phrygiús Graias hospés Amyclas   70
secuítque fretum pinús matri
sacrá Cybebae.
deciéns nivibus canúit Ide,
deciéns nostris nudáta rogis,
et Sígeis trepidús campis   75
decumás secuit messór aristas,
ut núlla dies maeróre caret.
sed nóva fletus causá ministrat:
ite ád planctus, miserámque leva,
regína, manum. vulgús dominam   80
vilé sequemur: non índociles
lugére sumus.
Hec. Fidaé casus nostrí comites,
solvíte crinem, per cólla fluant
maestá capilli tepidó Troiae   85

pulvére turpes: (102 b) compléte manus,
hoc éx Troia sumpsísse licet.   103
paret éxertos turbá lacertos;   87
vesté remissa substrínge sinus
uteróque tenus pateánt artus.
cui cóniugio pectóra velas,   90
captíve pudor?
cingát tunicas pallá solutas,
vacet ád crebri verbéra planctus
furibúnda manus — placet híc habitus,
placet: ágnosco Troáda turbam.   95
iterúm luctus redeánt veteres,
solitúm flendi vincíte morem:
Hectóra flemus.
CHOR. Solvímus omnes lacerúm multo
funére crinem; comá demissa est   100
libéra nodo sparsítque cinis
fervídus ora.
cadit éx umeris vestís apertis   104
imúmque tegit suffúlta latus;   105
iam núda vocant pectóra dextras:
nunc, núnc vires expróme, dolor.
Rhoetéa sonent litóra planctu,
habitánsque cavis montíbus Echo
non, út solita est, extréma brevis   110
verbá remittat, totós reddat
Troiaé gemitus: audíat omnis
pontús et aether.   saevíte, manus,
pulsú pectus tundíte vasto,
non súm solito conténta sono: 115
Hectóra flemus.
HEC. Tibi nóstra ferit dextrá lacertos

umerósque ferit tibi sánguineos,
tibi nóstra caput dextéra pulsat,
tibi máternis ubéra palmis   120
laniáta iacent: fluat ét multo
sanguíne manet quamcúmque tuo
funére feci ruptá cicatrix.
columén patriae, mora fátorum,
tu praésidium Phrygibús fessis,   125
tu múrus eras umerísque tuis
stetit ílla decem fultá per annos:
tecúm cecidit summúsque dies
Hectóris idem patriaéque fuit.

   Vertíte planctus: Priamó vestros   130
fundíte fletus, satis Héctor habet.
CHOR. Accípe, rector Phrygiaé, planctus,
accípe fletus, bis cápte senex.
nil Tróia semel te rége tulit,
bis púlsari Dardána Graio   135
moenía ferro bisqué pharetras
passa Hérculeas. post élatos
Hecubaé partus regúmque gregem
postréma pater funéra cludis
magnóque Iovi victíma caesus   140
Sigéa premis litóra truncus.
HEC. Alió lacrimas flectíte vestras:
non ést Priami miseránda mei
mors, Íliades — 'felíx Priamus'
dicíte cunctae: libér manes   145
vadít ad imos, nec féret umquam
victá Graium cervíce iugum;
non ílle duos videt Átridas
nec fállacem cernít Vlixen:

non Árgolici praedá triumphi   150
subiécta feret collá tropaeis;
non ádsuetas ad scéptra manus
post térga dabit currúsque sequens
Agamémnonios auréa dextra
vincúla gestans latís fiet   155
pompá Mycenis.
CHOR. 'Felíx Priamus' dicímus omnes:
secum éxcedens sua régna tulit;
nunc Élysii nemorís tutis
errát in umbris intérque pias   160
felíx animas Hectóra quaerit.
felíx Priamus, felíx quisquis
belló moriens omnía secum
consúmpta tulit.

TALTHYBIUS

O lónga Danais sémper in portú mora,
seu pétere bellum, pétere seu patriám volunt.   165
CHOR. Quae caúsa ratibus fáciat et Danaís moram,
effáre, reduces quís deus claudát vias.
TAL. Pavet ánimus, artus hórridus quassát tremor.
maióra veris mónstra vix capiúnt fidem —
vidi ípse, vidi. súmma iam Titán iuga   170
stringébat ortu, vícerat noctém dies,   170 b
cum súbito caeco térra mugitú fremens
concússa totos tráxit ex imó sinus;
movére silvae cápita et excelsúm nemus
fragóre vasto tónuit et lucús sacer;
Idaéa ruptis sáxa ceciderúnt iugis.   175
nec térra solum trémuit: et pontús suum

adésse Achillen sénsit ac stravít vada.
tum scíssa vallis áperit immensós specus
et hiátus Erebi pérvium ad superós iter
tellúre fracta praébet ac tumulúm levat.   180
emícuit ingens úmbra Thessalicí ducis,
Threícia qualis árma proludéns tuis
iam, Tróia, fatis strávit aut Ncptúnium
caná nitentem pérculit iuveném coma,
aut cum ínter acies Márte violentó furens   185
corpóribus amnes clúsit et quaeréns iter
tardús cruento Xánthus erravít vado,
aut cúm superbo víctor in currú stetit
egítque habenas Héctorem et Troiám trahens.
implévit omne lítus iratí sonus: 190
'ite, íte inertes, mánibus meis débitos
auférte honores, sólvite ingratás rates
per nóstra ituri mária — non parvó luit
irás Achillis Graécia et magnó luet.
despónsa nostris cíneribus Polýxene   195
Pyrrhí manu mactétur et tumulúm riget.'
haec fátus alta nócte divisít diem
repeténsque Ditem mérsus ingentém specum
coeúnte terra iúnxit.   immotí iacent
tranquílla pelagi, véntus abiecít minas   200
placidúmque fluctu múrmurat lení mare,
Tritónum ab alto cécinit hymenaeúm chorus.

PYRRHUS

Cum laéta pelago véla rediturús dares,
excídit Achilles cúius uniús manu
impúlsa Troia, quídquid adiecít morae   205
illó remoto, dúbia quo caderét stetit.

velís licet quod pétitur ac properés dare,
sero és daturus: iám suum cunctí duces
tulére pretium.   quaé minor mercés potest
tantaé dari virtútis?   an meruít parum   210
qui, fúgere bellum iússus et longá sedens
aevúm senecta dúcere ac Pylií senis
transcéndere annos, éxuit matrís dolos
falsásque vestes, fássus est armís virum?
inhóspitali Télephus regno ímpotens,   215
dum Mýsiae ferócis introitús negat,
rudém cruore régio dextram ímbuit
fortémque eandem sénsit et mitém manum.
cecidére Thebae, vídit Eetión capi
sua régna victus; cláde subversa ést pari   220
appósita celso párva Lyrnesós iugo,
captáque tellus nóbilis Briséide
et caúsa litis régibus Chrysé iacet
et nóta fama Ténedos et quae páscuo
fecúnda pingui Thrácios nutrít greges   225
Scyrós fretumque Lésbos Aegaeúm secans
et cára Phoebo Cílla; quid quas álluit
vernís Caÿcus gúrgitem attolléns aquis?
haec tánta clades géntium ac tantús pavor,
sparsaé tot urbes túrbinis vastí modo   230
altérius esset glória ac summúm decus:
iter ést Achillis; síc meus venít pater
et tánta gessit bélla, dum bellúm parat.
ut ália sileam mérita, non unús satis
Hectór fuisset?   Ílium vicít pater,   235
vos díruistis.   ínclitas laudés iuvat
et fácta magni clára genitorís sequi:
iacuít peremptus Héctor ante oculós patris

patruíque Memnon, cúius ob luctúm parens
pallénte maestum prótulit vultú diem;   240
suíque victor óperis exemplum hórruit
didicítque Achilles ét dea natós mori.
tum saéva Amazon últimus cecidít metus —
debés Achilli, mérita si digne aéstimas,
et si éx Myconis vírginem atque Argís petat.   245
dubitátur et iam plácita nunc subito ímprobas
Priamíque natam Pélei nató ferum
mactáre credis?   át tuam natám parens
Helenae ímmolasti: sólita iam et facta éxpeto.
AGAM. Iuveníle vitium est régere non posse ímpetum;   250
aetátis alios férvor hic primús rapit,
Pyrrhúm paternus.   spíritus quondám truces
minásque tumidi léntus Aeacidaé tuli:
quo plúra possis, plúra patientér feras.

   Quid caéde dira nóbiles clarí ducis   255
aspérgis umbras?   nóscere hoc primúm decet,
quid fácere victor débeat, victús pati.
violénta nemo impéria continuít diu,
moderáta durant; quóque Fortuna áltius
evéxit ac levávit humanás opes,   260
hoc sé magis supprímere felicém decet
variósque casus trémere metuentém deos
nimiúm faventes.   mágna momento óbrui
vincéndo didici.   Tróia nos tumidós facit
nimium ác feroces?   stámus hoc Danaí loco,   265
unde ílla cecidit.   fáteor, aliquando ímpotens
regno ác superbus áltius memét tuli;
sed frégit illos spíritus haec quaé dare
potuísset aliis caúsa, Fortunaé favor.
tu mé superbum, Príame, tu timidúm facis.   270

ego ésse quicquam scéptra nisi vanó putem
fulgóre tectum nómen et falsó comam
vincló decentem?   cásus haec rapiét brevis,
nec mílle forsan rátibus aut annís decem.
non ómnibus fortúna tam lenta ímminet.   275
equidém fatebor (páce dixisse hóc tua,
Argíva tellus, líceat) affligí Phrygas
vincíque volui: rúere et aequarí solo
utinam árcuissem.   séd regi frenís nequit
et íra et ardens hóstis et victória   280
commíssa nocti.   quídquid indignum aút ferum
cuiquám videri pótuit, hoc fecít dolor
tenebraéque, per quas ípse se irritát furor,
gladiúsque felix, cúius infectí semel
vecórs libido est.   quídquid eversaé potest   285
superésse Troiae, máneat: exactúm satis
poenárum et ultra est.   régia ut virgo óccidat
tumulóque donum détur et cinerés riget
et fácinus atrox caédis ut thalamós vocent,
non pátiar.   in me cúlpa cunctorúm redit: 290
qui nón vetat peccáre, cum possít, iubet.
PYRRH.   Nullúmne Achillis praémium manés ferent?
AGAM.   Ferént, et illum laúdibus cunctí canent
magnúmque terrae nómen ignotae aúdient.
quod sí levatur sánguine infusó cinis,   295
opíma Phrygii cólla caedantúr greges
fluátque nulli flébilis matrí cruor.
quis íste mos est?   quándo in inferiás homo est
impénsus hominis?   détrahe invidiám tuo
odiúmque patri, quém coli poená iubes.   300
PYRRH.   O túmide, rerum dúm secundarúm status
extóllit animos, tímide cum increpuít metus,

regúm tyranne! iámne flammatúm geris
amóre subito péctus ac venerís novae?
solúsne totiens spólia de nobís feres? 305
hac déxtra Achilli víctimam reddám suam.
quam sí negas retinésque, maiorém dabo
dignámque quam det Pýrrhus; et nimiúm diu
a caéde nostra régia cessát manus
parémque poscit Príamus. AGAM. Haud equidém nego 310
hoc ésse Pyrrhi máximum in belló decus,
saevó peremptus énse quod Priamús iacet,
suppléx paternus. PYRRH. Súpplices nostrí patris
hostésque eosdem nóvimus. Priamús tamen
praeséns rogavit; tú gravi pavidús metu, 315
nec ád rogandum fórtis, Aiací preces
Ithacóque mandas claúsus atque hostém tremens.
AGAM. At nón timebat túnc tuus, fateór, parens,
intérque caedes Graéciae atque ustás rates
segnís iacebat bélli et armorum ímmemor, 320
leví canoram vérberans plectró chelyn.
PYRRH. Tunc mágnus Hector, árma contemnéns tua,
cantús Achillis tímuit et tanto ín metu
naválibus pax álta Thessalicís fuit.
AGAM. Nempe ísdem in istis Théssalis naválibus 325
pax álta rursus Héctoris patrí fuit.
PYRRH. Est régis alti spíritum regí dare.
AGAM. Cur déxtra regi spíritum eripuít tua?
PYRRH. Mortém misericors saépe pro vitá dabit.
AGAM. Et núnc misericors vírginem bustó petis? 330
PYRRH. Iamne ímmolari vírgines credís nefas?
AGAM. Praeférre patriam líberis regém decet.
PYRRH. Lex núlla capto párcit aut poenam ímpedit.
AGAM. Quod nón vetat lex, hóc vetat fierí pudor.

PYRRH. Quodcúmque libuit fácere victorí licet.   335
AGAM. Minimúm decet libére cui multúm licet.
PYRRH. His ísta iactas, quós decem annorúm gravi
regnó subactos Pýrrhus exsolvít iugo?
AGAM. Hos Scýrus animos? PYRRH. Scélere quae fratrúm
    caret.
AGAM. Inclúsa fluctu — PYRRH. Némpe cognatí maris: 340
Atrei ét Thyestae nóbilem noví domum.
AGAM. Ex vírginis concépte furtivó stupro
et éx Achille náte, sed nondúm viro —
PYRRH. Illo éx Achille, génere qui mundúm suo
sparsús per omne caélitum regnúm tenet: 345
Thetide aéquor, umbras Aéaco, caelúm Iove.
AGAM. Illo éx Achille, quí manu Paridís iacet.
PYRRH. Quem néc deorum cómminus quisquám petit.
AGAM. Compéscere equidem vérba et audacém malo
poterám domare; séd meus captís quoque   350
scit párcere ensis. pótius interprés deum
Calchás vocetur: fáta si poscént, dabo.
    Tu quí Pelasgae víncla solvistí rati
morásque bellis, árte qui reserás polum,
cui víscerum secréta, cui mundí fragor   355
et stélla longa sémitam flammá trahens
dant sígna fati, cúius ingentí mihi
mercéde constant óra: quid iubeát deus
effáre, Calchas, nósque consilió rege.

CALCHAS

    Dant fáta Danais quó solent pretió viam: 360
mactánda virgo est Théssali bustó ducis;
sed quó iugari Théssalae cultú solent

Iónidesve vél Mycenaeaé nurus,
Pyrrhús parenti cóniugem tradát suo:
sic ríte dabitur.   nón tamen nostrás tenet   365
haec úna puppes caúsa: nobiliór tuo,
Polýxene, cruóre debetúr cruor.
quem fáta quaerunt, túrre de summá cadat
Priamí nepos Hectóreus et letum óppetat.
tum mílle velis ímpleat classís freta.   370

CHORUS

   Vérum est án timidós fábula décipit
   úmbras córporibús vívere cónditis,
   cúm coniúnx oculís ímposuít manum
   súpremúsque diés sólibus óbstitit
   ét tristís cinerés úrna coércuit?   375
   nón prodést animám trádere fúneri,
   séd restát miserís vívere lóngius?
   án totí morimúr núllaque párs manet
   nóstri, cúm profugó spíritus hálitu
   ímmixtús nebulís céssit in áera   380
   ét nudúm tetigít súbdita fáx latus?
      Quídquid sól oriéns, quídquid et óccidens
   nóvit, caéruleís Óceanús fretis
   quídquid bís veniéns ét fugiéns lavat,
   aétas Pégaseó córripiét gradu.   385
   quó bis séna volánt sídera túrbine,
   quó cursú properát vólvere saécula
   ástrorúm dominús, quó properát modo
   óbliquís Hecaté cúrrere fléxibus:
   hóc omnés petimús fáta nec ámplius,   390
   iúratós superís quí tetigít lacus,

úsquam est; út calidís fúmus ab ígnibus
vánescít, spatiúm pér breve sórdidus,
út nubés, gravidás quás modo vídimus,
árctoí Boreaé díssicit ímpetus: 395
síc hic, quó regimúr, spíritus éffluet.
póst mortém nihil ést ípsaque mórs nihil,
vélocís spatií méta novíssima;
spém ponánt avidí, sóllicití metum:
témpus nós avidúm dévorat ét chaos.   400
mórs indívidua ést, nóxia córpori
néc parcéns animaé: Taénara et áspero
régnum súb dominó límen et óbsidens
cústos nón facilí Cérberus óstio
rúmorés vacuí vérbaque inánia   405
ét par sóllicitó fábula sómnio.
quaéris quó iaceás póst obitúm loco?
quó non náta iacént. —

ANDROMACHA

Quid, maésta Phrygiae túrba, laceratís comas
miserúmque tunsae péctus effusó genas   410
fletú rigatis? lévia perpessaé sumus,
si flénda patimur. Ílium vobís modo,
mihi cécidit olim, cúm ferus curru íncito
mea mémbra raperet ét gravi gemerét sono
Pelíacus axis póndere Hectoreó tremens.   415
tunc óbruta atque evérsa quodcumque áccidit
torpéns malis rigénsque sine sensú fero.
iam erépta Danais cóniugem sequerér meum,
nisi híc teneret: híc meos animós domat
moríque prohibet; cógit hic aliquíd deos   420

adhúc rogare — témpus aerumnae áddidit.
hic míhi malorum máximum fructum ábstulit,
nihíl timere: prósperis rebús locus
eréptus omnis, díra qua veniánt habent.
misérrimum est timére, cum sperés nihil.   425

SENEX

Quis té repens commóvit afflictám metus?
ANDR. Exóritur aliquod máius ex magnó malum.
nondúm ruentis Ílii fatúm stetit.
SEN. Et quás reperiet, út velit, cladés deus?
ANDR. Stygís profundae claústra et obscurí specus   430
laxántur et, ne désit eversís metus,
hostés ab imo cónditi Dite éxeunt —
solísne retro pérvium est Danaís iter?
certe aéqua mors est: túrbat atque agitát Phrygas
commúnis iste terror; híc proprié meum   435
extérret animum nóctis horrendaé sopor.
SEN. Quae vísa portas? éffer in mediúm metus.
ANDR. Partés fere nox álma transierát duas
clarúmque septem vérterant stellaé iugum;
ignóta tandem vénit afflictaé quies   440
brevísque fessis sómnus obrepsít genis,
si sómnus ille est méntis attonitaé stupor:
cum súbito nostros Héctor ante oculós stetit,
non quális ultro bélla in Argivós ferens
Graiás petebat fácibus Idaeís rates,   445
nec caéde multa quális in Danaós furens
vera éx Achille spólia simulató tulit,
non ílle vultus flámmeum intendéns iubar,
sed féssus ac deiéctus et fletú gravis

similísque nostro, squálida obtectús coma.   450
iuvát tamen vidísse; tum quassáns caput:
'dispélle somnos' ínquit 'et natum éripe,
o fída coniunx: láteat, haec una ést salus.
omítte fletus — Tróia quod cecidít gemis?
utinám iaceret tóta.   festina, ámove   455
quocúmque nostrae párvulam stirpém domus.'
mihi gélidus horror ác tremor somnum éxpulit,
oculósque nunc huc pávida, nunc illúc ferens
oblíta nati mísera quaesivi Héctorem:
falláx per ipsos úmbra complexús abit.   460
    O náte, magni cérta progeniés patris,
spes úna Phrygibus, única afflictaé domus,
veterísque suboles sánguinis nimium íncliti
nimiúmque patri símilis: hos vultús meus
habébat Hector, tális incessú fuit   465
habitúque talis, síc tulit fortés manus,
sic célsus umeris, frónte sic torvá minax
cervíce fusam díssipans iactá comam —
o náte sero Phrýgibus, o matrí cito,
erítne tempus íllud ac felíx dies   470
quo Tróici defénsor et vindéx soli
redivíva ponas Pérgama et sparsós fuga
civés reducas, nómen et patriaé suum
Phrygibúsque reddas?   séd mei fatí memor
tam mágna timeo vóta — quod captís sat est,   475
vivámus.   heu me, quís locus fidús meo
erít timori quáve te sede ócculam?
arx ílla pollens ópibus et murís deum,
gentés per omnes clára et invidiaé gravis,
nunc púlvis altus, stráta sunt flamma ómnia   480
superéstque vasta ex úrbe ne tantúm quidem,

quo láteat infans — quém locum fraudí legam?
est túmulus ingens cóniugis carí sacer,
veréndus hosti, móle quem immensá parens
opibúsque magnis strúxit, in luctús suos   485
rex nón avarus: óptime credám patri —
sudór per artus frígidus totós cadit:
omén tremesco mísera feralís loci.   488
SEN. Miser óccupet praesídıa, securús legat.   497
ANDR. Quid quód latere síne metu magnó nequit,   496
ne pródat aliquis? SEN. Ámove testés doli.   492
ANDR. Si quaéret hostis? SEN. Úrbe in eversá perit: 493
haec caúsa multos úna ab interitu árcuit,   489
credí perisse. ANDR. Víx spei quicquam ést super:
grave póndus illum mágna nobilitás premit;   491
quid próderit latuísse redituro ín manus?   494
SEN. Victór feroces ímpetus primós habet.   495
ANDR. Quis té locus, quae régio seducta, ínvia   498
tutó reponet? quís feret trepidís opem?
quis próteget? qui sémper, etiam núnc tuos,   500
Hectór, tuere: cóniugis furtúm piae
serva ét fideli cínere victurum éxcipe.
succédc tumulo, náte — quid retró fugis
tutásque latebras spérnis? agnosco índolem:
pudét timere. spíritus magnós fuga   505
animósque veteres, súme quos casús dedit.
en íntuere, túrba quae simús super:
tumulús, puer, captíva: cedendum ést malis.
sanctás parentis cónditi sedés age
audé subire. fáta si miserós iuvant,   510
habés sa'utem; fáta si vitám negant,
habés sepulchrum. SEN. Claústra commissúm tegunt;
quem né tuus prodúcat in mediúm timor,

procul hínc recede téque diversam ámove.
ANDR. Leviús solet timére, qui propiús timet;   515
sed, sí placet, referámus hinc alió pedem.
SEN. Cohibé parumper óra questusque ópprime:
gressús nefandos dúx Cephallanum ádmovet.
ANDR. Dehísce tellus túque, coniunx, último
specú revulsam scínde tellurem ét Stygis   520
sinú profundo cónde depositúm meum.
adést Ulixes, ét quidem dubió gradu
vultúque: nectit péctore astus cállidos.

ULIXES

Duraé minister sórtis hoc primúm peto,
ut, óre quamvis vérba dicantúr meo,   525
non ésse credas nóstra: Graiorum ómnium
procerúmque vox est, pétere quos serás domos
Hectórea suboles próhibet: hanc fata éxpetunt.
sollícita Danaos pácis incertaé fides
sempér tenebit, sémper a tergó timor   530
respícere coget árma nec poní sinet,
dum Phrýgibus animos nátus eversís dabit,
Andrómacha, vester. aúgur haec Calchás canit;
et, sí taceret aúgur haec Calchás, tamen
dicébat Hector, cúius et stirpem hórreo: 535
generósa in ortus sémina exurgúnt suos.
sic ílle magni párvus armentí comes
primísque nondum córnibus findéns cutem
cervíce subito célsus et fronte árduus
gregém paternum dúcit ac pecori ímperat;   540
quae ténera caeso vírga de truncó stetit,
par ípsa matri témpore exiguó subit

umbrásque terris réddit et caeló nemus;
sic mále relictus ígne de magnó cinis
virés resumit. ést quidem iniustús dolor 545
rerum aéstimator: sí tamen tecum éxigas,
veniám dabis, quod bélla post hiemés decem
totidémque messes iám senex milés timet
aliásque clades rúrsus ac numquám bene
Troiám iacentem. mágna res Danaós movet, 550
futúrus Hector: líbera Graiós metu.
haec úna naves caúsa deductás tenet,
hac clássis haeret. néve crudelém putes,
quod sórte iussus Héctoris natúm petam:
petíssem Oresten. pátere quod victór tulit. 555
ANDR. Utinám quidem esses, náte, materna ín manu,
nossémque quis te cásus ereptúm mihi
tenéret, aut quae régio — non hostílibus
confóssa telis péctus ac vinclís manus
secántibus praestrícta, non acrí latus 560
utrúmque flamma cíncta maternám fidem
umquam éxuissem. nátc, quis te núnc locus,
fortúna quae possédit? errore ávio
vagus árva lustras? vástus an patriaé vapor
corrípuit artus? saévus an victór tuo 565
lusít cruore? númquid immanís ferae
morsú peremptus páscis Idaeás aves?
ULIX. Simuláta remove vérba; non facile ést tibi
decípere Ulixen: vícimus matrúm dolos
etiám dearum. cássa consilia ámove; 570
ubi nátus est? ANDR. Ubi Héctor? ubi cunctí Phryges?
ubi Príamus? unum quaéris: ego quaero ómnia.
ULIX. Coácta dices spónte quod fari ábnuis.
ANDR. Tuta ést, perire quaé potest debét cupit.

ULIX. Magnífica verba mórs prope admota éxcutit.   575
ANDR. Si vís, Ulixe, cógere Andromachám metu,
vitám minare: nám mori votum ést mihi.
ULIX. Verbéribus igni mórte cruciatu éloqui
quodcúmque celas ádiget invitám dolor
et péctore imo cóndita arcana éruet: 580
necéssitas plus pósse quam pietás solet.
ANDR. Propóne flammas, vúlnera et dirás mali
dolóris artes ét famem et saevám sitim
variásque pestes úndique, et ferrum índitum
viscéribus istis, cárceris caecí luem,   585
et quídquid audet víctor iratús timens:
animósa nullos máter admittít metus.   588
ULIX. Hic ípse, quo nunc cóntumax perstás, amor
consúlere parvis líberis Danaós monet.   590
post árma tam longínqua, post annós decem
minús timerem quós facit Calchás metus,
si míhi timerem: bélla Telemachó paras.
ANDR. Invíta, Ulixe, gaúdium Danaís dabo:
dandum ést; fatere quós premis luctús, dolor.   595
gaudéte, Atridae, túque laetifica, út soles,
refér Pelasgis: Héctoris prolés obit.
ULIX. Et ésse verum hoc quá probas Danaís fide?
ANDR. Ita quód minari máximum victór potest
contíngat et me fáta maturo éxitu   600
facilíque solvant ác meo condánt solo
et pátria tellus Héctorem levitér premat,
ut lúce cassus ínter extinctós iacet
datúsque tumulo débita exanimís tulit.
ULIX. Expléta fata stírpe sublata Héctoris   605
solidámque pacem laétus ad Danaós feram —
quid ágis, Ulixe?   Dánaidae credént tibi:

tu cuí? parenti — fíngit an quisquam hóc parens,
nec abóminandae mórtis auspiciúm pavet?
auspícia metuunt quí nihil maiús timent.   610
fidem álligavit iúre iurandó suam —
si péierat, timére quid graviús potest?
nunc ádvoca astus, ánime, nunc fraudés, dolos,
nunc tótum Ulixen; véritas numquám perit.
scrutáre matrem. maéret, inlacrimát, gemit;   615
sed et húc et illuc ánxios gressús refert
missásque voces aúre sollicita éxcipit:
magis haéc timet, quam maéret. ingenio ést opus.
    Aliós parentes álloqui in luctú decet:
tibi grátulandum est, mísera, quod nató cares,   620
quem mórs manebat saéva praecipitém datum
e túrre, lapsis sóla quae murís manet.
ANDR. Relíquit animus mómbra, quatiuntúr, labant
torpétque vinctus frígido sanguís gelu.
ULIX. Intrémuit: hac, hac párte quaerenda ést mihi;   625
matrém timor detéxit: iterabó metum —
ite, íte celeres, fraúde materna ábditum
hostém, Pelasgi nóminis pestem últimam,
ubicúmque latitat, érutam in mediúm date.
bene ést: tenetur. pérge, festina, áttrahe —   630
quid réspicis trepidásque? iam certó perit.
ANDR. Utinám timerem. sólitus ex longo ést metus:
dedíscit animus saépe quod didicít diu.
ULIX. Lustrále quoniam débitum murís puer
sacrum ántecessit néc potest vatém sequi   635
melióre fato ráptus, hoc Calchás ait
modó piari pósse rediturás rates,
si plácet undas Héctoris sparsí cinis
ac túmulus imo tótus aequetúr solo.

nunc ílle quoniam débitam effugít necem,   640
erit ádmovenda sédibus sacrís manus.
ANDR. Quid ágimus?   animum dístrahit geminús timor:
hinc nátus, illinc cóniugis sacrí cinis.
pars útra vincet?   téstor immités deos,
deósque veros cóniugis manés mei: 645
non áliud, Hector, ín meo nató mihi
placére quam te.   vívat, ut possít tuos
reférre vultus — prórutus tumuló cinis
mergétur?   ossa flúctibus spargí sinam
disiécta vastis?   pótius hic mortem óppetat. —   650
poterís nefandae déditum matér neci
vidére?   poteris célsa per fastígia
missúm rotari?   pótero, perpetiár, feram,
dum nón meus post fáta victorís manu
iactétur Hector. — híc suam poenám potest   655
sentíre, at illum fáta iam in tutó locant —
quid flúctuaris?   státue, quem poenae éxtrahas.
ingráta, dubitas?   Héctor est illínc tuus —
errás: utrimque est Héctor; hic sensús potens,
forsán futurus últor extinctí patris —   660
utríque parci nón potest: quid iám facis?
serva é duobus, ánime, quem Danaí timent.
ULIX. Respónsa peragam: fúnditus busta éruam.
ANDR. Quae véndidistis?   ULIX. Pérgam et e summo
      ággere
trahám sepulchra.   ANDR.   Caélitum appelló fidem   665
fidémque Achillis: Pýrrhe, genitorís tui
munús tuere.   ULIX. Túmulus hic campó statim
totó iacebit.   ANDR. Fúerat hoc prorsús nefas
Danaís inausum.   témpla violastís, deos
etiám faventes: bústa transierát furor.   670

resístam, inermes ófferam armatís manus,
dabit íra vires. quális Argolicás ferox
turmás Amazon strávit, aut qualís deo
percússa Maenas éntheo silvás gradu
armáta thyrso térret atque expérs sui   675
vulnús dedit nec sénsit, in mediós ruam
tumulóque cineris sócia defensó cadam.
　　Ulix. Cessátis et vos flébilis clamór movet
furórque cassus féminae?   iussa ócius
perágite. Andr. Me, me stérnite hic ferró prius.   680
repéllor, heu me.   rúmpe fatorúm moras,
molíre terras, Héctor, ut Ulixén domes.
vel úmbra satis es — árma concussít manu,
iaculátur ignes — cérnitis, Danai, Héctorem?
an sóla video? Ulix. Fúnditus cuncta éruam.   685
Andr. Quid agís?   ruina páriter et natum ét virum
prostérnis una?   fórsitan Danaós prece
placáre poteris.   cónditum illidét statim
immáne busti póndus — intereát miser
ubicúmque potius, né pater natum óbruat   690
premátque patrem nátus. — Ad genua áccido
suppléx, Ulixe, quámque nulliús pedes
novére dextram pédibus admoveó tuis.
miserére matris ét preces placidús pias
patiénsque recipe, quóque te celsum áltius   695
superí levarunt, mítius lapsós preme:
miseró datur quodcúmque, fortunaé datur.
sic té revisat cóniugis sanctaé torus,
annósque, dum te récipit, extendát suos
Laérta; sic te iúvenis aspiciát tuus,   700
et vóta vincens véstra felici índole
aetáte avum transcéndat, ingenió patrem.

miserére matris: únicum adflictaé mihi
solámen hic est.   ULIX.   Éxhibe natum ét roga.

    ANDR.   Huc é latebris procéde tuis,   705
flebíle matris furtúm miserae.
hic ést, hic est terrór, Ulixe,
millé carinis.   submítte manus
dominíque pedes supplíce dextra
stratús adora nec túrpe puta   710
quidquíd miseros fortúna iubet.
pone éx animo regés atavos
magníque senis iurá per omnes
inclúta terras, excídat Hector,
gere cáptivum positóque genu,   715
si túa nondum funéra sentis,
matrís fletus imitáre tuae.

    Vidít pueri regís lacrimas
et Tróia prior, parvúsque minas
trucis Álcidae flexít Priamus.   720
ille, ílle ferox, cuiús vastis
viríbus omnes cessére ferae,
qui pérfracto limíne Ditis
caecúm retro patefécit iter,
hostís parvi victús lacrimis: 725
'suscípe' dixit 'rectór habenas
patrióque sede celsús solio;
sed scéptra fide melióre tene.'
hoc fúit illo victóre capi:
discíte mites Hercúlis iras.   730
an sóla placent Hercúlis arma?
iacet ánte pedes non mínor illo
supplíce supplex vitámque petit —
regnúm Troiae quocúmque volet
        Fortúna ferat.   735

Ulix. Matrís quidem me maéror attonitaé movet,
magís Pelasgae mé tamen matrés movent,
quarum íste magnos créscit in luctús puer.
Andr. Has, hás ruinas úrbis in cinerém datae
hic éxcitabit? haé manus Troiam érigent?   740
nullás habet spes Tróia, si talés habet.
non síc iacemus Tróes, ut cuiquám metus
possímus esse. spíritus genitór facit?
sed némpe tractus. ípse post Troiám pater
posuísset animos, mágna quos frangúnt mala.   745
si poéna petitur, quaé peti graviór potest?
famuláre collo nóbili subeát iugum,
servíre liceat. áliquis hoc regí negat?
Ulix. Non hóc Ulixes, séd negat Calchás tibi.
Andr. O máchinator fraúdis et scelerum ártifex,   750
virtúte cuius béllica nemo óccidit,
dolís et astu máleficae mentís iacent
etiám Pelasgi, vátem et insontés deos
praeténdis? hoc est péctoris facinús tui.
noctúrne miles, fórtis in puerí necem   755
iam sólus audes áliquid et claró die.
Ulix. Virtús Ulixis Dánaidis nota ést satis
nimísque Phrygibus. nón vacat vanís diem
contérere verbis: áncoras classís legit.
Andr. Brevém moram largíre, dum officiúm parens   760
nató supremum réddo et amplexu último
avidós dolores sátio. Ulix. Misererí tui
utinám liceret. quód tamen solúm licet,
tempús moramque dábimus. arbitrió tuo
implére lacrimis: flétus aerumnás levat.   765
Andr. O dúlce pignus, ó decus lapsaé domus
summúmque Troiae fúnus, o Danaúm timor,

genetrícis o spes vána, cui deméns ego
laudés parentis béllicas, annós avi
deméns precabar, vóta destituít deus.　　　　77●
Ilíaca non tu scéptra regalí potens
gestábis aula, iúra nec populís dabis
victásque gentes súb tuum mittés iugum,
non Gráia caedes térga, non Pyrrhúm trahes;
non árma tenera párva tractabís manu　　　　775
sparsásque passim sáltibus latís feras
audáx sequeris néc stato lustrí die,
sollémne referens Tróici lusús sacrum,
puér citatas nóbilis turmás ages;
non ínter aras móbili velóx pede,　　　　780
reboánte flexo cóncitos cornú modos,
barbárica prisco témpla saltatú coles.
o Márte diro trístius letí genus!
flebílius aliquid Héctoris magní nece
murí videbunt.　ULIX. Rúmpe iam fletús, parens:　785
magnús sibi ipse nón facit finém dolor.
ANDR.　Lacrimís, Ulixe, párva quam petimús mora est;
concéde paucas, út mea condám manu
vivéntis oculos.　óccidis parvús quidem,
sed iám timendus.　Tróia te expectát tua:　790
i, váde liber, líberos Troás vide.
ASTYAN.　Miserére, mater.　ANDR.　Quíd meos retinés sinus
manúsque matris cássa praesidia óccupas?
fremitú leonis quális auditó tener
timidúm iuvencus ápplicat matrí latus,　795
at ílle saevus mátre summotá leo
praedám minorem mórsibus vastís tenens
frangít vehitque: tális e nostró sinu
te rápiet hostis.　óscula et fletús, puer,

*lacerósque crines éxcipe et plenús mei   800
occúrre patri; paúca maternaé tamen
perfér querelae vérba: 'si manés habent
curás priores néc perit flammís amor,
servíre Graio páteris Andromachén uiro,
crudélis Hector? léntus et segnís iaces?   805
redít Achilles.' súme nunc iterúm comas
et súme lacrimas, quídquid e miseró viri
funére relictum est, súme quae reddás tuo
oscúla parenti. mátris hanc solácio
relínque vestem: túmulus hanc tetigít meus   810
manésque cari. sí quid hic cinerís latet,
scrutábor ore. ULIX. Núllus est flendí modus:
abrípite propere clássis Argolicaé moram.

CHORUS

Quáe vocat sedés habitánda captas?
Théssali montés et opáca Tempe,   815
án viros tellús dare mílitares
áptior Phthié melíórque fetu
fórtis armentí lapidósa Trachin,
án maris vastí domitríx Iolcos?
úrbibus centúm spatiósa Crete,   820
párva Gortynís sterilísque Tricce,
án frequens rivís levibús Mothone,
quaé sub Oetaeís latebrósa silvis
mísit infestós Troiaé ruinis
          nón semel árcus?   825
Ólenos tectís habitáta raris,
vírgini Pleurón inimíca divae,
án maris latí sinuósa Troezen?

Pélion regnúm Prothoí superbum,
tértius caeló gradus? (híc recumbens   830
móntis exesí spatiósus antro
iám trucis Chirón puerí magister,
tínnulas plectró feriénte chordas,
túnc quoque ingentés acuébat iras
        bélla canéndo)   835
An ferax varií lapidís Carystos,
án premens litús maris ínquieti
sémper Euripó properánte Chalcis?
quólibet ventó facilés Calydnae,
án carens numquám Gonoéssa vento   840
quaéque formidát Boreán Enispe?
Áttica pendéns Peparéthos ora,
án sacris gaudéns tacitís Eleusin?
númquid Aiacís Salamína veri
aút fera notám Calydona saeva,   845
quásque perfundít subitúrus aequor
ségnibus terrás Titaréssos undis?
Béssan et Scarphén, Pylon án senilem?
Phárin an Pisás Iovis ét coronis
        Élida cláram?   850
Quólibet tristís miserás procella
míttat et donét cuicúmque terrae,
dúm luem tantám Troiae átque Achivis
quaé tulit, Sparté, procul ábsit, absit
Árgos et saeví Pelopís Mycenae,   855
Néritos parvá breviór Zacyntho
ét nocens saxís Ithacé dolosis.
    Quód manet fatúm dominúsque quis te,
aút quibus terrís, Hecubá, videndam
dúcet?   in cuiús moriére regno?   860

Helena

Quicúmque hymen funéstus, inlaetábilis
laménta caedes sánguinem gemitús habet
est aúspice Helena dígnus. eversís quoque
nocére cogor Phrýgibus: ego Pyrrhí toros
narráre falsos iúbeor, ego cultús dare   865
habitúsque Graios. árte capietúr mea
meáque fraude cóncidct Paridís soror.
fallátur; ipsi lévius hoc equidém reor:
optánda mors est síne metu mortís mori.
quid iússa cessas ágere? ad auctorém redit   870
scelerís coacti cúlpa. — Dardaniaé domus
generósa virgo, mélior afflictós deus
respícere coepit téque felicí parat
dotáre thalamo; tále coniugiúm tibi
non ípsa sospes Tróia, non Priamús daret.   875
nam té Pelasgae máximum gentís decus,
cui régna campi láta Thessalicí patent,   878
ad sáncta lecti iúra legitimí petit.   877
te mágna Tethys téque tot pelagí deae
placidúmque numen aéquoris tumidí Thetis   880
suám vocabunt, té datam Pyrrhó socer
Peleús nurum vocábit et Nereús nurum.
depóne cultus squálidos, festós cape,
dedísce captam; déprime horrentés comas
crinémque docta pátere distinguí manu.   885
hic fórsitan te cásus excelsó magis
solió reponet. prófuit multís capi.

Andromacha

Hoc dérat unum Phrýgibus eversís malum,
gaudére — flagrant stráta passim Pérgama:

o cóniugale témpus! an quisquam aúdeat   890
negáre? quisquam dúbius ad thalamós eat,
quos Hélena suadet? péstis exitiúm lues
utriúsque populi, cérnis hos tumulós ducum
et núda totis óssa quae passím iacent
inhumáta campis? haéc hymen sparsít tuus.   895
tibi flúxit Asiae, flúxit Europaé cruor,
cum dímicantes laéta prospicerés viros,
incérta voti — pérge, thalamos áppara.
taedís quid opus est quídve sollemní face?
quid ígne? thalamis Tróia praelucét novis.   900
celebráte Pyrrhi, Tróades, conúbia,
celebráte digne: plánctus et gemitús sonet.
HEL. Ratióne quamvis cáreat et flectí neget
magnús dolor sociósque nonnumquám sui
maeróris ipsos óderit: causám tamen   905
possúm tueri iúdice infestó meam,
gravióra passa. lúget Andromacha Héctorem
et Hécuba Priamum: sólus occulté Paris
lugéndus Helenae est. dúrum et invisum ét grave est
servítia ferre? pátior hoc olím iugum,   910
annís decem captíva. prostratum Ílium est,
versí penates? pérdere est patriám grave,
graviús timere. vós levat tantí mali
comitátus: in me víctor et victús furit.
quam quísque famulam tráheret incertó diu   915
casú pependit: mé meus traxít statim
sine sórte dominus. caúsa bellorúm fui
tantaéque Teucris cládis? hoc verúm puta,
Spartána puppis véstra si secuít freta;
sin rápta Phrygiis praéda remigibús fui   920
dedítque donum iúdici victríx dea,

ignósce praedae.   iúdicem iratúm mea
habitúra causa est: ísta Menelaúm manent
arbítria.   nunc hanc lúctibus paulúm tuis,
Andrómacha, omissis flécte — vix lacrimás queo   925
retinére.   ANDR. Quantum est Hélena quod lacrimát
    malum.
cur lácrimat autem?   fáre quos Ithacús dolos,
quae scélera nectat; útrum ab Idaeís iugis
iactánda virgo est, árcis an celsae édito
mitténda saxo?   núm per has vastum ín mare   930
volvénda rupes, látere quas scissó levat
altúm vadoso Sígeon spectáns sinu?
dic, fáre, quidquid súbdolo vultú tegis.
levióra mala sunt cúncta, quam Priamí gener
Hecubaéque Pyrrhus.   fáre, quam poenám pares   935
expróme et unum hoc déme nostris cládibus,
fallí: paratas pérpeti mortém vides.
HEL.   Utinám iuberet mé quoque interprés deum
abrúmpere ense lúcis invisaé moras
vel Achíllis ante bústa furibundá manu   940
occídere Pyrrhi, fáta comitantém tua,
Polýxene miseránda, quam tradí sibi
cinerémque Achilles ánte mactarí suum,
campó maritus út sit Elysió, iubet.
ANDR.   Vide ut ánimus ingens laétus audierít necem.   945
cultús decoros régiae vestís petit
et ádmoveri crínibus patitúr manum.
mortém putabat íllud, hoc thalamós putat.
at mísera luctu máter auditó stupet;
labefácta mens succúbuit.   assurge, álleva   950
animum ét cadentem, mísera, firma spíritum.
quam ténuis anima vínculo pendét levi —

minimum ést quod Hecubam fácere felicém potest.
spirát, revixit.   príma mors miserós fugit.
HEC. Adhúc Achilles vívit in poenás Phrygum?   955
adhúc rebellat?   ó manum Paridís levem.
cinis ípse nostrum sánguinem ac tumulús sitit.
modo túrba felix látera cingebát mea,
lassábar in tot óscula et tantúm gregem
divídere matrem; sóla nunc haec ést super   960
votúm, comes, levámen afflictaé, quies;
haec tótus Hecubae fétus, hac solá vocor
iam vóce mater.   dúra et infelíx age
elábere anima, dénique hoc unúm mihi
remítte funus.   ínrigat fletús genas   965
imbérque victo súbitus e vultú cadit.
ANDR. Nos Hécuba, nos, nos, Hécuba, lugendaé sumus, 969
quas móta classis húc et huc sparsás feret;   970
hanc cára tellus sédibus patriís teget.
HEL. Magis ínvidebis, sí tuam sortém scies.
ANDR. An áliqua poenae párs meae ignota ést mihi?
HEL. Versáta dominos úrna captivís dedit.
ANDR. Cui fámula trador?   éde; quem dominúm voco? 975
HEL. Te sórte prima Scýrius iuvenís tulit.
ANDR. Cassándra felix, quám furor sorti éximit
Phoebúsque. HEL. Regum hanc máximus rectór tenet. 978
HEC. Laetáre, gaude, náta.   quam vellét tuos   967
Cassándra thalamos, véllet Andromaché tuos.   968
estne áliquis, Hecubam quí suam dicí velit?   970
HEL. Ithaco óbtigisti praéda nolentí brevis.   980
HEC. Quis tam ímpotens ac dúrus et iniquaé ferus
sortítor urnae régibus regés dedit?
quis tám sinister dívidit captás deus?
quis árbiter crudélis et miserís gravis

elígere dominos néscit et matrem Héctoris 985
armís Achillis míscet ?   ad Ulixén vocor: 987
nunc vícta, nunc captíva, nunc cunctís mihı
obséssa videor cládibus — dominí pudet, 989
non sérvitutis.   stérilis et saevís fretis 991
inclúsa tellus nón capit tumulós meos —
duc, dúc, Ulixe, níl moror, dominúm sequor;
me méa sequentur fáta : non pelagó quies
tranquílla veniet, saéviet ventís mare, 995
          *   *   *   *   *   *   *   *
et bélla et ignes ét mea et Priamí mala,
dumque ísta veniant, ínterim hoc poenaé loco est:
sortem óccupavi, praémium eripuí tibi. —
    Sed én citato Pýrrhus accurrít gradu
vultúque torvo.   Pýrrhe, quid cessás ? age 1000
reclúde ferro péctus et Achillís tui
coniúnge soceros.   pérge, mactatór senum,
et híc decet te sánguis : abreptám trahe.
maculáte superos caéde funestá deos,
maculáte manes — quíd precer vobís ?   precor 1005
his dígna sacris aéquora : hoc classi áccidat
totí Pelasgae, rátibus hoc mille áccidat
meaé precabor, cúm vehar, quidquíd rati.

    Dúlce maerentí populús dolentum,
    dúlce lamentís resonáre gentes; 1010
    lénius luctús lacrimaéque mordent,
    túrba quas fletú similís frequentat.
    sémper ah sempér dolor ést malignus:
    gaúdet in multós sua fáta mitti

séque non solúm placuísse poenae.   1015
férre quam sortém patiúntur omnes,
    némo recúsat.
Tólle felicés: miserúm, licet sit,
némo se credét; removéte multo
dívites auró, removéte centum   1020
rúra qui scindúnt opulénta bubus:
paúperi surgént animí iacentes —
ést miser nemó nisi cómparatus.
dúlce in immensís positó ruinis,
néminem laetós habuísse vultus: 1025
ílle deplorát queritúrque fatum,
quí secans fluctúm rate síngulari
núdus in portús cecidit petítos;
aéquior casúm tulit ét procellas,
mílle qui pontó paritér carinas   1030
óbrui vidít tabuláque vectus
naúfraga, terrís mare dúm coactis
flúctibus Corús prohibét, revertit.
quéstus est Hellén cecidísse Phrixus,
cúm gregis ductór radiánte villo   1035
aúreo fratrém simul ác sororem
sústulit tergó medióque iactum
fécit in pontó; tenuít querelas
ét vir et Pyrrhá, mare cúm viderent,
ét nihil praetér mare cúm viderent   1040
únici terrís hominés relicti.
Sólvet hunc questúm lacrimásque nostras
spárget huc illúc agitáta classis,
       *   *   *   *   *   *   *   *
ét tuba iussí dare véla nautae
cúm simul ventís properánte remo   1045

prénderint altúm fugiétque litus.
quís status mentís miserís, ubi omnis
térra decrescét pelagúsque crescet,
célsa cum longé latitábit Ide?
túm puer matrí genetríxque nato,   1050
Tróia qua iaceát regióne monstrans,
dícet et longé digitó notabit:
'Ílium est illíc, ubi fúmus alte
sérpit in caelúm nebulaéque turpes.'
Tróes hoc signó patriam vidébunt.   1055

NUNTIUS, HECUBA, ANDROMACHA

O dúra fata, saéva miseranda hórrida!
quod tám ferum, tam tríste bis quinís scelus
Mars vídit annis?   quíd prius referéns gemam,
tuósne potius, án tuos luctús, anus?
HEC. Quoscúmque luctus fléveris, flebís meos: 1060
sua quémque tantum, me ómnium cladés premit;
mihi cúncta pereunt: quísquis est, Hecubae ést, miser.
NUNT. Mactáta virgo est, míssus e murís puer;
sed utérque letum ménte generosá tulit.
ANDR. Expóne seriem caédis, et dupléx nefas   1065
perséquere: gaudet mágnus aerumnás dolor
tractáre totas.   éde et enarra ómnia.
NUNT. Est úna magna túrris e Troiá super,
adsuéta Priamo, cúius e fastígio
summísque pinnis árbiter bellí sedens   1070
regébat acies.   túrre in hac blandó sinu
fovéns nepotem, cúm metu versós gravi
Danaós fugaret Héctor et ferro ét face,
patérna puero bélla monstrabát senex.

haec nóta quondam túrris et murí decus,   1075
nunc sóla cautes, úndique adfusá ducum
plebísque turba cíngitur; totúm coit
ratibús relictis vúlgus. his collís procul
aciém patenti líberam praebét loco,
his álta rupes, cúius in cacúmine   1080
erécta summos túrba libravít pedes.
hunc pínus, illum laúrus, hunc fagús gerit
et tóta populo sílva suspensó tremit.
extréma montis ílle praeruptí petit,
semústa at ille técta vel saxum ímminens   1085
murí cadentis préssit, atque aliquís (nefas)
tumuló ferus spectátor Hectoreó sedet.
per spátia late pléna sublimí gradu
incédit Ithacus párvulum dextrá trahens
Priamí nepotem, néc gradu segní puer   1090
ad álta pergit moénia. ut summá stetit
pro túrre, vultus húc et huc acrés tulit
intrépidus animo. quális ingentís ferae
parvús tenerque fétus et nondúm potens
saevíre dente iám tamen tollít minas   1095
morsúsque inanes témptat atque animís tumet:
sic ílle dextra prénsus hostilí puer
feróx superbe. móverat vulgum ác duces
ipsúmque Ulixen. nón flet e turba ómnium
qui flétur; ac, dum vérba fatidici ét preces   1100
concípit Ulixes vátis et saevós ciet
ad sácra superos, spónte desiluít sua
in média Priami régna. —
ANDR. Quis Cólchus hoc, quis sédis incertaé Scytha
commísit, aut quae Cáspium tangéns mare   1105
gens iúris expers aúsa? non Busíridis

puerílis aras sánguis aspersít feri,
nec párva gregibus mémbra Diomedés suis
epulánda posuit.   quís tuos artús leget
tumulóque tradet?   Nunt. Quós enim praecéps locus 1110
relíquit artus?   óssa disiecta ét gravi
elísa casu; sígna clari córporis,
et óra et illas nóbiles patrís notas,
confúdit imam póndus ad terrám datum;
solúta cervix sílicis impulsú, caput   1115
ruptúm cerebro pénitus expressó — iacet
defórme corpus.   Andr. Síc quoque est similís patri.
Nunt. Praecéps ut altis cécidit e murís puer
flevítque Achivum túrba quod fecít nefas,
idem ílle populus áliud ad facinús redit   1120
tumulúmque Achillis.   cúius extremúm latus
Rhoetéa leni vérberant fluctú vada;
advérsa cingit cámpus et clivó levi
erécta medium vállis includéns locum.
crescít theatri móre concursús frequens,   125
implévit omnc lítus: hi classís moram
hac mórte solvi réntur, hi stirpem hóstium
gaudént recidi.   mágna pars vulgí levis
odít scelus, spectátque; nec Troés minus
suúm frequentant fúnus et pavidí metu   130
partém ruentis últimam Troiaé vident:
cum súbito thalami móre praecedúnt faces
et prónuba illi Týndaris, maestúm caput
demíssa. ' tali núbat Hermioné modo'
Phrygés precantur ' síc viro turpís suo   1135
reddátur Helena.'   térror attonitós tenet
utrósque populos.   ípsa deiectós gerit
vultús pudore, séd tamen fulgént genae

magísque solito spléndet extremús decor,
ut ésse Phoebi dúlcius lumén solet   1140
iam iám cadentis, ástra cum repetúnt vices
premitúrque dubius nócte viciná dies.
stupet ómne vulgus — ét fere cunctí magis
peritúra laudant.   hós movet formaé decus,
hos móllis aetas, hós vagae rerúm vices;   1145
movet ánimus omnes fórtis et leto óbvius.
Pyrrhum ántecedit; ómnium mentés tremunt,
mirántur ac miserántur.   ut primum árdui
sublíme montis tétigit atque alte édito
iuvenís paterni vértice in bustí stetit,   1150
audáx virago nón tulit retró gradum;
convérsa ad ictum stát truci vultú ferox.
tam fórtis animus ómnium mentés ferit
novúmque monstrum est Pýrrhus ad caedém piger.
ut déxtra ferrum pénitus exactum ábdidit,   1155
subitús recepta mórte prorupít cruor
per vúlnus ingens.   néc tamen moriéns adhuc
depónit animos: cécidit, ut Achillí gravem
factúra terram, próna et irato ímpetu.
utérque flevit coétus; at timidúm Phryges   1160
misére gemitum, clárius victór gemit.
hic órdo sacri.   nón stetit fusús cruor
humóve summa flúxit: obduxít statim
saevúsque totum sánguinem tumulús bibit.
Hec. Ite, íte, Danai, pétite iam tutí domos;   1165
optáta velis mária diffusís secet
secúra classis: cóncidit virgo ác puer;
bellúm peractum est.   quó meas lacrimás feram?
ubi hánc anilis éxpuam letí moram?
natam án nepotem, cóniugem an patríam fleam?   1170

an ómnia an me sóla? Mors votúm meum,
infántibus, violénta, virginibús venis,
ubíque properas, saéva: me solám times
vitásque, gladios ínter ac tela ét faces
quaesíta tota nócte, cupientém fugis.   1175
non hóstis aut ruína, non ignís meos
absúmpsit artus: quám prope a Priamó steti.
NUNT. Repétite celeri mária, captivaé, gradu:
iam véla puppis láxat et classís movet.

MEDEA

DRAMATIS PERSONAE

Medea
Nutrix
Creo
Iason
Nuntius
Chorus

Scaena Corinthi

THE PARTS TAKEN BY EACH ACTOR

I Medea
II Jaso
Creo
III Nutrix
Nuntius

MEDEA

Di cóniugales túque genialís tori,
Lucína, custos quaéque domiturám freta
Tiphýn novam frenáre docuistí ratem,
et tú, profundi saéve dominatór maris,
clarúmque Titan díividens orbí diem,   5
tacitísque praebens cónscium sacrís iubar
Hecaté triformis, quósque iuravít mihi
deós Iason, quósque Medeaé magis
fas ést precari : nóctis aeternaé chaos,
avérsa superis régna manesque ímpios   10
dominúmque regni trístis et dominám fide
melióre raptam, vóce non faustá precor.
nunc, núnc adeste, scéleris ultricés deae,
criném solutis squálidae serpéntibus,
atrám cruentis mánibus amplexaé facem,   15
adéste, thalamis hórridae quondám meis
qualés stetistis : cóniugi letúm novae
letúmque socero et régiae stirpí date.
mihi péius aliquid, quód precer sponsó, manet :
vivát.   per urbes érret ignotás egens   20
exúl pavens invísus incertí laris,
iam nótus hospes límen alienum éxpetat,
me cóniugem optet quóque non aliúd queam
peiús precari, líberos similés patri
similésque matri — párta iam, parta últio est :   25
peperí.   querelas vérbaque in cassúm sero ?
115

non íbo in hostes? mánibus excutiám faces
caelóque lucem — spéctat hoc nostrí sator
Sol géneris, et spectátur, et curru ínsidens
per sólita puri spátia decurrít poli?   30
non rédit in ortus ét remetitúr diem?
da, dá per auras cúrribus patriís vehi,
commítte habenas, génitor, et flagrántibus
ignífera loris tríbue moderarí iuga:
geminó Corinthos lítore opponéns moras   35
cremáta flammis mária committát duo.
hoc réstat unum, prónubam thalamó feram
ut ípsa pinum póstque sacrificás preces
caedám dicatis víctimas altáribus.
per víscera ipsa quaére supplició viam,   40
si vívis, anime, sí quid antiquí tibi
remanét vigoris; pélle femineós metus
et inhóspitalem Caúcasum mente índue.
quodcúmque vidit Póntus aut Phasís nefas,
vidébit Isthmos.   éffera, ignota, hórrida,   45
treménda caelo páriter ac terrís mala
mens íntus agitat: vúlnera et caedem ét vagum
funús per artus — lévia memoraví nimis:
haec vírgo feci; grávior exurgát dolor:
maióra iam me scélera post partús decent.   50
accíngere ira téque in exitiúm para
furóre toto.   pária narrentúr tua
repúdia thalamis: quó virum linqués modo?
hoc quó secuta es.   rúmpe iam segnés moras:
quae scélere parta est, scélere linquenda ést domus.   55

Chorus

Ád regúm thalamós númine próspero
quí caelúm superí quíque regúnt fretum
ádsint cúm populís ríte favéntibus.
prímum scéptriferís cólla Tonántibus
taúrus célsa ferát térgore cándido;   60
Lúcinám niveí fémina córporis
íntemptáta iugó plácet, et ásperi
Mártis sánguineás quaé cohibét manus,
quaé dat bélligerís foédera géntibus
ét cornú retinét dívite cópiam,   65
dónetúr tenerá mítior hóstia.
ét tu, quí facibús légitimís ades,
nóctem díscutiéns aúspice déxtera
húc incéde gradú márcidus ébrio,
praécingéns roseó témpora vínculo.   70
ét tu quaé, geminí praévia témporis,
tárde, stélla, redís sémper amántibus:
té matrés, avidé té cupiúnt nurus
quám primúm radiós spárgere lúcidos.

Víncit vírgineús decor   75
lónge Cécropiás nurus,
ét quas Táÿgetí iugis
éxercét iuvenúm modo
múris quód caret óppidum,
ét quas Áoniús latex   80
Álpheósque sacér lavat.

sí formá velit áspici,
cédent Aésonió duci

próles fúlminis ímprobi
áptat quí iuga tígribus,   85
néc non, quí tripodás movet,
fráter vírginis ásperae,
cédet Cástore cúm suo
Póllux caéstibus áptior.

síc, sic, caélicolaé, precor,   9●
víncat fémina cóniuges,
vír longé superét viros.

Haéc cum fémineó cónstitit ín choro,
úniús faciés praénitet ómnibus.
síc cum sóle perít sídereús decor,   95
ét densí latitánt Pléiadúm greges
cúm Phoebé solidúm lúmine nón suo
órbem círcuitís córnibus álligat.

   *   *   *   *   *   *   *

óstro síc niveús púniceó color
pérfusús rubuít, síc nitidúm iubar   100
pástor lúce nová róscidus áspicit.

éreptús thalamís Phásidis hórridi,
éffrenaé solitús péctora cóniugis
ínvitá trepidús préndere déxtera,
félix Aéoliám córripe vírginem   105
núnc primúm socerís, spónse, voléntibus.
cóncessó, iuvenés, lúdite iúrgio,
hínc illínc, iuvenés, míttite cármina:
rára est ín dominós iústa licéntia.

Cándida thyrsigerí proles generósa Lyaei,   110
múltifidam iam témpus erat succéndere pinum:
éxcute sollemném digitis marcéntibus ignem.
fésta dicax fundát convicia féscenninus,
sólvat turba iocós — tacitis eat ílla tenebris,
sí qua peregrinó nubit fugitíva marito.   115

Medea

Occídimus, aures pépulit hymenaeús meas.
vix ípsa tantum, víx adhuc credó malum.
hoc fácere Iason pótuit, ereptó patre
patria átque regno sédibus solam éxteris
desérere durus?   mérita contempsít mea   120
qui scélere flammas víderat vinci ét mare?
adeóne credit ómne consumptúm nefas?
incérta vaecors ménte vaesaná feror
partés in omnes; únde me ulciscí queam?
utinam ésset illi fráter!   est coniúnx: in hanc   125
ferrum éxigatur.   hóc meis satis ést malis?
si quód Pelasgae, sí quod urbes bárbarae
novére facinus quód tuae ignorént manus,
nunc ést parandum.   scélera te hortentúr tua
et cúncta redeant: ínclitum regní decus   130
raptum ét nefandae vírginis parvús comes
divísus ense, fúnus ingestúm patri
sparsúmque ponto córpus et Peliaé senis
decócta aëno mémbra: funestum ímpie
quam saépe fudi sánguinem, et nullúm scelus   135
iráta feci: móvit infelíx amor.
Quid támen Iason pótuit, alieni árbitri
iurísque factus?   débuit ferro óbvium
offérre pectus — mélius, ah meliús, dolor

furióse, loquere. sí potest, vivát meus,   140
ut fúit, Iason; sí minus, vivát tamen
memórque nostri múneri parcát meo.
culpa ést Creontis tóta, qui sceptro ímpotens
coniúgia solvit quíque genetricem ábstrahit
natís et arto pígnore astrictám fidem   145
dirimít: petatur, sólus hic poenás luat
quas débet. alto cínere cumulabó domum;
vidébit atrum vérticem flammís agi
Maléa longas návibus flecténs moras.
NUTR. Sile, óbsecro, questúsque secreto ábditos   150
mandá dolori. grávia quisquis vúlnera
patiénte et aequo mútus animo pértulit,
reférre potuit: íra quae tegitúr nocet;
proféssa perdunt ódia vindictaé locum.
MED. Levis ést dolor qui cápere consiliúm potest   155
et clépere sese: mágna non latitánt mala.
libet íre contra. NUTR. Síste furialem ímpetum,
alúmna: vix te tácita defendít quies.
MED. Fortúna fortes métuit, ignavós premit.
NUTR. Tunc ést probanda, sí locum virtús habet.   160
MED. Numquám potest non ésse virtutí locus.
NUTR. Spes núlla rebus mónstrat adflictís viam.
MED. Qui níl potest speráre, desperét nihil.
NUTR. Abiére Colchi, cóniugis nulla ést fides
nihílque superest ópibus e tantís tibi.   165
MED. Medéa superest, híc mare et terrás vides
ferrúmque et ignes ét deos et fúlmina.
NUTR. Rex ést timendus. MED. Réx meus fuerát pater.
NUTR. Non métuis arma? MED. Sínt licet terra édita.
NUTR. Moriére. MED. Cupio. NUTR. Prófuge. MED.
      Paenituít fugae.   170

NUTR. Medéa — MED. Fiam. NUTR. Máter es. MED.
  Cui sím vides.
NUTR. Profúgere dubitas? MED. Fúgiam, at ulciscár
  prius.
NUTR. Vindéx sequetur. MED. Fórsan inveniám moras.
NUTR. Compésce verba, párce iam, deméns, minis
animósque minue: témpori aptarí decet.   175
MED. Fortúna opes auférre, non animúm potest.
sed cúius ictu régius cardó strepit?
ipse ést Pelasgo túmidus imperió Creo.

                        CREO

  Medéa, Colchi nóxium Aeetaé genus,
nondúm meis expórtat e regnís pedem?   180
molítur aliquid: nóta fraus, nota ést manus,
cui párcet illa quémve securúm sinet?
abolére propere péssimam ferró luem
equidém parabam: précibus evicít gener.
concéssa vita est, líberet finés metu   185
abeátque tuta.   fért gradum contrá ferox
mináxque nostros própius affatús petit.
arcéte, famuli, táctu et accessú procul,
iubéte sileat.   régium imperiúm pati
aliquándo discat.   váde velocí fuga   190
monstrúmque saevum horríbile iamdudum ávehe.
MED. Quod crímen aut quae cúlpa multatúr fuga?
CR. Quae caúsa pellat, ínnocens muliér rogat.
MED. Si iúdicas, cognósce. si regnás, iube.
CR. Aequum átque iniquum régis imperiúm feras.   195
MED. Iníqua numquam régna perpetuó manent.
CR. I, quérere Colchis. MED. Rédeo: qui avexít, ferat.

Cr. Vox cónstituto séra decretó venit.

Med. Qui státuit aliquid párte inaudita áltera,
aequúm licet statúerit, haud aequús fuit.   200

Cr. Audítus a te Pélia suppliciúm tulit?
sed fáre, causae détur egregiaé locus.

Med. Difficile quam sit ánimum ab ira fléctere
iam cóncitatum quámque regale hóc putet
sceptrís superbas quísquis admovít manus,   205
qua coépit ire, régia didicí mea.

quamvís enim sim cláde miseranda óbruta,
expúlsa supplex sóla deserta, úndique
afflícta, quondam nóbili fulsí patre
avóque clarum Sóle deduxí genus.   210

quodcúmque placidis fléxibus Phasís rigat
Pontúsque quidquid Scýthicus a tergó videt,
palústribus qua mária dulcescúnt aquis,
armáta peltis quídquid exterrét cohors
inclúsa ripis vídua Thermodóntiis,   215
hoc ómne noster génitor imperió regit.

generósa, felix, décore regalí potens
fulsí: petebant túnc meos thalamós proci,
qui núnc petuntur.   rápida fortuna ác levis
praecépsque regno erípuit, exilió dedit.   220

confíde regnis, cúm levis magnás opes
huc férat et illuc cásus — hoc regés habent
magníficum et ingens, núlla quod rapiát dies:
prodésse miseris, súpplices fidó lare
protégere.   solum hoc Cólchico regno éxtuli,   225
decus íllud ingens Graéciae et florem ínclitum,
praesídia Achivae géntis et prolém deum
servásse memet.   múnus est Orpheús meum,
qui sáxa cantu múlcet et silvás trahit,

geminíque munus Cástor et Pollúx meum est   230
satíque Borea quíque trans Pontúm quoque
summóta Lynceus lúmine immissó videt,
omnésque Minyae: nám ducem taceó ducum,
pro quó nihil debétur: hunc nulli ímputo;
vobís revexi céteros, unúm mihi.   235
incésse nunc et cúncta flagitia íngere.
fatébor: obici crimen hoc solúm potest,
Argó reversa.   vírgini placeát pudor
patérque placeat: tóta cum ducibús ruet
Pelásga tellus, híc tuus primúm gener   240
taurí ferocis óre flammanti óccidet.
fortúna causam quaé volet nostrám premat,
non paénitet servásse tot regúm decus.
quodcúmque culpa praémium ex omní tuli,
hoc ést penes te.   sí placet, damná ream;   245
sed rédde crimen.   súm nocens, fateór, Creo:
talém sciebas ésse, cum genua áttigi
fidémque supplex praésidis dextraé petí;
iterúm miseriis ángulum ac sedém rogo
latebrásque viles: úrbe si pellí placet,   250
detúr remotus áliquis in regnís locus.
CR. Non ésse me qui scéptra violentús geram
nec quí superbo míserias calcém pede,
testátus equidem vídeor haud claré parum
generum éxulem legéndo et afflictum ét gravi   255
terróre pavidum, quíppe quem poenae éxpetit
letóque Acastus régna Thessalica óptinens.
senió trementem débili atque aevó gravem
patrém peremptum quéritur et caesí senis
discíssa membra, cúm dolo captaé tuo   260
piaé sorores ímpium auderént nefas.

potést Iason, sí tuam causam ámoves,
suám tueri: núllus innocuúm cruor
contáminavit, áfuit ferró manus
procúlque vestro púrus a coetú stetit.   265
tu, tú malorum máchinatrix fácinorum,
femínea cui nequítia ad audenda ómnia,
robúr virile est, núlla famae mémoria,
egrédere, purga régna, letalés simul
tecum aúfer herbas, líbera civés metu,   270
aliá sedens tellúre sollicitá deos.
MED. Profúgere cogis? rédde fugientí ratem
et rédde comitem — fúgere cur solám iubes?
non sóla veni. bélla si metuís pati,
utrúmque regno pélle. cur sontés duos   275
distínguis? illi Pélia, non nobís iacet;
fugám, rapinas ádice, desertúm patrem
lacerúmque fratrem, quídquid etiam núnc novas
docét maritus cóniuges, non ést meum:
totiéns nocens sum fácta, sed numquám mihi.   280
CR. Iam exísse decuit. quíd seris fandó moras?
MED. Suppléx recedens íllud extremúm precor,
ne cúlpa natos mátris insontés trahat.
CR. Vade: hós paterno ut génitor excipiám sinu.
MED. Per ego aúspicatos régii thalamí toros,   285
per spés futuras pérque regnorúm status,
Fortúna varia dúbia quos agitát vice,
precór, brevem largíre fugientí moram,
dum extréma natis máter infigo óscula,
fortásse moriens. CR. Fraúdibus tempús petis.   290
MED. Quae fraús timeri témpore exiguó potest?
CR. Nullum ád nocendum témpus angustum ést malis.
MED. Parúmne miserae témporis lacrimís negas?

CR. Etsí repugnat précibus infixús timor,
unús parando dábitur exilió dies.   295
MED. Nimis ést, recidas áliquid ex istó licet:
et ípsa propero.   CR. Cápite suppliciúm lues
clarúm priusquam Phoébus attollát diem
nisi cédis Isthmo.   sácra me thalamí vocant,
vocát precari féstus Hymenaeó dies.   300

CHORUS

Audáx nimium qui fréta primus
rate tám fragili perfída rupit
terrásque suas post térga videns
animám levibus credídit auris,
dubióque secans aequóra cursu   305
potuít tenui fidére ligno
intér vitae mortísque vias
nimiúm gracili limíte ducto.

Candída nostri saecúla patres   329
vidére, procul fraudé remota.   330
sua quísque piger litóra tangens
patrióque senex factús in arvo,
parvó dives, nisi quás tulerat
natále solum, non nórat opes: 334
nondúm quisquam sidéra norat,   309
stellísque quibus pingítur aether   310
non érat usus, nondúm pluvias
Hyadás poterat vitáre ratis,
non Óleniae lumína caprae,
nec quaé sequitur flectítque senex
Attíca tardus plaustrá Bootes;   315
nondúm Boreas, nondúm Zephyrus

nomén habebant.

Ausús Tiphys pandére vasto
carbása ponto legésque novas
scribére ventis: nunc lína sinu   320
tendére toto, nunc prólato
pede tránsversos captáre Notos;
nunc ántemnas medió tutas
ponére malo, nunc ín summo
religáre loco, cum iám totos   325
avidús nimium navíta flatus
optát et alto rubicúnda tremunt
sipára velo.   328
bene díssaepti foedéra mundi   335
traxít in unum Thessála pinus
iussítque pati verbéra pontum,
partémque metus fierí nostri
mare sépositum.
dedit ílla graves impróba poenas   340
per tám longos ductá timores,
cum dúo montes, claustrá profundi,
hinc átque illinc subito ímpulsu
velut aétherio gemerént sonitu,
spargéret arces nubésque ipsas
mare déprensum.   345
pallúit audax Tiphýs et omnes
labénte manu misít habenas,
Orpheús tacuit torpénte lyra
ipsáque vocem perdídit Argo.
quid cúm Siculi virgó Pelori,   350
rabidós utero succíncta canes,
omnés pariter solvít hiatus?
quis nón totos horrúit artus

totiéns uno latránte malo?
quid cum Aúsonium diraé pestes   355
vocé canora mare múlcerent,
cum Píeria resonáns cithara
Thracíus Orpheus solitám cantu
retinére rates paené coegit
Siréna sequi? quod fúit huius   360
pretiúm cursus? auréa pellis
maiúsque mari Medéa malum,
mercés prima digná carina.

Nunc iám cessit pontús et omnes
patitúr leges: non Pálladia   365
compácta manu regúmque ferens
inclíta remos quaerítur Argo —
quaelíbet altum cumbá pererrat;
termínus omnis motús et urbes
murós terra posuére nova,   370
nil quá fuerat sedé reliquit
perviús orbis:
Indús gelidum potát Araxen,
Albín Persae Rhenúmque bibunt —
veniént annis saecúla seris,   375
quibus Óceanus vincúla rerum
laxét et ingens pateát tellus
Tethýsque novos detégat orbes
nec sít terris ultíma Thule.

Nutrix

Alúmna, celerem quó rapis tectís pedem?   380
resíste et iras cómprime ac retine ímpetum.
Incérta qualis éntheos gressús tulit

cum iám recepto maénas insanít deo
Pindí nivalis vértice aut Nysaé iugis,
talís recursat húc et huc motu éffero,   385
furóris ore sígna lymphatí gerens.
flammáta facies spíritum ex altó citat,
proclámat, oculos úberi fletú rigat,
renídet : omnis spécimen affectús capit.   389
quo póndus animi vérgat, ubi ponát minas,   391
haerét : minatur aéstuat queritúr gemit.   390
ubi se íste fluctus fránget ?   exundát furor.   392
non fácile secum vérsat aut mediúm scelus ;
se víncet : irae nóvimus veterís notas.
magnum áliquid instat, éfferum immane ímpium :   395
vultúm furoris cérno.   di fallánt metum !

MEDEA

Si quaéris odio, mísera, quem statuás modum :
imitáre amorem.   régias egone út faces
inúlta patiar ?   ségnis hic ibít dies,
tantó petitus ámbitu, tantó datus ?   400
dum térra caelum média libratúm feret
nitidúsque certas múndus evolvét vices
numerúsque harenis dérit et solém dies,
noctém sequentur ástra, dum siccás polus
versábit Arctos, flúmina in pontúm cadent,   405
numquám meus cessábit in poenás furor
crescétque semper — quaé ferarum immánitas,
quae Scýlla, quae Charýbdis Ausoniúm mare
Siculúmque sorbens quaéve anhelantém premens
Titána tantis Aétna fervebít minis ?   410
non rápidus amnis, nón procellosúm mare

Pontúsve Coro saévus aut vis ígnium
adiúṭa flatu póssit imitari ímpetum
irásque nostras: stérnam et evertam ómnia.
    Timuít Creontem ac bélla Thessalicí ducis?   415
amór timere néminem verús potest.
sed césserit coáctus et dederít manus:
adíre certe et cóniugem extremo álloqui
sermóne potuit — hóc quoque extimuít ferox;
laxáre certe témpus immitís fugae   420
generó licebat — líberis unús dies
daṭus ést duobus.   nón queror tempús breve:
multúm patebit.   fáciet hic faciét dies
quod núllus umquam táceat — invadám deos
et cúncta quatiam.   Nutr. Récipe turbatúm malis,   425
era, péctus, animum mítiga.   Med. Sola ést quies,
mecúm ruina cúncta si video óbruta:
mecum ómnia abeant.   tráhere, cum pereás, libet.
Nutr. Quam múlta sint timénda, si perstás, vide:
nemó potentes ággredi tutús potest.   430

Iason

    O dúra fata sémper et sortem ásperam,
cum saévit et cum párcit ex aequó malam!
remédia quotiens ínvenit nobís deus
perículis peióra: si vellém fidem
praestáre meritis cóniugis, letó fuit   435
caput ófferendum; sí mori nollém, fide
miseró carendum.   nón timor vicít fidem,
sed trépida pietas: quíppe sequeretúr necem
prolés parentum.   sáncta si caelum íncolis
Iustítia, numen ínvoco ac testór tuum: 440

natí patrem vicére. quin ipsám quoque,
etsí ferox est córde nec patiéns iugi,
consúlere natis málle quam thalamís reor.
constítuit animus précibus iratam ággredi.
atque écce, viso mémet exiluít, furit,   445
fert ódia prae se: tótus in vultu ést dolor.
MED. Fugímus, Iason: fúgimus — hoc non ést novum,
mutáre sedes; caúsa fugiendí nova est:
pro té solebam fúgere. discedo éxeo,
penátibus profúgere quam cogís tuis: 450
at quó remittis? Phásin et Colchós petam
patriúmque regnum quaéque fraternús cruor
perfúdit arva? quás peti terrás iubes?
quae mária monstras? Póntici faucés freti
per quás revexi nóbilem regúm manum   455
adúlterum secúta per Symplégadas?
parvámne Iolcon, Théssala an Tempé petam?
quascúmque aperui tíbi vias, clausí mihi —
quo mé remittis? éxuli exilium ímperas
nec dás. eatur. régius iussít gener: 460
nihíl recuso. díra supplicia íngere:
meruí. cruentis paélicem poenís premat
regális ira, vínculis onerét manus
clausámque saxo nóctis aeternae óbruat:
minóra meritis pátiar — ingratúm caput,   465
revólvat animus ígneos tauri hálitus
hostísque subiti téla, cum iussú meo   469
terrígena miles mútua caede óccidit;   470
adice éxpetita spólia Phrixei árietis
somnóque iussum lúmina ignotó dare
insómne monstrum, tráditum fratrém neci
et scélere in uno nón semel factúm scelus,

ausásque natas fraúde deceptás mea 475
secáre membra nón revicturí senis:
per spés tuorum líberum et certúm larem, 478
per vícta monstra, pér manus, pro té quibus
numquám peperci, pérque praeteritós metus, 480
per caélum et undas, cóniugi testés mei,
miserére, redde súpplici felíx vicem. 482
aliéna quaerens régna deseruí mea: 477
ex ópibus illis, quás procul raptás Scythae 483
usque á perustis Índiae populís agunt,
quas quía referta víx domus gazá capit, 485
ornámus auro némora, nil exúl tuli
nisi frátris artus: hós quoque impendí tibi;
tibi pátria cessit, tíbi pater, fratér, pudor —
hac dóte nupsi. rédde fugientí sua.
IAS. Perímere cum te véllet infestús Creo, 490
lacrimís meis evíctus exiliúm dedit.
MED. Poenám putabam: múnus ut video ést fuga.
IAS. Dum lícet abire, prófuge teque hinc éripe:
gravis íra regum est sémper. MED. Hoc suadés mihi,
praestás Creusae: paélicem invisam ámoves. 495
IAS. Medéa amores óbicit? MED. Et caedem ét dolos.
IAS. Obícere tandem quód potes crimén mihi?
MED. Quodcúmque feci. IAS. Réstat hoc unum ínsuper,
tuís ut etiam scéleribus fiám nocens.
MED. Tua ílla, tua sunt ílla: cui prodést scelus 500
is fécit — omnes cóniugem infamem árguant,
solús tuere, sólus insontém voca:
tibi ínnocens sit quísquis est pro té nocens.
IAS. Ingráta vita est cúius acceptaé pudet.
MED. Retinénda non est cúius acceptaé pudet. 505
IAS. Quin pótius ira cóncitum pectús doma,

placáre natis.   Med. Ábdico eiuro ábnuo —
meís Creusa líberis fratrés dabit?
Ias. Regína natis éxulum, afflictís potens.
Med. Non véniat umquam tám malus miserís dies   51c
qui próle foeda mísceat prolem ínclitam,
Phoebí nepotes Sísyphi nepótibus.
Ias. Quid, mísera, meque téque in exitiúm trahis?
abscéde quaeso.   Med. Súpplicem audivít Creo.
Ias. Quid fácere possim, lóquere.   Med. Pro me?   vél
    scelus.   515
Ias. Hinc réx et illinc — Med. Ést et his maiór metus:
Medéa. nos conflígere.   certemús sine:
sit prétium Iason.   Ias. Cédo defessús malis.
et ípsa casus saépe iam expertós time.
Med. Fortúna semper ómnis infra mé stetit.   520
Ias. Acástus instat.   Med. Própior est hostís Creo:
utrúmque profuge.   nón ut in socerúm manus
armés nec ut te caéde cognata ínquines
Medéa cogit: ínnocens mecúm fuge.
Ias. Et quís resistet, gémina si bella íngruant,   525
Creo átque Acastus árma si iungánt sua?
Med. His ádice Colchos, ádice et Aeetén ducem,
Scythás Pelasgis iúnge: demersós dabo.
Ias. Alta éxtimesco scéptra.   Med. Ne cupiás vide.
Ias. Suspécta ne sint, lónga colloquia ámputa.   530
Med. Nunc súmme toto Iúppiter caeló tona,
inténde dextram, víndices flammás para
omnémque ruptis núbibus mundúm quate.
nec déligenti téla librentúr manu
vel mé vel istum: quísquis e nobís cadet   535
nocéns peribit, nón potest in nós tuum
erráre fulmen.   Ias. Sána meditari íncipe

et plácida fare. sí quod ex socerí domo
potést fugam leváre solamén, pete.
MED. Contémnere animus régias, ut scís, opes   540
potést soletque; líberos tantúm fugae
habére comites líceat in quorúm sinu
lacrimás profundam.   té novi natí manent.
IAS. Parére precibus cúpere me fateór tuis;
pietás vetat: namque ístud ut possím pati,   545
non ípse memet cógat et rex ét socer.
haec caúsa vitae est, hóc perusti péctoris
curís levamen.   spíritu citiús queam
carére, membris, lúce.   MED. Sic natós amat?
bene ést, tenetur, vúlneri patuít locus. —   550
supréma certe líceat abeuntém loqui
mandáta, liceat últimum amplexúm dare:
gratum ést et illud.   vóce iam extremá peto,
ne, sí qua noster dúbius effudít dolor,
maneánt in animo vérba: meliorís tibi   555
memória nostri sédeat; haec iraé data
oblítterentur.   IAS. Ómnia ex animo éxpuli
precórque et ipse, férvidam ut mentém regas
placidéque tractes: míserias lenít quies.
MED. Discéssit. itane est? vádis oblitús mei   560
et tót meorum fácinorum? excidimús tibi?
numquam éxcidemus. hóc age, omnes ádvoca
virés et artes. frúctus est scelerúm tibi
nullúm scelus putare. víx fraudi ést locus:
timémur. hac aggrédere, qua nemó potest   565
quicquám timere. pérge nunc, aude, íncipe
quidquíd potest Medéa, quidquid nón potest.
    Tu, fída nutrix, sócia maerorís mei
variíque casus, mísera consilia ádiuva.

est pálla nobis, múnus aetheriúm, domus   570
decúsque regni, pígnus Aeetaé datum
a Sóle generis, ést et auro téxtili
moníle fulgens quódque gemmarúm nitor
distínguit aurum, quó solent cingí comae.
haec nóstra nati dóna nubentí ferant,   575
sed ánte diris ínlita ac tincta ártibus.
vocétur Hecate.   sácra letifica áppara:
statuántur arae, flámma iam tectís sonet.

Chorus

Núlla vis flammaé tumidíve venti
tánta, nec telí metuénda torti,   580
quánta cum coniúnx viduáta taedis
        árdet et odit;

nón ubi hibernós nebulósus imbres
Aúster advexít properátque torrens
Híster et iunctós vetat ésse pontes   585
        ác vagus errat;

nón ubi impellít Rhodanús profundum,
aút ubi in rivós nivibús solutis
sóle iam fortí medióque vere
        tábuit Haemus.   590

caécus est ignís stimulátus ira
néc regi curát patitúrve frenos
aút timet mortém: cupit íre in ipsos
        óbvius enses.

párcite, o diví, veniám precamur,   595
vívat ut tutús mare quí subegit.
séd furit vincí dominús profundi
    régna secunda.

aúsus aeternós agitáre currus
ímmemor metaé iuvenís paternae   600
quós polo sparsít furiósus ignes
    ípse recepit.

cónstitit nullí via nóta magno:
váde qua tutúm populó priori,
rúmpe nec sacró, violénte, sancta   605
    foédera mundi.

Quísquis audacís tetigít carinae
nóbiles remós nemorísque sacri
Pélion densá spoliávit umbra,
quísquis intravít scopulós vagantes   610
ét tot emensús pelagí labores
bárbara funém religávit ora
ráptor externí reditúrus auri,
éxitu diró temeráta ponti
    iúra piavit.   615

éxigit poenás mare próvocatum:
Típhys in primís, domitór profundi,
líquit indoctó regimén magistro;
lítore externó, procul á paternis
óccidens regnís tumulóque vili   620
téctus ignotás iacet ínter umbras.
Aúlis amissí memor índe regis
pórtibus lentís retinét carinas
    stáre querentes.

ílle vocalí genitús Camena,   625
cúius ad chordás modulánte plectro
réstitit torréns, siluére venti,
cúm suo cantú volucrís relicto
ádfuit totá comitánte silva,
Thrácios sparsús iacuít per agros,   630
át caput tristí fluitávit Hebro:
cóntigit notám Styga Tártarumque,
    nón rediturus.

strávit Alcidés Aquilóne natos,
pátre Neptunó genitúm necavit   635
súmere innumerás solitúm figuras:
ípse post terraé pelagíque pacem,
póst feri Ditís patefácta regna,
vívus ardentí recubáns in Oeta
praébuit saevís sua mémbra flammis,   640
tábe consumptús geminí cruoris
    múnere nuptae.

strávit Ancaeúm violéntus ictu
saétiger; fratrém, Meleágre, matris
ímpius mactás morerísque dextra   645
mátris irataé. meruére cuncti
mórte quod crimén tener éxpiavit
Hérculi magnó puer ínrepertus,
ráptus, heu, tutás puer ínter undas.
íte nunc fortés peraráte pontum   650
    fónte timendo.

Ídmonem, quamvís bene fáta nosset,
cóndidit serpéns Libycís harenis;
ómnibus veráx, sibi fálsus uni

cóncidit Mopsús caruítque **Thebis.**   655
ílle si veré cecinít futura,
éxul errabít Thetidís maritus.   657
fúlmine et pontó moriéns **Oileus;**   661
. . . patrióque pendet   660
    crímine poenas.

ígne fallací nocitúrus Argis   658
Naúplius praecéps cadet ín profundum;   659
cóniugis fatúm rediméns Pheraei   662
úxor, impendés animám marito.
ípse qui praedám spoliúmque iussit
aúreum primá revehí carina,   665
ústus accensó Peliás aeno
ársit angustás vagus ínter undas.
iám satis, diví, mare víndicastis:
    párcite iusso.

NUTRIX

    Pavet ánimus, horret, mágna perniciés **adest.**   670
immáne quantum augéscit et semét dolor
accéndit ipse vímque praeteritam íntegrat.
vidí furentem saépe et aggressám deos,
caelúm trahentem: máius his, maiús parat
Medéa monstrum.   námque ut attonitó **gradu**   675
evásit et penetrále funestum áttigit,
totás opes effúndit et quidquíd diu
etiam ípsa timuit prómit atque omnem **éxplicat**
turbám malorum, arcána secreta ábdita,
et tríste laeva cómprecans sacrúm manu   680
pestés vocat quascúmque ferventís creat

haréna Libyae quásque perpetuá nive
Taurús cohercet frígore Arctoó rigens,
et ómne monstrum.   trácta magicis cántibus
squamífera latebris túrba desertís adest.   685
hic saéva serpens córpus immensúm trahit
trifidámque linguam exértat et quaerít quibus
mortífera veniat: cármine auditó stupet
tumidúmque nodis córpus aggestís plicat
cogítque in orbes.   'párva sunt' inquít 'mala   690
et víle telum est, íma quod tellús creat:
caeló petam venéna.   iam iam témpus est
aliquíd movere fraúde vulgari áltius.
huc ílle vasti móre torrentís iacens
descéndat anguis, cúius immensós duae,   695
maiór minorque, séntiunt nodós ferae
(maiór Pelasgis ápta, Sidoniís minor)
pressásque tandem sólvat Ophiuchús manus
virúsque fundat; ádsit ad cantús meos
lacéssere ausus gémina Python númina.   700
et Hýdra et omnis rédeat Herculeá manu
succísa serpens, caéde se reparáns sua.
tu quóque relictis pérvigil Colchís ades,
sopíte primum cántibus, serpéns, meis.'

    Postquam évocavit ómne serpentúm genus,   705
congérit in unum frúgis infaustaé mala:
quaecúmque generat ínvius saxís Eryx,
quae fért opertis híeme perpetuá iugis
sparsús cruore Caúcasus Prométhei,
et quís sagittas dívites Arabés linunt   711
pharetráque pugnax Médus aut Parthí leves,   710
aut quós sub axe frígido sucós legunt   712
lucís Suebae nóbiles Hercýniis;

quodcúmque tellus vére nidificó creat
aut rígida cum iam brúma discussít decus   715
nemorum ét nivali cúncta constrinxít gelu,
quodcúmque gramen flóre mortiferó viret,
quicúmque tortis súcus in radícibus
causás nocendi gígnit, attrectát manu.
Haemónius illas cóntulit pestés Athos,   720
has Píndus ingens, ílla Pangaeí iugis
tenerám cruenta fálce deposuít comam;
has áluit altum gúrgitem Tigrís premens,
Danúvius illas, hás per arentés plagas
tepidís Hydaspes gémmifer curréns aquis,   725
noménque terris quí dedit Baetís suis
Hespéria pulsans mária languentí vado.
haec pássa ferrum est, dúm parat Phoebús diem,
illíus alta nócte succisús frutex;
at húius ungue sécta cantató seges.   730
   Mortífera carpit grámina ac serpéntium
saniem éxprimit miscétque et obscenás aves
maestíque cor bubónis et raucaé strigis
exsécta vivae víscera.   haec scelerum ártifex
discréta ponit; hís rapax vis ígnium,   735
his gélida pigri frígoris glaciés inest.
addít venenis vérba non illís minus
metuénda.   sonuit écce vesanó gradu
canítque.   mundus vócibus primís tremit.

MEDEA

Cómprecor vulgús silentum vósque feralés deos   740
ét Chaos caecum átque opacam Dítis umbrosí domum,
Tártari ripís ligatos squálidae Mortís specus.

súpplicis, animaé, remissis cúrrite ad thalamós novos:
róta resistat mémbra torquens, tángat Ixión humum,
Tántalus secúrus undas haúriat Pirénidas.   745
grávior uni poéna sedeat cóniugis soceró mei:
lúbricus per sáxa retro Sísyphum volvát lapis.
vós quoque, urnis quás foratis ínritus ludít labor,
Dánaides, coíte: vestras híc dies quaerít manus. —
núnc meis vocáta sacris, nóctium sidús, veni   750
péssimos indúta vultus, frónte non uná minax.

Tibi móre gentis vínculo solvéns comam
secréta nudo némora lustraví pede
et évocavi núbibus siccís aquas
egíque ad imum mária, et Oceanús graves   755
intérius undas aéstibus victís dedit;
paritérque mundus lége confusa aétheris
et sólem et astra vídit, et vetitúm mare
tetigístis, ursae.   témporum flexí vices:
aestíva tellus flóruit cantú meo,   760
coácta messem vídit hibernám Ceres;
violénta Phasis vértit in fontém vada
et Híster, in tot óra divisús, truces
compréssit undas ómnibus ripís piger.
Sonuére fluctus, túmuit insanúm mare   765
tacénte vento; némoris antiquí domus
amísit umbras, vócis imperió meae
dié reducto; Phoébus in medió stetit
Hyadésque nostris cántibus motaé labant:
adésse sacris témpus est, Phoebé, tuis.   770

tibi haéc cruenta sérta texuntúr manu,
    novéna quae serpéns ligat,

tibi haéc Typhoeus mémbra quae discórs tulit,
    qui régna concussít Iovis.
vectóris istic pérfidi sanguís inest,   775
    quem Néssus expiráns dedit.
Oetaéus isto cínere defecít rogus,
    qui vírus Herculeúm bibit.
piaé sororis, ímpiae matrís, facem
    ultrícis Althaeaé vides.   780
relíquit istas ínvio plumás specu
    Harpyía, dum Zetén fugit.
his ádice pinnas saúciae Stymphálidos
    Lernaéa passae spícula.
sonuístis, arae, trípodas agnoscó meos   785
    favéntc commotós dea.

    Videó Triviae currús agiles,
non quós pleno lucída vultu
pernóx agitat, sed quós facie
lurída maesta, cum Théssalicis   790
vexáta minis caelúm freno
propióre legit.   sic fáce tristem
pallída lucem fundé per auras,
horróre novo terré populos
inque aúxilium, Dictýnna, tuum   795
pretiósa sonent aerá Corinthi.
tibi sánguineo caespíte sacrum
sollémne damus, tibi dé medio
raptá sepulchro fax nócturnos
sustúlit ignes, tibi móta caput   800
flexá voces cervíce dedi,
tibi fúnereo de móre iacens
passós cingit vittá capillos,

tibi iáctatur tristís Stygia
ramús ab unda, tibi núdato   805
pectóre maenas sacró feriam
bracchía cultro.   manét noster
sanguís ad aras: assuésce, manus,
stringére ferrum carósque pati
possé cruores — sacrúm laticem   810
percússa dedi.
quodsí nimium saepé vocari
quererís votis, ignósce precor:
causá vocandi, Perséi, tuos
saepíus arcus una átque eadem est   8, 5
sempér, Iason.
tu núnc vestes tingé Creusae,
quas cúm primum sumpsérit, imas
urát serpens flammá medullas.
ignís fulvo clusús in auro   820
latet óbscurus, quem míhi caeli
qui fúrta luit viscére feto
dedit ét docuit condére vires
arté, Prometheus.   dedit ét tenui
sulphúre tectos Mulcíber ignes,   825
et vívacis fulgúra flammae
de cógnato Phaethónte tuli.
habeó mediae doná Chimaerae,
habeó flammas ustó tauri
guttúre raptas, quas pérmixto   830
fellé Medusae tacitúm iussi
serváre malum.
addé venenis stimulós, Hecate,
donísque meis semína flammae
condíta serva.   fallánt visus   835

tactúsque ferant, meet ín pectus
venásque calor, stillént artus
ossáque fument vincátque suas
flagránte coma nova núpta faces.
  Votá tenentur: ter látratus   840
audáx Hecate dedit ét sacros
edídit ignes face lúcifera.

Perácta vis est ómnis: huc natós voca,
pretiósa per quos dóna nubentí feras.
ite, íte, nati, mátris infaustaé genus,   845
placáte vobis múnere et multá prece
dominam ác novercam.   vádite et celerés domum
reférte gressus, último amplexu út fruar.

CHORUS

  Quonám cruenta maénas
praecéps amore saévo   850
rapitúr?   quod impoténti
facinús parat furóre?
vultús citatus íra
riget ét caput feróci
quatiéns superba mótu   855
regí minatur últro.
quis crédat exulém?

flagránt genae rubéntes,
pallór fugat rubórem,
nullúm vagante fórma   860
servát diu colórem.
huc fért pedes et ílluc,

ut tígris orba nátis
cursú furente lústrat
Gangéticum nemús.   865

frenáre nescit íras
Medéa, non amóres;
nunc íra amorque caúsam
iunxére: quid sequétur?
quando éfferet Pelásgis   870
nefánda Colchis árvis
gressúm metuque sólvet
regnúm simulque réges?
nunc, Phoébe, mitte cúrrus
nulló morante lóro,   875
nox cóndat alma lúcem,
mergát diem timéndum
dux nóctis Hesperús.

NUNTIUS

Periére cuncta, cóncidit regní status.
nata átque genitor cínere permixtó iacent.   880
CHOR. Qua fraúde capti? NUNT. Quá solent regés capi:
donís. CHOR. In illis ésse quis potuít dolus?
NUNT. Et ípse miror víxque iam factó malo
potuísse fieri crédo. CHOR. Quis cladís modus?
NUNT. Avidús per omnem régiae partém furit   885
ut iússus ignis: iám domus tota óccidit,
urbí timetur. CHOR. Únda flammas ópprimat.
NUNT. Et hóc in ista cláde mirandum áccidit:
alit únda flammas, quóque prohibetúr magis,
magis árdet ignis: ípsa praesidia óccupat.   890

Nutrix

Effér citatum séde Pelopeá gradum,
Medéa, praeceps quáslibet terrás pete.

Medea

Egone út recedam? sí profugissém prius,
ad hóc redirem. núptias spectó novas.
quid, ánime, cessas? séquere felicem ímpetum.   895
pars últionis ísta, qua gaudés, quota est?
amás adhuc, furióse, si satis ést tibi
caelébs Iason. quaére poenarúm genus
haut úsitatum iámque sic temét para:
fas ómne cedat, ábeat expulsús pudor;   900
vindícta levis est quám ferunt puraé manus.
incúmbe in iras téque languentem éxcita
penitúsque veteres péctore ex imo ímpetus
violéntus hauri. quídquid admissum ést adhuc,
pietás vocetur. hóc age et faxís sciant   905
quam lévia fuerint quámque vulgarís notae
quae cómmodavi scélera. prolusít dolor
per ísta noster: quíd manus poteránt rudes
audére magnum? quíd puellarís furor?
Medéa nunc sum; crévit ingeniúm malis.   910
    Iuvát, iuvat rapuísse fraternúm caput;
artús iuvat secuísse et arcanó patrem
spoliásse sacro, iúvat in exitiúm senis
armásse natas. quaére materiám, dolor:
ad ómne facinus nón rudem dextram ófferes.   915
    Quo te ígitur, ira, míttis, aut quae pérfido
inténdis hosti téla? nescio quíd ferox

L

decrévit animus íntus et nondúm sibi
audét fateri. stúlta properaví nimis:
ex paélice utinam líberos hostís meus   920
aliquós haberet — quídquid ex illó tuum est,
Creúsa peperit. plácuit hoc poenaé genus,
meritóque placuit: últimum, agnoscó, scelus
animó parandum est — líberi quondám mei,
vos pró paternis scéleribus poenás date.   925
　Cor pépulit horror, mémbra torpescúnt gelu
pectúsque tremuit. íra discessít loco
matérque tota cóniuge expulsá redit.
egone út meorum líberum ac prolís meae
fundám cruorem? mélius, ah, deméns furor!   930
incógnitum istud fácinus ac dirúm nefas
a mé quoque absit; quód scelus miserí luent?
scelus ést Iason génitor et maiús scelus
Medéa mater — óccidant, non súnt mei. —
pereánt? mei sunt; crímine et culpá carent. —   935
sunt ínnocentes: fáteor, et fratér fuit.
quid, ánime, titubas? óra quid lacrimaé rigant
variámque nunc huc íra, nunc illúc amor
didúcit? anceps aéstus incertám rapit;
ut saéva rapidi bélla cum ventí gerunt   940
utrímque fluctus mária discordés agunt
dubiúmque fervet pélagus, haut alitér meum
cor flúctuatur. íra pietatém fugat
irámque pietas — céde pietatí, dolor.
　Huc, cára proles, únicum afflictaé domus   945
solámen, huc vos férte et infusós mihi
coniúngite artus. hábeat incolumés pater,
dum et máter habeat — úrget exilium ác fuga.
iam iám meo rapiéntur avulsi é sinu,

flentés, gementes ósculis — pereánt patri,   950
periére matri. rúrsus increscít dolor
et férvet odium, répetit invitám manum
antíqua Erinys — íra, qua ducís, sequor.
utinám superbae túrba Tantalidós meo
exísset utero bísque septenós parens   955
natós tulissem ! stérilis in poenás fui —
fratrí patrique quód sat est, peperí duos.
   Quonam ísta tendit túrba Furiarum ímpotens?
quem quáerit aut quo flámmeos ictús parat,
aut cuí cruentas ágmen infernúm faces   960
inténtat? ingens ánguis excussó sonat
tortús flagello. quém trabe infestá petit
Megaéra? — cuius úmbra dispersís venit
incérta membris? fráter est, poenás petit —
dabimús, sed omnes. fíge luminibús faces,   965
laniá, perure, péctus en Furiís patet.
   Discédere a me, fráter, ultricés deas
manésque ad imos íre securás iube:
mihi mé relinque et útere hac, fratér, manu
quae strínxit ensem — víctima manés tuos   970
placámus ista. quíd repens affért sonus?
parántur arma méque in exitiúm petunt.
excélsa nostrae técta conscendám domus
caede íncohata. pérge tu mecúm comes.
tuúm quoque ipsa córpus hinc mecum áveham.   975
nunc hóc age, anime: nón in occultó tibi est
perdénda virtus; ápproba populó manum.

IASON

Quicúmque regum cládibus fidús doles,
Concúrre, ut ipsam scéleris auctorem hórridi
Capiámus. huc, huc fórtis armiferí cohors   980
Conférte tela, vértite ex imó domum.
MED. Iam iám recepi scéptra, germanúm, patrem,
spoliúmque Colchi pécudis aurataé tenent;
rediére regna, rápta virginitás redit.
o plácida tandem númina, o festúm diem,   985
o núptialem! váde, perfectum ést scelus;
vindícta nondum: pérage, dum faciúnt manus.
quid núnc moraris, ánime? quid dubitás potens?
iam cécidit ira. paénitet factí, pudet.
quid, mísera, feci? mísera? paeniteát licet,   990
fecí — voluptas mágna me invitám subit,
et écce crescit. dérat hoc unúm mihi,
spectátor iste. níl adhuc factí reor:
quidquíd sine isto fécimus scelerís perit.
IAS. En ípsa tecti párte praecipiti ímminet.   995
huc rápiat ignes áliquis, ut flammís cadat
suís perusta. MED. Cóngere extremúm tuis
natís, Iason, fúnus, ac tumulúm strue:
coniúnx socerque iústa iam functís habent,
a mé sepulti; nátus hic fatúm tulit,   1000
hic té vidente dábitur exitió pari.
IAS. Per númen omne pérque communés fugas
torósque, quos non nóstra violavít fides,
iam párce nato. sí quod est crimén, meum est:
me dédo morti; nóxium mactá caput.   1005
MED. Hac quá recusas, quá doles, ferrum éxigam.
i núnc, superbe, vírginum thalamós pete,

relínque matres. IAS. Únus est poenaé satis.
MED. Si pósset una caéde satiari haéc manus,
nullám petisset. út duos perimám, tamen   1010
nimium ést dolori númerus angustús meo.
IAS. Iam pérage coeptum fácinus, haut ultrá precor,   1014
morámque saltem súpplicis doná meis.   1015
MED. Perfrúere lento scélere, ne properá, dolor:
meús dies est; témpore accepto útimur.
IAS. Infésta, memet périme. MED. Misererí iubes.
bene ést, peractum' est. plúra non habuí, dolor,
quae tíbi litarem. lúmina huc tumida álleva,   1020
ingráte Iason. cóniugem agnoscís tuam?
sic fúgere soleo. pátuit in caelúm via:
squamósa gemini cólla serpentés iugo
summíssa praebent. récipe iam natós, parens;
ego ínter auras áliti currú vehar.   1025
IAS. Per álta vade spátia sublimi aéthere,
testáre nullos ésse, qua veherís, deos.

THE STORY OF HERCULES

Hercules was the son of Jupiter and Alcmena, afterward wife of Amphitryon. The goddess Juno, always jealous of her rivals in Jupiter's affections, was bitterly hostile to Alcmena and her son from the first. As it had been foretold that a child born at a certain time would have the mastery over his neighbors, Juno as Lucina delayed the birth of Hercules and hastened that of Eurystheus, son of Sthenelus, so that the latter was the elder and so master of the other.

Her persecution of the infant Hercules began in his very cradle. Two serpents were sent to destroy him, but the child of a few hours seized them and strangled them to death. When he reached maturity he was made servant to Eurystheus for a certain time and required to perform whatever tasks he might impose. With Juno's aid tasks were assigned which seemed impossible of performance, and these are known as "the twelve labors." They were: (1) killing the Nemean lion; (2) the hydra; (3) capturing the hind of Maenalus; (4) the boar of Erymanthus; (5) cleansing the stables of Augeas; (6) killing the Stymphalian birds; (7) capturing the Cretan bull; (8) the mares of Diomede; (9) the girdle of Hippolyte, queen of the Amazons; (10) Geryon and his cattle; (11) the apples of the Hesperides; (12) the capture of Cerberus.

Besides these assigned labors he performed many voluntary exploits, known as *parerga*, and constituted himself the champion of the oppressed and the foe of tyrants. In this capacity he is represented as bringing about peace and happiness throughout the world.

Meantime he had married Megara, daughter of Creon, king of Thebes, who was left at home with her three children during his absence on the last adventure. While he was in the infernal world Creon and his sons were killed and the royal power usurped by Lycus, an adventurer from Euboea.

At this point begins the action of the play, which is introduced by a soliloquy of Juno's, expressing her disgust at his constant success and resolving to turn his might against himself and so destroy him.

NOTES ON THE HERCULES FURENS

ACT I

Dramatis Personae: In the Greek drama the rule was strictly observed that not more than three speaking characters might appear on the stage at once. The classification here given — which is borrowed from Richter — shows how Seneca probably had the same rule in mind. It was violated constantly by Plautus and Terence in their comedies. All the parts were taken by men, as female actors were unheard of.

SCENE 1 (vv. 1–124). — The goddess Juno expresses her vexation at her husband's infidelity and the honors shown her rivals. Especially is she troubled by the prowess of Hercules, the son of Alcmena, who has overcome every monster that can be sent against him, and even has invaded the lower world and captured its guard, the three-headed dog Cerberus. She resolves to make him his own destroyer, and summons the Furies to her aid.

1. soror: appositive to the subject of *deserui*, 3. — **Tonantis**: Jupiter.

2. nomen: *soror*. She regards her claim to the title of wife as vitiated by her husband's infidelity (cf. Dido's words, Vergil, A. 4. 323): *Hospes, hoc solum nomen quoniam de coniuge restat — Guest, since only this name remains from that of husband.* — **semper alienum:** *always another's lover.* — **Iovem:** this and *templa* are objects of *deserui*. She is leaving her home in heaven.

5. colenda est: sc. *mihi — I must dwell on the earth.* — **paelices:** the mortal women whom Jupiter had loved, and who as constellations had been given place in the skies; she names or describes Callisto (6), Europa (9), the Pleiades (11), Danae (13), Leda (14), Latona (15), Semele (16) and Alcmena (22).

6–15. hinc, hinc, illinc, hinc, hinc: *on this side and on that,* pointing to the constellations which immortalized her rivals. —

153

Arctos: nom. sing. Ursa Major, which according to one account is the translated nymph Callisto, who had been loved by Jupiter Their son Arcas was placed in the heavens with his mother as the constellation Arctophylax. Ursa Major was known to the Greeks very early, and hence is said (7) to *guide the fleet of Argolis.*

8. hinc . . . nitet: *on this side, where the day is lengthened in the early spring, shines the bearer of Tyrian Europa over the seas.* The sun passes out of the zodiacal sign Aries into Taurus about April 20, *when the spring is young.*

9. vector: the snow-white bull which carried off Europa from Sidon to Crete (Ovid, M. 2. 833–875), and by way of reward was made the constellation Taurus.

10. timendum . . . gregem: the Pleiades, daughters of Atlas (called *Atlantides* in 11), three of whom — Maia, Electra and Taygete — had enjoyed the favor of Jove, and were the mothers respectively of Mercury, Dardanus and Lacedaemon. The poet here ascribes to them the malign influence upon the weather which ordinarily belonged to the Hyades (see note on Med. 311), who also were daughters of Atlas. As their times of rising and setting varied with the seasons, and they thus appeared to change position, they are called, in 11, *vagantes.*

11. exerunt: for *exserunt,* the superfluous *s* being omitted after *x.*

12. Orion: for his adventures on earth see Classical Dictionary. As a constellation he is represented as a giant armed with club and sword and continuing in the heavens the pursuit of the Pleiades which he had begun while a mortal. Though not a son of Jupiter, like Arcas, Perseus and the others here mentioned, he is looked upon by Juno as an interloper.

13. *Perseus the golden has his own stars.* The allusion in *suas stellas* may be to the constellation Perseus alone, or to Andromeda with it, as her rescue from the sea-monster was one of his greatest exploits. He was a son of Jupiter and Danae, whom the god visited in a shower of gold (hence *aureus*).

14. Tyndaridae: Castor and Pollux, sons of Jupiter and Leda, known in the heavens as the constellation Gemini, which the ancients always associated with fair weather (*clara signa;* cf. *fratres Helenae, lucida sidera,* Horace, C. 1. 3. 2).

15. quibus: sc. *ii*. Apollo and Diana were the twin children of Jupiter and Latona. As the time of their birth drew near the ever watchful Juno secured from the earth a pledge that she would grant the mother no resting-place. In her distress Latona appealed to the sea, and the island Ortygia, which hitherto had floated beneath the surface of the Aegean, emerged and became stationary (*mobilis tellus stetit*). This island, on account of its having first appeared at this time, was known thenceforth as *Delos* (from δηλῶ, *appear*), and was a favorite resort of the twin deities.

16. Bacchi parens: Semele, translated to the skies by her son.

18. *The universe wears the wreath of the Cretan maid.* This was Ariadne, daughter of Minos. Having saved the life of Theseus by giving him a clew to the windings of the labyrinth, she fled with him and was abandoned on the island Naxos, where she was found and loved by Bacchus. Her bridal wreath (*serta*) was hung in the heavens as the constellation Corona. Thus not only Bacchus and his mother (16) but his mistress, too, had invaded the skies.

20. nuribus: in its wider sense of *women*, with especial reference to Jupiter's favorites.

21. novercam fecit: Juno calls herself the *stepmother* of all the sons of Jupiter who were not her own; of these Bacchus the son of Semele, Amphion and Zethus the sons of Antiope, and Hercules the son of Alcmena all were Thebans. — **escendat:** not merely *mount up to* heaven (which would be *ascendat*), but *rise out of* her proper sphere.

22. The catalogue of Juno's grievances against her faithless husband reaches its climax in the mention of Alcmena, the mother of Hercules. The name here appears in its Greek form Alcmene, for the sake of long ultima. She is *victrix* in the person of her invincible son. Translate, *Though Alcmena, victorious, should . . . hold my place, and her son with her possess the promised stars*, etc.

24. impendit diem: at Hercules' conception the sun, *bidden to keep his brightness sunk in the ocean*, failed to rise at all one day.

27. non sic abibunt: apodosis of *escendat licet* (22) and *occupet* (23). — **odia:** sc. *mea*, and *meus* with *animus* (28).

30. quae bella: sc. *saevus dolor geret*.

32. A striking case of the asyndeton which is so marked a characteristic of Seneca's style (cf. 1260, where six nouns without connectives constitute the line).

33. fractum . . . est: sc. *ab Hercule.* Hercules is to be understood as subject of the verbs that follow — *superat, crescit, fruitur, vertit.* — **crescit malis:** *he thrives upon misfortune.*

34. ira fruitur: cf. *fruitur dis iratis* (Juvenal, Sat. 1. 49), *enjoys the wrath of the gods.* — **in laudes . . . vertit:** *he turns my hate to his own glory* by succeeding in spite of it. Throughout his career Juno was the bitter foe of Hercules, devising for him labors that seemed impossible and doing her utmost to prevent his success.

36. patrem probavi: *I have succeeded only in proving Jove his father.*

38. binos . . . Aethiopas: in the *Odyssey* (1. 22–24) we read of "The Ethiopians, most remote of men. Two tribes there are: one dwells beneath the rising, one beneath the setting sun." — (Bryant's translation.)

40. monstra . . . desunt: the most fearful monsters in the universe — lion, hydra, and now Cerberus — had fallen before him, and the goddess was in despair of finding new ones to take their place.

41. minorque . . . iubere: *'tis a less task for Hercules to do my bidding than for me to bid* (cf. Hercules' own words in Ovid, M. 9. 198: *Defessa iubendo est Iovis coniunx, ego sum indefessus agendo — weary of commanding is Jupiter's wife, but I am unwearied in doing).* — **Herculi:** dat.

43. tyranni: Eurystheus, to whom it was fated that Hercules should be subject for a time. — **violento:** *forceful, mighty.*

45. armatus . . . hydra: after slaying the Nemean lion the hero constantly carried its impenetrable skin as a shield (cf. 797, 1150), while his arrows were poisoned by dipping into the hydra's gall (cf. 1195). Hence he is said in 44 to carry as weapons *what he had feared and afterward defeated.*

47. inferni Iovis: Pluto (cf. *diro Iovi,* 608; *Iovi Stygio,* Vergil A. 4. 638).

48. opima: for *spolia opima* (see 51; and for the origin of the phrase cf. Livy, 1. 10); or perhaps used substantively as in Pliny's panegyric, 17, in the sense *spoils of honor.* — **ad superos:** to the

land of the living as contrasted with the subterranean abode of the
dead (cf. Vergil, A. 6. 481).

50. inferum: gen. plu., here contrasted with *superos*, 48: *I
saw him, myself I saw him, after having riven the darkness of the
underworld and vanquished Pluto, displaying to his father the spoils
of that father's brother.*

51. iactantem: sc. *Herculem*, object of *vidi*. — **patri**: Jupiter,
who was Hercules' father and Pluto's brother (hence *fraterna*, 52).

53. ipsum: Pluto. — **paria sortitum**: in the *Iliad* (15. 184 ff.)
Neptune says : —

> "We are three brothers — Jupiter and I
> And Pluto, regent of the realms below.
> Three parts were made of all existing things,
> And each of us received his heritage.
> The lots were shaken, and to me it fell
> To dwell forever in the hoary deep;
> And Pluto took the gloomy realm of night;
> And, lastly, Jupiter the ample heaven
> And air and clouds." — (Bryant's translation.)

In the same connection the sea-god Neptune claims "rights equal
to Jove's own." His domain repeatedly in these tragedies is called
regna secunda (*e.g.* Med. 598; cf. *secundo sceptro*, 599), and Pluto's
"the third lot" (*tertiae sortis*, 609).

49. foedus: the agreement whereby each of the three domains
was to be inviolable (cf. *foedera mundi*, Med. 606 n.). A son of
Jupiter now had invaded Pluto's kingdom and carried off the
three-headed dog, thus violating the compact.

55. *A way back from deepest Hades has been opened, and the
mysteries of grim death have been revealed*, since Hercules has returned unharmed.

57. ille: Hercules. — **ferox**: *exultant.*

58. superbifica: a word found nowhere else, lit., *pride-creating*,
but perhaps not greatly different in force from *superba.*

59. atrum: an attribute rather of the underworld itself, but
transferred by a common license to persons and things belonging
there (cf. *ater Cocytus*, Horace, C. 2. 14. 17; *furvae Proserpinae*,
Horace, C. 2. 13. 21).

60. At any surpassingly unnatural sight the sun was supposed to hide his face or retrace his course in horror (cf. 941, 1333), notably at the feast of Thyestes (cf. Med. 28 n.).

63. **timui imperasse:** *I was alarmed at having given such command.* All the labors of Hercules were imposed upon him by Eurystheus, but at Juno's suggestion. — **levia:** *trifling* when compared with what may come (cf. Med. 906).

64. **caelo:** *we must fear for heaven itself.* — **summa . . . ima:** Olympus and Hades, the respective abodes of the *di superi* and *di inferi*.

65. **patri:** *Hercules will snatch away the scepter from his father, as he from Saturn.*

66. **lenta:** with *via*. Bacchus had established his divinity by a relatively peaceful conquest, and been admitted to Olympus by the gods. Juno fears that Hercules will force his way thither by violence.

70. **ferendo:** *by bearing it up he has learned that heaven can be overmatched by his strength.* When Hercules, in quest of the apples of the Hesperides, had come to where Atlas stood supporting the heavens, the latter volunteered to procure the golden fruit if Hercules would meantime take his place. The hero consented and received the burden, which he bore with ease; hence, *melius . . . sedit,* 72 (cf. 425, 528, 1101).

72. **melius:** better than on the shoulders of Atlas.

74. **me prementem:** Juno, in heaven, had lent her weight in the hope of crushing the upstart. — **meditantem:** sc. *Herculem.*

75. **Perge, ira, perge :** *on, wrath, on! Crush him as he meditates great plans! Meet him! Tear him yourself with your own hands! Why do you commit the satisfaction of such hate (to any one else)?*

77. **ferae:** the monsters overcome (see the labors detailed, 222–248).

78. **vacet:** *be relieved* of his precarious mastery over Hercules. For Eurystheus see 43 n. — **fessus:** cf. 41 n., especially the quotation from Ovid.

79. **Titanas:** the sons of Caelus and Terra (Heaven and Earth), who overthrew their father and set up in his place the youngest of their number, Kronos or Saturn. Later the majority of the Titans, including descendants of the original twelve, supported

Jupiter in his successful attempt to dethrone Saturn. Only the
family of Iapetus, embracing Prometheus, Epimetheus and their
descendants, dared oppose him, and it is to them that reference
is made here.

80. laxa: imperative. — **Siculi verticis:** Mt. Aetna.

81. tellus . . . Doris: Sicily, which was colonized largely by
Dorians from Corinth. — **gigante:** Enceladus, who, in his flight
after the defeat of the giants in their attack on Jupiter, was buried
under the island of Sicily, cast upon him by Minerva (cf. Med.
410 n., where he is called a Titan; Vergil, A. 3. 578–582). Hercules
had been Jupiter's ally on that occasion; hence *vicit ista*, 83. — **tremens:** cf. Vergil, A. 3. 581: (*Fama est) fessum quotiens mutet
latus, intremere omnem . . . Trinacriam — The story is that whenever
he turns his weary body, all Sicily shakes.* — **monstri:** Enceladus.

85. bella . . . gerat: an intimation of Juno's plan, serving to
make the hero's madness the natural climax of the plot and to give
unity to the whole. *Do you seek a match for Hercules? There is
none but himself; then let him wage war with himself.*

89–91. The speaker apostrophizes Hercules.

91. fugisse: sc. *te* as subject. — **hic:** *here, on earth.*

93. discordem deam: Furor, the personification of madness
(see 98), corresponding to Lyssa, introduced by Euripides as an
acting character in his *Herakles Mainomenos*, which most likely
was Seneca's immediate model. Farnabius suggests that *deam*
refers to the fury Megaera (102), and this is consistent with the
idea in 94, *whom a great cavern of the mountain, set over her, guards*,
for in an Orphic hymn the Furies are represented as dwelling in
caverns near the waters of the Styx.

96. quidquid relictum est: *whatever is left* in Hades since Cerberus has been dragged forth. — **Scelus, Impietas, Error, Furor:**
personifications summoned as more terrible than any concrete
being (cf. Vergil's description of the horrid forms met at the
entrance to the infernal world, A. 6. 273–281). All these now
are to assail the hero and contribute to the horror of his obsession
and his crime

98. in se armatus: *Madness, ever armed against itself.* Here,
as in 85, we have an intimation of the form Juno's vengeance was
to take.

100. famulae Ditis: the Furies — Alecto, Megaera, Tisiphone.

101. pinum: the blazing torch carried by each Fury (cf. *trabem,* 103). — **agmen:** *company,* a term often used in speaking of the three sisters.

103. rogo: a torch taken from a funeral pyre would be of evil omen, and hence appropriate to the fiendish work now contemplated (cf. *de medio rapta sepulchro fax,* Med. 798; *faces de funere raptas,* Ovid, M. 6. 430).

104. hoc agite: *this do,* to the exclusion of all else (cf. Med. 562 n.).

105. pectus, mentem: *your heart and mind.* — **excoquat:** the subject is *ignis.*

107. animo captus: *possessed, maddened.* — **ut possit . . . insaniendum est:** for both thought and form cf. Horace's dictum, A.P. 102: *Si vis me flere dolendum est primum ipsi tibi — If you would have me weep, you first must grieve yourself.*

110. sorores: not *my sisters,* but *ye sisters three* — the Furies.

112. dignum noverca: cf. *vota te digna,* 1038, said by Hercules to the same goddess Juno. The cruelty of a stepmother was proverbial. — **vota mutentur:** hitherto her desire has been to effect Hercules' destruction; now it is that he may live to return and meet a more fearful fate.

114. manu fortis: *strong of hand* to do the deed I purpose for him. — **inveni:** perfect tense.

116. cupiat mori: see 1245, 1263, 1278.

117. hic: the adverb.

119. tela: the shafts that were to be aimed at his children (991 ff.). — **librabo manu:** *I will aim the arrows with my own hand.*

122. genitor: *though when the crime is done his father may admit those hands to heaven* (cf. *promissa astra occupet,* 23; *astra promittit pater,* 959).

124. croceo: a stock poetic epithet of dawn (cf. Vergil, A. 4. 585).

SCENE 2 (vv. 125–204). — The chorus describes the approach of day and is led to think of the various activities to which men awake, and so to speak of the last daring labor of Hercules. It closes with a eulogy of a life spent in repose and retirement. The measure is the anapestic dimeter.

125. **rara:** fewer stars are visible as the daylight brightens. —
prono: *descending*, describing the western sky where the stars are
setting (cf. Ovid, M. 2. 67: *ultima prona via est*).

126. **languida:** *growing dim.* — **vagos** . . . **ignes:** the plan-
ets.

128. **Phosphoros:** a Greek noun in nom. sing.   Both this word
and its Latin synonym *Lucifer* have the literal meaning *light-
bringer*, and refer to the morning star, which, immediately preceding the advancing sun, *brings up the rear* (*cogit . . . agmen*) of the
starry host as it retreats.

129. **signum:** *Ursa Major*, often thought of as a wagon on account of the figure outlined by its brightest stars (see note on Med.
315).   This accounts for *temone*, 131.

131. **verso temone:** in its apparent revolution about the pole.

133. **Titan:** the sun, as often (cf. Med. 5). — **Oeta:** Mt. Oeta
was not east but west from Thebes, where the scene of this play
is laid, and was more than sixty miles distant.   In Herc. Oet. 1440
it is called *cubile noctis*.   No doubt its inconsistent introduction
here as the scene of the sun's rising is due to its constant and close
association with the life and death of Hercules.   We must not
scrutinize too closely a poet's geography — or history either.

134. *Now the thickets famed for the bacchantes, daughters of Cadmus, flooded with daylight are blushing.*   Mt. Cithaeron is meant,
which Ovid (M. 3. 702) calls *Cithaeron, electus facienda ad sacra
— set apart for celebrating the rites (of Bacchus).* — **Bacchis:** the
bacchantes, Agave, etc.

136. **soror:** Phoebe, the moon goddess. — **reditura:** to return
at night.

137. **labor:** the day's toil for men.

139. Observe the quantities and agreement of the words ending
in *a* — *gelida, cana, pruina, pabula.*

140. **dimisso:** from the fold, where they had been kept over-
night.

142. **nondum rupta:** by the growth of horns (cf. *nondum cornibus
findens cutem*, Tro. 538; *frons turgida cornibus*, Horace, C. 3.
13. 4).

143. *The kine at leisure fill again (with milk) their udders,* which
were drained this morning.

146–149. *The nightingale, shrill-voiced, hangs upon the topmost boughs and yearns, amid her chirping young, to spread her wings to the new morning.*

149. **Thracia paelex:** the nightingale. Philomela, fleeing with her sister Procne from the latter's husband Tereus, was changed into a nightingale (Ovid, M. 6. 667–670). — **turba . . . confusa sonat:** cf. Chaucer, *Parlament of Foules*, 190 ff.

154. **hic:** a fisherman.

156. **instruit:** *either rebaits his hooks, robbed of their lure (deceptos), or excitedly (suspensus) gazes upon his catch, his hand closed tight upon it.*

158. **linea:** nom.

159. **haec:** sc. *agunt ii — these are the occupations of those who enjoy the tranquil repose of a guileless life and a home that is happy with a little, all its own.* For *laeta . . . parvo,* cf. Horace, C. 3. 16. 43.

162. With this the chorus now contrasts the complicated life of the city. Note in 164–173 the precise alternation of demonstratives — *ille, hic, illum, hic,* and cf. Med. 720–725.

164. **ille:** the courtier or client. — **superbos aditus regum:** cf. Horace, Epod. 2. 7: *superba civium potentiorum limina — the proud thresholds of the more influential citizens.*

165. **expers somni:** clients at Rome in Seneca's day rose very early in order to be among the first in paying their respects to their patrons (cf. Juvenal, 5. 19: *Trebius . . . is worried lest the whole throng of clients may have finished the round of visits while the stars are just growing faint, or even at midnight;* also 3. 126–130).

166. **hic:** the miser. — **beatas:** cf. *beatis gazis,* Horace, C. 1. 29. 1.

167. **inhians:** cf. *saccis indormis inhians,* Horace, S. 1. 1. 70.

168. Cf. Horace, C. 3. 16. 28: *magnas inter opes inops.*

169. **illum:** the politician.

170. *The mob, more changeful than the sea* (cf. *mobilium turba quiritium,* Horace, C. 1. 1. 7).

171. **tumidum:** *puffed up —* acc. agreeing with *illum.*

172. **hic:** the advocate. — **clamosi . . . fori:** cf. Pliny's description of the centumviral court, Epist. 2. 14.

173. **vendens:** originally at Rome an advocate received no fee for his services, but felt he was rewarded by the devotion and political support of his client. In time this custom was modified by the offering and accepting of gifts, and finally pleading became a profession which many entered for the sake of gain (see Quintilian's discussion of the proper charge, I.O. 12. 7. 8–12). — **iras . . . locat:** *offers for hire his words and his emotions.*

176. tempora numquam reditura: a thought which is common in all of Seneca's writings, *e.g.* Brev. Vitae, 8. 5; cf. 182 below.

177. dum . . . laeti: Horace's philosophy exactly, *e.g.* C. 1. 9. 13–18; 2. 3. 13–16, and often.

180. rota: nom., *cycle.*

181. peragunt: *carry through to the end.* — **pensa:** tasks assigned for spinning, here with reference to the thread of life spun by the Fates. — **sorores:** the three Fates, not the Furies as in 110. The Fates, while hard (*durae*) and implacable, were not malicious like the Furies.

185. quaerimus: alluding to Hercules' invasion of the lower world, as is seen from what follows.

187. properas . . . visere: *i.e.* before your time. — **maestos:** the same epithet is applied to the *manes* in 647, and is used often by Vergil in the sixth book of his *Aeneid.*

189. iusso: *when summoned.*

190. scriptum: *appointed*; lit., *written* in the book of fate.

191. urna: a change of figure. Horace (C. 2. 3. 26 ff.; 3. 1. 16) represents the Fates as shaking an urn in which is a lot for every living man, who must die when his lot falls out. According to Vergil (Aen. 6. 432) it is Minos the judge who shakes the urn.

192 ff. A favorite theme with the author of these tragedies (*e.g.* Oed. 882–913; Ag. 57–107; Oct. 379–386): *Let glory hand down another to many lands, and prattling fame praise him throughout the cities and extol him as on a plane with the sky and the stars.*

198. pigros: *unambitious* (cf. Med. 331).

199. *In lowly sphere, yet safe, abides the mean lot of the dweller in a cottage.*

201. alte: *far.* The idea is either "from a great height" or "to a great depth." — **animosa:** *high-spirited, ambitious.* For the thought cf. Horace, C. 2. 10. 9–12: *'Tis the great pine that is shaken oftener by the winds, and lofty towers fall with a heavier crash, and thunderbolts smite the mountain tops.*

203. parvum gregem: her three small children. The acc. may be regarded as the object of *comitata* deponent, or an imitation (with *comitata* passive) of the construction with *induta*. — **Megara:** nom., here scanned with long *a* in the ultima, as a Greek noun.

204. Alcidae parens: Amphitryon, who was the husband of Alcmena and putative father of Hercules. In the *Amphitryon* of Plautus, where the dramatic time is before the birth of Hercules, Amphitryon is represented as a strong and vigorous warrior; here he is old and relatively feeble.

ACT II

SCENE 1 (vv. 205–278). — Amphitryon reviews the labors of Hercules, laments his absence on the desperate quest of Cerberus, and prays for his safe return.

207. cladi: this, like *aerumnis*, refers to the evil fate that allowed Hercules no peace or repose.

209. futuri: used instead of *alterius*, which we should expect as correlative to *alterius* in 208. The end of one misfortune only marks the approach of its successor. — **reduci:** the adjective, as shown by *ŭ*; sc. *Herculi*.

211. contingat . . . meat: sc. *Hercules.*

213. dum iubetur: the brief interval in which he is receiving his new orders. — **a primo:** *from his very birth.* As is told in the following verses, two serpents were sent by Juno to destroy the infant Hercules, but were seized by him and strangled to death.

216. cristati caput: *crested as to head, with crested head.*

218. reptabat: frequentative for simple verb, common in the Silver Age.

219. remisso lumine: *with eye not strained* by fear, *i.e. with fearless gaze and calm.*

221. *Crushing their swelling necks with tender hand.*

222. Cf. the review of the twelve labors by the chorus, 527–546 (Ag. 808–866; Ovid, M. 9. 182–199). The order is given variously by various authors, but the numbers assigned the labors in these notes are those of Apollodorus. — **prolusit hydrae:** *practiced beforehand for his battle with the great serpent, the hydrae* (cf. *proludens*

fatis, Tro. 182; *prolusit per ista*, Med. 907). *Hydrae* is dat. —
fera: the third labor was the taking alive of the hind of Mt. Maenalus, which was sacred to Diana. The chase lasted a year and extended as far as the upper Danube, but was finally successful. The
hind had horns of gold and hoofs of brass.

225. leo: the first labor. As the lion's skin was impenetrable,
Hercules killed it by strangling (*pressus lacertis*).

226. Bistonii gregis: the eighth labor was to bring the man-
eating mares of Diomede, king of the Thracian Bistones (not the
Homeric hero), to Mycenae. The king had been in the habit of
feeding these animals with the flesh of strangers who entered his
land. Hercules overcame him and made him the victim of his
own custom (227).

229. suem: the boar of Erymanthus — the fourth labor. *Suem*
is modified by *solitum* and *hispidum* in the preceding line as well
as by *Maenalium* here. This verse is notable for its large proportion of short syllables, the scheme being, —

$$\_ \; \acute{\cup} \cup \; | \; \cup \cup \cup \; | \; \cup \acute{\cup} \cup \; | \; \cup \_ \; | \; \cup \cup \acute{\diagup} \; | \; \cup \cup.$$

230. taurum: the seventh labor. A mad bull which had been
ravaging Crete was brought by Hercules to Mycenae and there
released. — **centum . . . populis:** dat. The island of Crete,
early settled and thickly populated, often is called "the land of
a hundred cities" (*e.g. urbibus centum spatiosa Crete*, Tro. 820; cf.
Phaed. 150; H.O. 27). In the *Odyssey* (19. 174) it is ninety.

231. greges: as his tenth labor the hero sought the scarlet
cattle of Geryon, the three-bodied monster who dwelt on the island
of Erytheia in the western ocean (*occasu ultimo*). Having found
the object of his search he slew the giant keeper (*pastor triformis*),
and with many adventures drove the cattle through Spain and
Gaul, Illyricum and Thrace, to Mycenae.

234. pavit: from *pasco*. As his course naturally would take
him through Boeotia, his cattle are said here to have grazed upon
the Boeotian mountain. *Cithaeron* is subject and *pecus* object of
pavit.

235. solis . . . plagas: Apollodorus (2. 5. 10) tells us that Hercules came to the place of the sun's setting and obtained from
him the use of the golden bowl in which as in a boat he crossed the
western sea. Of course the next verse — *the parched realms which*

the midday sun scorches — would naturally suggest the south, but 237 fixes the scene of this adventure at Gibraltar, and reminds us that the places of sunrise and sunset were thought of as exposed to the sun's greatest heat (cf. 38 n.).

237. There is a myth to the effect that in the earliest times there was no communication between the Mediterranean Sea and the ocean, and that the passage now known as the Strait of Gibraltar was made by Hercules' tearing of the mountains asunder (Pliny, N.H., proem. to 3). With this compare the similar exploit in opening the Vale of Tempe (283–288).

240. spolia: the golden apples of the Hesperides — the eleventh labor. They were guarded by a sleepless dragon (*vigilis serpentis*).

241. Lernae monstra: the hydra — second labor. The plural *monstra* and the words *numerosum malum* allude to the creature's having had nine heads and to the fact that when one was lopped off two sprang up in its place. By searing the wound (*igne*, 242) as each was cut off the hero finally was able to check the multiplication and *teach it to die.*

243. condere: complement of *solitas.* The killing of these birds was the sixth labor.

244. petit: perfect, contracted from *petiit*, as often in these tragedies (cf. *adit*, 321; *perit*, Med. 994, etc.).

245. caelibis . . . tori: gen. of quality. The same idea is repeated in *vidua* (246; cf. *viduis gentibus*, 542), which means no more nor less than *unmarried*, not necessarily *widowed.* The ninth labor was the obtaining of the girdle worn by Hippolyte, queen of the Amazons, who dwelt beside the Thermodon River (cf. Med. 214).

247. ad . . . facinus: after *audaces — bold for every glorious deed.* Note the antithesis between *clarum* and *turpis* (248).

248. Cleansing the stables of Augeas was the fifth labor.

249. orbe defenso: the same phrase recurs in 633. — **caret:** after having defended the world from these monsters and the oppression of many tyrants, whose destruction constituted his numerous *parerga* or *side-labors*, Hercules himself is banished from it and sent to the underworld.

251. rursus: as before his achievements.

252. virtus: predicate. The reference is to Lycus' successful usurpation, as is shown in what follows.

255. natos: the sons of Creon, king of Thebes and father of Megara.

256. ipsumque: Creon.

257. capiti decus: the crown.

259. ferax deorum: Bacchus, Amphion, Hercules (cf. 21 n.). — **quem:** for *qualem*, used contemptuously of Creon (cf. *sordido iugo*, 267; *tremitis ignavum exulem*, 269). Though Lycus was a son of Neptune, he speaks of himself (338) as being of lowly origin as compared with Megara, who was a descendant of Cadmus, characterized in 256 as *nobilis*.

261. iuventus: the *terrigenae,* who sprang full-armed from the earth on the sowing of the dragon's teeth by Cadmus (Ovid, M. 3. 101 ff.).

262. In the days of Cadmus, its founder, Thebes had no fortifications. Amphion charmed the stones with his music and led them to their places, and so reared the walls (Ovid, M. 6. 178).

264. non semel: *not once,* but often (cf. 20) — a common litotes.

265. haec: sc. *terra,* from 259, antecedent of *cuius* in 260, 262, 264.

266. fecit: *has given birth to gods;* so *faciet,* 267. For a different sense of *facere deos,* cf. Oct. 449, where Nero says: *Stulte verebor, ipse cum faciam, deos — I shall be foolish to reverence the gods, when I create them myself,* i.e. *when I can decree the deification of whom I will.*

267. sordido: *mean, degrading,* because imposed by the low-born Lycus.

268. Ophionium genus: descendants of Ophion, one of the *terrigenae.*

269. exulem: the same term is repeated in 274. It refers to Lycus, who was a native of Euboea (cf. *suis carentem finibus,* 270; Euripides, H.F. 32).

271. qui: the antecedent is *Hercules,* subject of *servit* and of *fert,* 273.

272. Agreements can be determined by scansion.

273. servit: sc. *Eurysthei.* — **quae . . . vetat:** oppression (cf. 272, 249 n.).

275. The subject of *tenebit* is *Lycus;* of the next five verbs *Hercules*.

276. **ad astra:** not *to heaven*, but from the darkness of the underworld to the light of the stars which shine on the earth (cf. note on *ad superos*, 48, and Shakespeare's "glimpses of the moon," Hamlet, 1. 4. 53).

277. **adsis:** an apostrophe to the absent hero.

278. Note the alliteration and cf. Med. 360 n.

Scene 2 (vv. 279–331). — Megara, the wife of Hercules, unites with Amphitryon in bewailing the woes of their house and country and the absence of their natural defender.

280. **tenebras:** the darkness of Hades. — **retro via:** cf. 55 n.

281. **orbe diducto:** abl. abs., *rend the earth asunder and return*.

283. **dirutis . . . iugis:** it was a common belief that originally the Vale of Tempe was separated from the sea by the range of which Olympus and Ossa are peaks, and that some terrific convulsion of nature cleft the barrier and so gave the Peneus River an outlet. Here and often the change is ascribed to Hercules. In his *Naturales Quaestiones* Seneca gives this (6. 25. 2): " If you care to believe it, they say that Olympus once was attached to Ossa, then was separated from it by an earthquake and the one great mountain cleft in two. Then the Peneus found an outlet, and dried up the marshes under which Thessaly had labored, draining their water into itself." For another like exploit of Hercules see 237 n.

284. **praeceps:** adverbial modifier of *citato — the headlong-rushing river*. — **flumini:** the Peneus; so *Thessalus torrens*, 288.

290. **terminos:** object of *efferens*. Its meaning may be literally the physical boundary between the living and the dead (cf. 280–283), or, figuratively, the limitations imposed on man's activity by nature and precedent.

293. **lucisque pavidos:** cf. Cerberus' fear of the unfamiliar light, 814. — **populos:** the races of dead men.

294. **indigna . . . est:** the great labors imposed on Hercules had usually been accompanied by incidental voluntary exploits (see Cl. Dict., artt. "Antaeus," "Busiris," "Cacus," etc.). These were called *parerga* (see note on *caret*, 249).

296. illum . . . diem: object of some verb understood, perhaps *petam* or *exspectem* (cf. Horace, S. 2. 5. 102: *Unde mihi tam fortem tamque fidelem — Where shall I seek one so strong and so faithful?*) So here, *Whence shall I seek that day on which I may clasp thee?*

298. nec . . . memores: with *reditus, thy return, tardy and forgetful of me.*

299. deorum ductor: Jupiter, to whom the appropriate sacrifice was a white bull which had never been " broken " to work (*indomiti*). — **ferent colla:** *shall yield their hundred throats* — a hecatomb is promised.

300. frugum potens: Ceres or Demeter, goddess of growth in nature. Her special worship was celebrated at the Attic village of Eleusin, and came to be one of the most famous cults of antiquity (see 844 n.). For many centuries it was considered a high privilege to receive initiation into the " Eleusinian mysteries." The revelation of any of the secrets of the initiation was visited with vengeance of the gods (hence *secreta sacra, muta fide, Eleusin tacita;* cf. *sacris gaudens tacitis Eleusin,* Tro. 843). Hercules had sought initiation before setting out on his last labor.

302. longas: alluding to the great procession of torch-bearing initiates (see 838 ff.).

303. fratribus: the sons of Creon, slain by Lycus (254 ff.).

304. ipsum: here as in 256 refers to Creon.

305. maior: *greater than yourself.* — **te:** object of *tenet.*

306. sequimur: to death; present for future, after the analogy of *ire.*

308. Her speech ends in a wail of despair.

313. nimis: with *volunt,* as with *metuunt* in 314.

318. ad superos: as in 48.

319. quam: the antecedent is *viam.* — **plagam:** *the desert;* perhaps to be compared with *solis aestivi plagas,* 235. In this and the following verses are gathered a group of Hercules' adventures in or near Africa.

321. adit: perfect (cf. *petit,* 244 n.); *the way he had when he went through the burning desert and the sands surging like a stormy sea, and through the sea twice ebbing and twice flowing; and when, caught in the shoals of the Syrtes, he came to a standstill, and leaving his vessel aground overpassed the seas on foot.*

323. **Syrtium:** a famous reach of quicksands north of Africa (Pliny, N.H. 5. 4; Vergil, A. 1. 111, 146).

324. **fixā:** with *puppe*. — **pedes:** nom. sing.

330. *Such in gait as he is in spirit.*

SCENE 3 (vv. 332–523). — The tyrant Lycus, feeling the disadvantage of his low origin, proposes to marry Megara, whose high birth would add strength to his position. On her spirited refusal he threatens her and hers with destruction.

333. *All that slanting Phocis bounds with its rich lands.*

334. **obliqua:** suggested by the sinuosities of its coast. See the map.

337. *Though master (by usurpation) of all these regions, I have not the ancient rights of an ancestral line (patriae domus).* The same thought is continued in the next two lines.

339. **titulis:** a Roman word and idea, hence an anachronism here. — **clara virtus:** *I have not birth, but brilliant courage.*

340. **qui . . laudat:** this idea is developed at length and illustrated in Juvenal's eighth satire.

341. **rapta:** *power usurped is held with trembling hand, i.e.* in constant fear of losing it by another revolution or by assassination.

343. **scias:** the " general " second person — *what you know you keep against your subjects' will, the sword protects.*

345. **haut:** *haud.* — **una:** with *Megara* — *only Megara.* This plan of Lycus to strengthen himself by means of a marriage with the Theban princess is not found in Euripides. It may be an invention of the Latin author, or he may have borrowed it from some intervening version.

348. **novitas:** probably suggested to Seneca by his familiarity with the suspicion the Roman patricians had of any *novus homo* who rose to prominence.

351. **stat:** *my determination is fixed.* — **tollere:** as he already had destroyed King Creon and his sons (254–258).

352. *Will the people's hate and comment check the deed?*

353. Cf. Oed. 703: *Odia qui nimium timet regnare nescit* — *he knows not how to reign who too much fears men's hatred.* The line as it stands involves an unusual hiatus, but no sure emendation has been offered.

354. *Then let me try, since chance has given me opportunity* (*locum*, as in Med. 160). It is at this point that he first sees Megara, his speech thus far having been soliloquy.

356. velata: *her head veiled* (*veiled as to her head*) *with the dismal covering of her raiment*, as it is not unheard of to-day for a woman to throw her apron over her head in her grief. — **praesides**: *protecting*.

357. verus sator: the usurper was very willing to think of Hercules as mortal, and therefore calls Amphitryon his *true father*.

359. novi: partitive with *quidnam*. — **trahens**: *deriving, inheriting*.

364. *The victors retain, the vanquished prepare their weapons*, for a renewal of the conflict.

365. relinquent: the future indicative in the conclusion after the subjunctive condition represents the result as more imminent and vivid (cf. Med. 238–241).

366. tectis: dat. after *subdita*.

368. reduci: contrast this passive infinitive with the adjective of like spelling in 209, and note the quantity of the *u*. — **expedit**: *it is expedient*.

369. regno: the rare dat. with *particeps*. — **veni**: imperative.

371. He offers her his hand, which she refuses to touch.

. **372. Egone ut contingam**: a question of surprise and horror, *Am I to touch that hand ?* (cf. *egone ut recedam*, Med. 893).

374. *Sooner will the sun reverse his course!*

376. *And Scylla unite the Sicilian to the Italian shore*, at the Strait of Messina, where Scylla and Charybdis were supposed to lurk on opposite sides.

378. Euripus: the strait between Euboea and the mainland of Greece. Its waters were constantly shifting the direction of their flow, under the influence of various winds and currents, and the ancients had the idea that the tide there ebbed and flowed (*vicibus alternis*, 377) seven times each day (Tro. 838; H.O. 779 : "Euripus shifts its wandering waters, and rolls up seven tides and ebbs as often"). Livy (28. 6. 10) gives this more rational account of it: "The strait of Euripus does not ebb and flow, as the story goes, seven times a day at stated hours, but as the sea turns now in this direction, now in that after the fashion of the wind, it hurries along like a torrent rolling down a precipitous mountain side. Thus no rest is given vessels sailing there, either night or day."

382. odium tui: *my hate of you!* appositive to *res*, 380. — **quod . . . doleo:** Farnabius gives two suggestions as to the meaning of this: (1) that Megara wishes the universal hatred of Lycus might be concentrated in herself, so that her loathing of him might be adequate; and (2) that she grieves over the oppression of her people, which arouses them to hatred and may bring down further wrath upon them.

383. *How small a part of it is mine!* For *quota*, cf. Med. 896 n.

385. *Pride goeth before destruction.*

386. novi: from *nosco.* — **quid . . . scelᵔra:** *why should I name the (Theban) matrons who have dared or suffered wrong?* — Ino, Agave, etc.

388. coniugis, nati, patris: by his marriage with Jocasta Oedipus became his mother's husband and his own stepfather — hence *husband, son and father* (cf. Oed. 1009, 1039).

389. fratrum: Eteocles and Polynices, sons of Oedipus and Jocasta. Polynices, deprived of his rights by his brother, returned with the hosts of the "seven against Thebes" (*bina castra*). When all the other leaders were slain the war was ended by a single combat between the two brothers, in which each killed the other. Their mutual hatred was so implacable that when their bodies were laid on the pyre for burning the very flames parted, and consumed the bodies separately (*totidem rogos*); cf. Statius, Theb. 12. 429 ff.: "Behold, the brothers again! When the devouring flame touched their bodies the pile quivered and the newcomer was thrust from the pyre. The flames surged with divided crest."

390. riget . . . Tantalis: Niobe, daughter of Tantalus and wife of Amphion, tauntingly contrasted her family of seven sons and seven daughters (cf. Med. 954–956 n.) with Latona's two, Apollo and Diana. To avenge the insult to his mother Apollo with his arrows shot to death all the children of Niobe, and she in her grief hardened (*riget*) into a rock down whose face trickled (*manat*) "tears" of spring water (Ovid, M. 6. 301–312). Mt. Sipylus in Phrygia, presenting from one point of view the rude outline of a woman's form, used to be pointed out as the petrified Niobe.

392–394. Cadmus finally left the Thebes which he had founded, became king of Illyricum, and at last both he and his wife Harmonia were transformed into serpents (Ovid, M. 4. 563–603).

394. notas: the mark of a serpent's body dragged on the ground.

395. haec . . . exempla: *these instances,* and hence the fate they illustrate, will befall you, like all the other kings of Thebes. — **dominare . . . vocent:** *lord it as you will, till the wonted fate of our kingdom overtakes you.*

397–398. rabida: voc.; *come, now, mad woman, learn submission from your husband, Hercules,* who is and has been the slave of Eurystheus (430, 432).

399. *Though I wield a scepter seized by a victor's hand, and govern all things without fear of the laws, which force overcomes, I will say a few words for my own cause.* — **victrici:** abl., in agreement with *manu,* which is implied in *dextra.*

402. He claims that Creon and his sons fell in battle.

406. sed: for *at,* introducing an anticipated objection to his reasoning. — **ille:** *pater,* 402. Creon, of course, is meant. Supply the proper forms of *pugnare* with *ille* and *nos.*

407. quaeritur . . . causa: *the issue of a war is asked, not its justice,* a bit of specious argument not without its illustrations in history, ancient and modern.

409. et: *also,* introducing the main clause.

411. petimus: *I do not demand that you do homage to me on bended knee as your sovereign.* — **hoc:** explained by the clause *quod capis,* in apposition.

413. exangues: for *exsangues* (cf. *exerunt,* 11 n.).

418. thalamos tremesco: *I do shudder at the thought of marriage.*

420. mors . . . lenta: *a lingering death.* The subjunctives in *gravent* and *protrahatur* are concessive in effect (cf. Med. 417).

421. Alcide: voc. She apostrophizes the absent Hercules, who is referred to also in *coniunx,* next line.

423. supera: the reference here is not, as in 48, to the earth's surface as contrasted with the infernal world, but to the heavens above, which he was to reach through his promised apotheosis (cf. 23, 122, etc.). For the antithesis of *inferna* and *supera,* cf. note on *summa,* 64.

425. qui caelum tulit: cf. 70 n.

426. cogĕre: future, as is *moriere*, 429.

427. quod . . . parem: indirect question; *parem* is from *parare*.

429. coniugi: Hercules, who though living was already in the world of the dead. The thought is, *if, as you say, I am to die, I shall simply be going to rejoin my husband.*

430. sceptro: abl. after the comparative. — **famulus:** Lycus dwells persistently on Hercules' subjection to Eurystheus as the only counterpoise to his own inferiority of birth (398, 432, 450). — **potior:** *more to be desired.*

431. iste: *that slave, as you call him.* Note the accurate reference of *iste*, the "demonstrative of the second person."

432. ergo: the short *o* is rare in the later poets. — **regi:** Eurystheus.

433. Here we meet a case of parataxis — two coördinate clauses to convey a thought more usually expressed by a complex sentence. The imperative suggests a condition of which *quid . . . erit* is the conclusion — *take away the harsh commands, and where will be the valor ?*

434. *Do you suppose that valor is wasted upon* (lit. *thrown away upon*) *wild animals and monsters ?* The implication is that the hero's conquests over inferior animals were less glorious than victories won in war.

435. Virtutis: predicate gen. — *'tis valor's part.*

436. loquentem magna: *boaster, braggart.* — **magna:** cognate acc. (cf. *dulce ridentem, dulce loquentem,* Horace, C. 1. 22. 23; Catullus, 51. 5). — **premunt:** cf. *premit,* 424.

438. quo patre: cf. 36, 118, 122, 357 n. — **domos:** *mansions.* Here the dialogue between Lycus and Megara is interrupted by the aged Amphitryon, who claims the right to speak for his house (*partes meae sunt*).

442. post pacatum: *after the conquest by his hand of whatever the risen and the sinking sun beholds. Pacatum* agrees with the antecedent of *quodcumque.* — **memoranda:** *memorable.*

444. Phlegram: one of the three parallel peninsulas on the coast of Macedonia. Its later name was Pallene (979). This was the scene of the battle between the giants and the gods, in which Hercules supported the latter (*defensos deos,* 445; cf. 81 n.).

446. mentimur: *do we falsely claim Jove as his sire? Why then does Juno hate him so?*

449. ista causa: *that condition (of servitude, see famuli, 450, and cf. 430) which you are harping on is common to many gods,* i.e. many have been in the same position. Observe again the force of *ista,* referring the idea to the person addressed (cf. 431 n.).

451. pastor . . . Delius: Apollo, who as punishment for having slain the Cyclopes was required to tend the flocks of Admetus, king of Pherae (*Pheraeos greges*) for a year.

453. profuga: nom. with *mater.* — terra errante: see note on 15.

455. imbuit: *stained* with blood. — draco: the python at Delphi.

456. Having been answered in every attempt to show that the career of Hercules had been inconsistent with divinity, Lycus reminds Amphitryon of the misfortunes that had pursued him from his very infancy (cf. 213 ff. and note). In reply the elder shows that Bacchus and even Jove himself had suffered similar trials. The subject of *tulerit,* of course, is *Hercules.*

457. puer: Bacchus. His mother Semele, daughter of Cadmus, beguiled by Juno, desired that Jove should visit her as he visited his sister wife; but when he did appear to her in the midst of thunderings and lightning flashes she perished of fright. The child was cared for by Ino, his mother's sister, and afterward by the nymphs at Nysa, whence he was called Dionysus. In Med. 84 Bacchus is called *proles fulminis improbi.*

460. infans: Jupiter, who was hidden in his infancy from his father Saturn in a cave near the Cretan Mt. Ida.

461. tanti . . . natales: *such high birth.*

462. *It has ever been costly to be born a god.* — magno: abl. of price (see note on Med. 603).

465. leo: *the lion's skin.* As atonement for having killed Iphitus, son of Eurytus (see 477 n.), Hercules bound himself for three years as a servant to Omphale, queen of Lydia. She took from him and wore herself the lion's skin (hence *donum puellae factus*), while he was clad in soft raiment (*veste Sidonia,* 467) and spun among her maids (cf. Phaed. 317 ff.: "The son of Alcmena laid aside his quiver and the menacing hide of the huge lion . . . and with his hand, in which but now he had carried the club, he drew out the threads as the shuttle flew"). The verses that follow here describe the effeminacy of the hero's habit at that time. Amphitryon in his rejoinder (472–476) points out the fact that Bacchus, whose divinity was not questioned, had indulged in the very same luxuries which Lycus had cited as evidence of Hercules' unworthiness.

470. non: with *virilem — unmasculine, effeminate.*

471. barbara: *not Greek* (cf. Med. 612 n.).

473. sparsisse: *to have sprinkled his flowing locks* with perfume.

474. thyrsum: the thyrsus was the wand and weapon of Bacchus and the bacchantes. It was a rod ornamented with leaves of the grape or ivy, and is supposed to have been originally a spear with its point thus concealed (cf. 904, *bearing a spearpoint covered with the green thyrsus*). *Vibrare thyrsum* is *to wave or brandish the thyrsus.* — **parum forti:** not the bold, free step of a warrior, but the languid movement of a debauchee.

475. barbarico: *outlandish* (cf. *barbara*, 471 n.).

477. Euryti . . . eversi: Eurytus was a king of Oechalia who refused his daughter Iole to Hercules after the latter had fulfilled the conditions imposed, and who was slain by him, with all his house. — **Hoc fatetur:** a sarcastic indorsement of Amphitryon's last statement, that valor must be relaxed.

478. pecorum ritu: *like the beasts of the field.* — **virginum greges:** the fifty daughters of Thespius, king of Thespiae, all of whom were given to Hercules.

480. ipsius: sc. *Herculis.* Note the sneer — *no Juno, no Eurystheus imposed this task; these are labors of his own.*

482. Eryx: a son of Butes and Venus, who challenged all comers to fight with the caestus (at boxing). Hercules on his way home with the cattle of Geryon accepted the challenge and in the fight killed Eryx *suis caestibus* — that is, with the weapons of Eryx's own choosing. His name was given to a mountain in western Sicily, made famous afterward by Hamilcar's defense in the first Punic war (Med. 707 n.). — **Antaeus:** an African (*Libys*) giant, invincible as long as he was in contact with his mother earth. Hercules wrestled with him and overcame and killed him by lifting him up and strangling him.

483. qui: in agreement with its antecedent *foci*, here incorporated in the relative clause. — **hospitali caede:** Busiris, to insure good harvests, offered on the altar of Jupiter all strangers who entered Egypt. Hercules, visiting there, was about to be sacrificed when he burst his bonds and laid the king on his own altar (*iustum sanguinem*).

484. bibēre: perfect, with *qui foci* as subject. — **iustum:** *justly shed*.

486. Cycnus: our author here confuses two mythical characters of this name. The first was a son of Mars and was killed by Hercules with a spear; while the second was a son of Neptune, slain at the siege of Troy by Achilles (Tro. 183; Ag. 215). It was the second who was invulnerable (*vulneri . . . invius*, 485), and Achilles was obliged to strangle him (hence *integer, unwounded;* see Ovid, M. 12. 72–145 for the story in detail).

487. Nec unus: Geryon had three bodies (*pastor triformis*, 232). — **una . . . manu:** *single-handed*.

488. eris inter istos: *you will share their fate.* — **tamen:** yet they were less guilty, for they never assailed his honor, as you are doing.

489. quod Iovi: sc. *licet*.

490. *You gave your wife (Alcmena) up to Jove, he (Hercules) shall give up his to a king (Lycus).*

491. hoc: explained by the infinitive clause *meliorem sequi*, appositive to it. — **nurus:** Megara.

493. taedis: *in lawful wedlock*.

495. Labdaci: a Theban king, father of Laius. An evil fate pursued the whole line, culminating in the incestuous marriage, blindness and death of Oedipus (388 n.).

496. Oedipodae: an *a*- declension form for the more regular *Oedipodis* (Oed. 943).

498. nurūs: the daughters of Danaus, who slew their husbands (Med. 749 n.).

499 manūs: acc. of specification.

500. dest: for *deest* (cf. *derat*, 832). — **una:** one of the fifty Danaides, Hypermnestra, had spared her husband. Megara determines, in case of being forced into a marriage with Lycus, to take his life and so qualify herself to take her place with the guilty forty-nine (cf. H.O. 948: *Vacat una Danais, has ego explebo vices — one of the Danaides is missing; I will fill her place.*

502. terres: *attempt to terrify* by your threat — conative use of present.

503. complectere: said tauntingly as he sees Megara lay her hand upon the altar, claiming the right of asylum.

504. nec: *not even.* — **remolito:** a passive use of the participle from the deponent *remolior.* In Tro. 682 the simple verb has its regular active force, *molire terras — force open the earth.*

506. congerite silvas: said to his attendants. For the phrase cf. *congeriem silvae* in Ovid's account of Hercules' cremation on Oeta (M. 9. 235), and *nemore congesto,* 1216. — **templa:** though plural (so in 521, 616, etc.) this refers to the one temple in which she was seeking to take refuge with her children. *Let the temple be cast down upon its suppliant worshipers, and let one pyre, with fire applied, consume his (Hercules') wife and children.* — **gregem:** the children.

509. genitor Alcidae: appositive to the subject of *peto.* *Hoc munus* anticipates the clause *ut . . . cadam.*

512. diversa inroga: *impose various penalties — forbid the wretched man to die, but compel the happy man.* These imperatives are in the "general" second person and are used to enunciate the policy of a tyrant.

513. *While the pyre is being built by my servants I will pay to Neptune the offerings I vowed for the success of my war against Creon.* — **trabibus:** abl. of means or of material. Lycus had appealed for success to Neptune, his own father, as Iarbas prayed to Jupiter Hammon (Vergil, A. 4. 205 ff.), and as Hercules does to his father in 914 ff.

516. pro: the interjection, often spelled *proh* (cf. *O* and *oh*).

518. telis: the thunderbolts.

520. nate: Hercules, *Why do I make vain appeal to the gods? Where'er thou art, hear thou, my son!* — **cur:** he hears the sound of Hercules' approach. — **mugit solum:** an expression often used to describe the sounds attending the coming of one from the lower world (cf. *terra mugitu fremens,* Tro. 171; *sub pedibus mugire solum,* Vergil, A. 6. 256).

SCENE 4 (vv. 524–591). — The chorus recounts the deeds of Hercules, recalls the return of Orpheus from the land of shadows,

and expresses the hope that Hercules also will come back.   The
measure is the minor asclepiadean.

525. quam non aequa . . . praemia: *what unequal favors.*

528. caeliferam manum: *the hand that bore the heavens* (cf.
70 n.;   425).   Vergil (A. 6. 796) applies the same epithet to
Atlas.

529. serpentis: the hydra. — colla feracia: see 241 n.

530. māla: *apples* (Greek μῆλα). — sororibus: the Hesperides
(240).

533. multivagas: *nomadic* (cf. *vagi passim Scythae*, Thy. 631).

534. patriis . . . hospitas: *strangers to the homes of their fathers.*
For *hospita* see Harper's Dictionary under *hospes*, II. D. β.   The
statement under *hospitus* in the same dictionary that "only the
form *hospita*, fem. sing. and neut. plu., occurs," is manifestly in-
correct.

535. terga rigentia: *the frozen surface.*   The adjectives in the
next two lines, *mutis, tacitum, dura,* also express effects of the
intense cold.   With this description cf. Ovid, T. 3. 10: *Quaque rates
ierant, pedibus nunc itur, et undas | frigore concretas ungula pulsat
equi; . . . durum calcavimus aequor — where vessels had gone we
now go afoot, and the horse's hoof pounds the waters made solid by
the cold; . . . I have walked on the hardened sea.*

539. intonsis: *unshorn,* hence uncivilized, barbarous.   The
Romans of the late republican and imperial days as a rule were
smooth-shaven — though Seneca himself wore a beard — and
often spoke of their forefathers by contrast as *intonsi* (Ovid, F. 2.
30).   The elder Pliny (N.H. 7. 59. 211) says that "Barbers came to
Rome in the year of the city 454 (300 B.C.), and before that the
Romans were *intonsi.*"   It is a Roman idea unconsciously assigned
by the author to a Greek chorus. — semita: a footpath across the
frozen sea (541).

540. vicibus mobilis: *changing with the seasons.*

541. facilis pati: *easily able to bear now the ship, now the horse-
man.*   For the construction of *pati* cf. *facilis perrumpi,* Tac. H.
4. 39; *audax ire,* 548.

542. quae . . . imperat: Hippolyte, queen of the Amazons
(cf. 245 n.).

544. **spolium nobile**: *the far-famed spoil* — the girdle (*balteo,* 543) of Hippolyte, given her by Mars on account of her surpassing bravery.   When a Roman leader killed his foe in battle he would strip off the dead man's armor and carry it home in triumph as *spolia opima* (48 n.).   Our author here employs the same term, though in the singular, to designate the prize taken by Hercules from a woman.

546. *Looking up, on bended knee, to her conqueror.*

547. **praecipites**: the epithet is transferred from the road (cf. 675 ff.) that must be traveled to the travelers themselves, the spirits of the dead.

548. **vias**: cognate object with *ire*. — **irremeabiles**: cf. Vergil, A. 6. 126 ff.: *Facilis descensus Averni; sed revocare gradum super-asque evadere auras, hɔc opus, hic labor est.* — **audax ire**: cf. *audax perpeti,* Horace, C. 1. 3. 25.

549. **vidisti**: the subject is Hercules, here apostrophized. — **Siculae**: so called because stolen from Sicily by Pluto (Ovid, M. 5. 385 ff.).

550. There is no breeze; the air, like all else in that world of the dead, is sluggish and heavy (cf. 703). — **Noto**: not the participle of *nosco.*

552. **geminum Tyndaridae genus**: a favorite arrangement of appositives in Seneca (cf. *fortis armiferi cohors,* Med. 980; *turba captivae mea,* Tro. 63).   *Sidera* is another appositive.   For the meaning of 553 see 14 n.; Horace, C. 1. 3. 2.

554. **pelagus**: the Styx. — **nigro**: cf. note on *atrum,* 59. — **languidum**: see note on 550 and for the adjective cf. *languido flumine,* Horace, C. 2. 14. 17.

555. **Mors pallida**: Horace uses the same phrase (C. 1. 4. 13).

556. **manibus**: dat. Note the quantity of *a.* — **innumeras**: Vergil (A. 6. 706) has *innumerae gentes.*

557. **remige**: Charon (Vergil, A. 6. 298–304).

558. *O that thou mayst overcome the laws of the cruel Styx and the irreversible spinning of the Fates.*   The reference is to the thread of life, whose length was determined by the Fates with no possibility of appeal.

560. **hic**: Pluto. This incident is mentioned by Apollodorus (2. 7. 3. 1), who says that Hercules wounded Hades (Pluto) as the latter was bearing aid to the Pylians. Homer (Il. 5. 395) tells us the god was wounded by the arrows of Hercules ἐν πύλῳ, which some have interpreted as meaning not at the city of Pylos but in the gateway of Inferno. — **populis pluribus:** cf. 556.

562. *Conseruit manus* is common enough in the sense *joined battle;* the novel thing here is the adjective with *manus,* making it *loathsome battle.*

563. tergemina cuspide: abl. of quality. The trident properly belonged to Neptune (*triplice cuspide,* Ovid, M. 12. 594).

567. prospectus . . . lucis: *a view of the light.*

572–574. Cf. Med. 625–629.

575. non solitis: *unwonted.*

576. surdis: *silent* (lit. *deaf;* cf. the double sense of *caecus*).

577. Threiciae: the reading is doubtful and the sense obscure. Farnabius suggests that the souls of Thracian women, Eurydice's neighbors, are meant.

578. lacrimis: dat. with *difficiles* (cf. *difficilem precibus,* Ovid, Ex Ponto, 2. 2. 20). The whole expression is not very different from Horace's *illacrimabilem Plutona* (C. 2. 14. 6). — **dei:** Pluto and Proserpina, of course.

579. qui: relating to *iuridici,* 581. — **nimis:** with *tetrica,* the phrase meaning *with brow too stern.*

580. Cf. 727–729; Vergil, A. 6. 567–569.

581. Eurydicen: acc. sing. (Greek), object of *flentes.* — **iuridici:** Minos, Rhadamanthus and Aeacus.

582. mortis . . . arbiter: Pluto.

583. lege: *condition.*

584, 585. tu, tu: Eurydice, Orpheus. — **ante:** the adverb, followed by *quam* in 586.

586. deos: the heavens, with the divinities of the sun, moon and stars.

587. Taenari: the Greeks placed the entrance to the lower world at Taenarus, a promontory in Laconia (cf. 663), as the Romans did near Cumae (Vergil, A. 6. 441–460).

589. perdidit: Orpheus *did* look back as they neared the entrance, and so lost the wife he had regained.

591. viribus: the strength of Hercules; *what a mere song could accomplish, his power can surely do.*

ACT III

SCENE 1 (vv. 592–617). — Hercules enters, rejoicing at his escape from the horrors of the underworld.

592. rector, decus: the sun-god, Phoebus (595).

593. alterna . . . spatia: *above the earth by day, beneath it at night.*

594. exeris: *exseris* (see 11 n.).

595. si . . . videre: *if thine eyes have seen aught that is not permitted.* The eyes of the sun were supposed to see all that is on earth, but never to penetrate the realm of Pluto. The reference here is to Cerberus, whom the speaker had brought with him from below (cf. 60–63, 813–827, and *arcana mundi*, 597).

596. iussus: under orders (cf. *iusso*, Med. 669 n.).

598. parens: Jupiter. — **visus . . . tege:** *veil thine eyes behind a thunderbolt.*

599. Neptune (cf. 53 n.).

600. imas . . . undas: *hide in deepest ocean to escape this sight.* — **quisquis ex alto:** *whoever from on high looks upon the things of earth, let him, fearing to be defiled by this strange sight, turn back his gaze.*

604. qui, quae: Hercules and Juno, respectively.

605. non . . . patent: Juno's own words (46).

607. ignota Phoebo: cf. 595 n. — **quae . . . Iovi:** *dark regions which a lower heaven has yielded to a grim Jove.* The comparison of the infernal king with the king of heaven is a common one (cf. *inferni Iovis*, 47 n.; *nigri Iovis*, H.O. 1705; *Iovi Stygio*, Vergil, A. 4. 638).

609. tertiae sortis: see 53 n., 833. — **placerent:** sc. *mihi.*

612. redi: for *redii.*

614. Just returned from his greatest labor the speaker challenges his persecutor: *if there is any task greater than this, impose it,* and adds, ironically, *you have let my hands rest idle too long, Juno* (cf. 208).

616. He sees the unwonted condition of things and takes alarm.

SCENE 2 (vv. 618–640). — Hercules learns from Amphitryon what has happened and leaves the stage in search of Lycus.

618. vota: *desires* (cf. *quod . . . credunt*, 313).

620. *That silent abode, with its dismal atmosphere* — Hades.

622. sera: because he had not returned in time to save Creon and his sons.

623. editum: sc. *te.* — **vana umbra:** *empty apparition.*

625. trunco: the great club, cut in the Nemean wood.

626. squalor: *mournful sight.* — **lugubribus:** *mourning garb.*

630. leto: dat. of end or purpose.

633. defensus orbis: cf. *orbe defenso*, 249; *ingrata tellus*, 631. — **tero:** *why do I waste the day in idle lamentation ?*

634. Hercules' contempt for Lycus is shown in several strokes here. He calls him not *hostis*, but *hostia, helpless victim; notam* suggests that he considers it a shameful thing to deal with such a foe; and the sentence ends with their two names in anticlimax — *Alcidae Lycus* — *let this victim be offered up, let my valor accept this mark of shame, and let the last and greatest foe of Hercules be* — *Lycus!*

637. Theseu: voc. Euripides does not introduce Theseus till near the close of his tragedy (v. 1154), after the madness of Hercules has passed away. — **resiste:** in its literal sense, *stand back, stay here*, and the reason is added, *lest any sudden violence assail my wife and children.*

638. me: emphatic; *'tis I the war demands.* — **differ:** *postpone.*

639. nuntiet Diti: a common figure in such threats (cf. 988: *This hand will restore you to your hated father*, who was dead; Vergil, A. 2. 547–549: " You shall be my messenger to my dead father . . . now die ").

SCENE 3 (vv. 640–829). — Theseus, at the request of Amphitryon, gives an account of the lower world and the capture of Cerberus.

640. fugā: imperative — *drive that mournful look from your eyes.*

641. regina: Megara. — **tu:** Amphitryon.

644. dabit: subject of *est*, with *lentum* as predicate. Though not yet accomplished the deed is so certain that Theseus is not satisfied to say it will be done, or even that it is doing — *It has been done.*

645. *May the god who can second our desire and favor our fallen estate.*

647. virtutum: *his valorous deeds,* abstract for concrete.

648, 649. Indirect question clauses, *how long a road leads down* and *how* (*ut*) *Cerberus bore his bonds.*

650. securae . . . menti: *dreadful even to a mind at ease.* Theseus long before this time had aided his friend Pirithous in an attempt to carry off Proserpina, but they had been detected and placed by Pluto on an enchanted rock from which they could not stir. Hercules on his visit to the underworld released Theseus, but could not do the same for Pirithous. Theseus here represents his escape as too recent to enable him to contemplate the affair calmly.

655. fructu optimo: *do not cheat yourself out of the best fruit of your sufferings,* the recalling of them. With this passage to *dulce est* cf. Vergil, A. 1. 203: *forsan et haec olim meminisse iuvabit.*

658. Fas omne: here almost in the sense of *numen,* divinity (cf. *audiat fas,* Livy 1. 32. 6). — **te:** Pluto.

659. regno: dat. after *dominantem.* — **te:** Proserpina. — **amotam:** *carried away* by Pluto. — **inrita:** nom. with *mater;* translate *vainly sought.* The Latin often uses an adjective with the subject where we should use an adverb.

660. Enna: abl. of place from which. Enna was the chief seat of the worship of Ceres in Sicily, and it was near there that her daughter Proserpina was seized and carried off by Pluto (Ovid, M. 5. 385–401). The mother sought far and wide and finally learned from the tale of Arethusa where her daughter was (Ovid, M. 5. 504). — **ut liceat:** cf. Vergil's prayer, A. 6. 264–267.

663. Taenarus: see note on 587. — **premit:** *borders close upon the sea.*

664. ora solvit: *opens its jaws,* affords an entrance. This expression together with *hiat, vorago* and *faucibus* in the following lines represents the unseen world as a voracious monster eager to devour the nations (*populis*). — **invisi:** "Ἀιδης, *unseen;* to be distinguished from the participle met in 824.

668. Cf. Vergil, A. 6. 268–272, where the light is described as like that of the moon half hidden by the clouds.

671. ludit aciem: *mocks the sight.* — **nocte sic mixta**: *the night thus mingled with the day* — twilight (cf. *gemini temporis*, Med. 71).

672. primus . . . dies: dawn or evening.

675. See 548 n.

677. pronus aer: *downward current.* — **avidum**: see 664 n.

679. umbrae: *shadows* or shadowy regions, not shades of the dead. — **tenaces**: unwilling to yield up what has come into their embrace. — **immensi sinus**: gen. of quality, *of measureless sweep* (cf. Tro. 178 n.).

680. With the cumulative idea in *placido, quieta, labitur,* cf. 762 and Vergil's *aequora tuta silent,* A. 1. 168. For Lethe and its function cf. Vergil, A. 6. 703–715, 749–751.

682. gravem . . . amnem: *winds its sluggish stream.*

684. Maeander: the well-known stream in Asia Minor, famous for its winding course and taken by classic writers as the type of sinuosity (Strabo, 577). — **cedit sibi**: *makes way for itself,* one bend appearing to have no other purpose than to leave space for another within it.

687. For the horrors of the entrance to Hades cf. Vergil, A. 6. 273–289, where many of the personified ills here named (*Sopor, Fames, Metus, Luctus, Morbus, Bellum, Senectus*), together with others (*Curae, Egestas, Letum, Labor*), and various mythological monsters, such as the centaurs, Scylla, the hydra, the chimaera, the gorgons and the harpies, are given. — **vultur**: repulsive, as being a carrion bird. — **bubo**: the horned owl, whose presence was of evil omen (Pliny, N.H. 10. 16; cf. Vergil, A. 4. 462, *ferali carmine bubo*). Both the *bubo* and the *strix* (688) were associated with the lower world and the powers of darkness, and were addressed in incantations (Med. 733; Ovid, M. 7. 269).

689. opaca, nigrantes: note how the idea of darkness is dwelt upon and reiterated in this scene and the following chorus. We meet *furvus* (693), *ater* (694), *obscurus* (709), *caligo* (710), *umbrante* (718), *caecos* (834), *nigra* (836), *noctem* (856). — **comae**: the foliage, as often.

690. Cf. Vergil's elm, with a dream under every leaf (A. 6. 283).

691. tabido rictu: *with starving mouth agape.*

692. serus: because the virtue should have been practiced in life and not left till after death (cf. Vergil, A. 6. 569).

697. Cereris aut Bacchi: *grain or wine.* Lucretius (R.N. 2. 652 ff.), in protesting against the superstitious belief of men in the gods, says: " If one has determined to call the sea Neptune and grain Ceres, and prefers to misuse the name of Bacchus rather than to utter the appropriate word ' wine,' let us grant him the privilege, provided he refrains in fact from defiling his mind with base superstition."

699. Zephyro: in 550 the absence of wind is noted, here the want of both wind and fields of grain (cf. 704). Note the aptness of the verb *fluctuat.*

702. situ: probably with suggestion of a twofold thought — *repulsive* in appearance, and abhorrent for its uselessness (Harper's Dict. *s.v.* II. A. 1; II. B. 1.).

708. leves: *incorporeal* (cf. Vergil, A. 6. 292). Of course *ille qui regit* is Pluto.

712. quieto: sc. *latici* — *like a stream asleep.* — hunc iurant dei: the only oath that was binding on the gods above was one sworn by the Styx (Vergil, A. 6. 324); hence *sacram Styga.*

714. hic: for *alter*, correlative with *alter* in 712; agrees with *Acheron.*

716. renavigari: an instance of the rare complementary infinitive with *invius.* — duplici vado: *with double moat.* — adversa: *turned toward*, i.e. *facing* those who approached.

719. hoc . . . iter: *this is the road for the spirits.*

721. digerit: *separates*, appoints each to his place.

722. recentes: *newly come* (cf. *recens Dido*, Vergil, A. 6. 450). — dira maiestas dei: Claudian (*de Raptu Proserpinae*, 1. 79–83) thus describes Pluto : *Ipse rudi fultus solio nigraque verendus maiestate sedet; squalent immania foedo sceptra situ, sublime caput maestissima nubes asperat et dirae riget inclementia formae; terrorem dolor augebat* — *Pluto himself sits supported on a rude throne, a being to be feared for his dark dignity; his enormous scepter is covered with foul grime, a gloomy cloud adds fierceness to his lofty head, and the sternness of his grim form is unchanging; his own gloomy expression augments the terror he inspires.*

723. fratrum: Jupiter and Neptune. — **quae . . . gerat:** a characteristic clause modifying *frons*.

725. fulminantis: *he has the face of Jove — but Jove when hurling his thunderbolts, i.e.* Jove in anger.

726. aspectūs: acc. plu.

727. quidquid timetur: the monsters of Inferno.

728. reddi iura: their dues are awarded, rewards to the pious, punishment to the guilty (cf. Vergil, A. 6. 566–627, especially 567–569).

732. sera: *tardy*, not following immediately upon the sin (cf. 728 n.). — **sortitur:** *allots.*

733. foro: a Roman word and idea (cf. *titulis*, 339). As the Roman courts were about the *forum* (hence " forensic ") it is a natural word for Seneca to use. — **illo, illo, hoc:** *this, that, the other.* The three judges here named were traditional.

734. Thetidis socer: Aeacus, father of the Peleus who married Thetis, the goddess of the sea, and became father of Achilles.

735. quod . . . patitur: *what each has done he suffers* (Vergil, A. 6. 743 : *quisque suos manes patimur — we suffer each his penalty*); the doctrine of stern retribution, retaliation, " eye for eye, tooth for tooth." — **auctorem . . . repetit:** cf. our proverb, " Curses are like young chickens, and still come home to roost."

738. terga . . . tyranni: *the back of à tyrant scourged by a plebeian hand* in retaliation for oppression.

740. innocuas: predicate, *has kept his hands free of guilt.*

741. imperium: cognate — *wields power without bloodshed.*

742. animo parcit: *spares his own soul*, guards it from the contamination of wrong doing. Another reading here is *animae, spares life.*

743. caelum petit: *is deified*, like Bacchus, Castor and Pollux, etc.

745. futurus iudex: like Minos, Aeacus and Rhadamanthus, all of whom had lived on earth. — **sanguine . . . vestra:** *abstain from bloodshed, ye who reign; your sins are judged more sternly* than those of men in humbler station.

750 ff. These are the stock examples of punishment in the after life, and are repeated over and over by the poets (*e.g.* Med. 744–749; Oct. 619–623; H.O. 942–948, 1068–1078; Vergil, A. 6.

595 ff., etc.), and to them Theseus now adds the names of Theban women who had sinned — Agave, Ino and Autonoë — and also Phineus, a brother of Cadmus, the founder of Thebes.

750. rapitur: emphatic from its position — *it is true that Ixion is whirled*, etc.; so *praebet*, 756.

752. senex: Tantalus.

754. decepto: dat. — *when it has held out its promise (of drink) to him, already often disappointed.*

756. aeternas dapes: his liver, which grew as fast as it was consumed by the vulture (cf. *viscere feto*, Med. 822; *fecundum iecur*, Ag. 18; *fibris renatis*, Vergil, A. 6. 600).

758. Cadmeides: Agave, Autonoë and Ino, daughters of Cadmus. When the worship of Bacchus was introduced they became his devotees, and when Pentheus, son of Agave and king of Thebes, opposed the new cult they tore him to pieces in their frenzy (Ovid, M. 3. 511–733). Here they are represented as wandering forever in their madness in the other world.

759. avis: the harpy (Vergil, A. 3. 210–218). — **mensas Phineas:** the table of Phineus, whose food the harpies either stole or defiled.

761. patrui: Pluto, as the brother of Jove, of course was *patruus* to Hercules. It is noteworthy that Amphitryon in 760 says *nati mei*, and in the very next line calls Hercules the nephew of Pluto and so the son of Jove. Like inconsistencies are common throughout the play. — **volentis:** Amphitryon assumes that Hercules has been successful, and asks only whether he received the dog as a willing gift of his uncle or had to take it by force as from an enemy in war (*spolium*).

762. Note the cumulative effect of *tardis, stupent, segne, torpescit,* and cf. 680 n.

765. vectat: frequentative. — **senex:** Charon (Vergil. A. 6. 298–304).

767. nodus: *a knot confines his ill-fitting tunic.* — **squalent:** *are rough, unshaven, shaggy.* The reading is doubtful, and for *squalent* various editors have conjectured *lurent, lucent* or *fulgent.*

769. onere: abl. of separation with *vacuam.*

770. poscit . . . turba: *Hercules cries out, " Make way ! " as the throng of spirits falls back before him.*

775. cumba . . . bibit: The boat had carried whole nations of disembodied spirits, but the fleshly body of one man was too heavy for it (cf. Vergil, A. 6. 413). Our author has followed Vergil in many details throughout this description.

777. Lethen: here confused with the Styx (see also 680), from which Vergil is careful to distinguish it (A. 6. 323, 705).

779. Lapithae: a rude Thessalian people. At the marriage of their king Pirithous with Hippodamia some of the centaurs present, being heated with wine, tried to carry off the bride, and a fierce battle ensued (Ovid, M. 12. 210 ff.). Here the shades of both parties are pictured as trembling at sight of Hercules, who often had defeated the centaurs. Cf. the terror of the ghosts of the Greeks at seeing their old foe Aeneas (Vergil, A. 6. 489–493).

781. fecunda . . . capita: cf. *colla feracia*, 529; *numerosum malum*, 241. — **Lernaeus labor:** the hydra, whose ghost now, at sight of its conqueror, flees to the farthest pools of the Styx.

782. avari: so called because he keeps the precious metals close in the earth. Cf. the Greek name Πλούτων, Pluto, " rich," and the Latin *Dis, Dives*, which has the same meaning. Cicero (N.D. 2. 26. 66) says, " He is called Dives, among the Greeks Pluto, because all things fall to the earth and spring from the earth." Possibly allusion is made in *avari* to the fact that none of the dead who came under his sway were released.

783. territat: frequentative (cf. 765). — **canis:** Cerberus. With the line cf. Vergil's *ingens ianitor . . . terreat umbras* (A. 6. 400). Like the Furies and the Gorgons he had live serpents for hair (786).

791. sentire et umbras: *wont to hear even the shades.*

794. muta: any one who has visited a great cavern, like those found for example in the Ohio valley, can appreciate the stress laid upon the two features of darkness and silence by the poets who try to describe the underworld.

795. per armos: *all over his shoulders*, the serpents in his mane (*iubae*, 786).

796. felices quoque: *even the blest*, who had no need to fear him.

798. ipse: Hercules. — **rictus:** acc., lit. *the open jaws* of the lion, whose hide and head he wore as a shield on his left arm (*a laeva*, 797; cf. 1150). — **Cleonaeum:** Nemean.

799. tegmine: cf. *tegimen,* 1151, the lion's hide, which was impenetrable.

800. robur: the club (cf. *trunco,* 625; *clava,* 1024; *tela,* 1153).

802. domitus: with *canis,* subject of the next three verbs. In the preceding sentence the subject was Hercules.

805. uterque . . . dominus: Pluto and Proserpina. — duci: sc. *canem — bade him take the dog.*

806. me: cf. 650 n. — munus: appositive to *me.* According to Apollodorus (2. 5. 12. 6) Hercules released Theseus without Pluto's permission, and was deterred only by an earthquake from freeing Pirithous in the same manner.

808. vincit: from *vincire,* not *vincere.*

809. Note the alternation of the words in agreement.

812. cauda . . . anguifera: quantities determine the case.

813. Taenari: the gateway of Hades (663 n.).

814. oculos: sc. *canis.*

818. respexit: *looked to me for aid.*

821. orbi: for *orbi terrarum* (Med. 5), here the earth's surface as distinguished from the underworld.

824. invisum: *hated.* For the other *invisus* see 664.

825. petit: perfect. — omni . . . cervice: cf. *ore summisso,* 811.

827. umbras: *Hercules' shadow,* the old "plural of preëminence." — venit: present. Theseus has finished his narrative and now sees the throng of jubilant Thebans approaching.

Scene 4 (vv. 830–894). — Thinking of the scene of the hero's latest exploit the chorus is led to sing of the countless number of the dead and to pray for long life on earth; and then celebrates the return of peace and happiness under the rule of Hercules. The measure to 874 is the sapphic, from there to the end glyconic.

830. properante partu: through the agency of Juno as Lucina the birth of Eurystheus had been hastened and that of Hercules retarded in order that the former might be the senior and so master of the other.

832. derat: for *deerat,* a common contraction (cf. *dest,* 500).

833. tertiae . . . sortis: see 53 n.; 609.

834. caecos aditus: *dark entrance.* With the double meaning of *caecus, blind* and *dark,* cf. *surdis locis,* 576 n.

836. nigra . . . silva: abl., giving the cause of *metuenda.*
Both *metuenda* and *frequens* modify *via.*

838–847. The crowds thronging to the games of the amphi-
theater (*quantus populus*, 838), to the Olympic games (*quantus*,
840), and to the celebration of the Eleusinian mysteries (*quanta
. . . turba*, 842), are used by the poet to convey to the minds
of his (Roman) readers some idea of the multitudes of spirits constantly traveling the road to Pluto's domain.   All this is in illustration of *frequens*, 837.

840. Eleum . . . Tonantem: the Olympian Jove, represented
in classic art by a famous chryselephantine statue, the work of
Phidias, which was counted one of the seven wonders of the world.
The temple of Zeus (Jupiter) stood in Elis, near which town the
Olympic games were celebrated, and it is to these games that the
crowd is supposed to be hastening in this verse.

841. quinta . . . aestas: the olympiad consisted of four years,
yet *quinta aestas* is correct according to the Roman method of
counting, which reckoned both the summer of its beginning and
that of its close.   On the same principle they would call a week,
say from Sunday to Sunday, eight days (*e.g.* Gospel of St. John
20: 26).   In music we still retain a like notation, speaking of
"thirds," "fifths" and "octaves." — **sacrum:** the Olympic
games, which were sacred to Jupiter.

842. cum . . . crescere: *when the season returns for the night
to lengthen.* — **longae:** proleptic. — **hora:** equivalent to *tempus*
with the following infinitive.   The time of the autumnal equinox
is meant, when the nights begin to exceed the days in length.

844. libra . . . aequa: *the even balance* between day and night,
which then are equal.   *Libra* is subject of *tenet*, and is modified
by *cupiens.*   It can be said to be *desirous of peaceful slumber*
in the sense that the longer nights conduce to rest. — **Phoebeos
currus:** the chariots of both sun and moon.   The celebration of
the Eleusinian mysteries (see 300 n.) was in commemoration of
Proserpina's descent to Hades as the bride of Pluto (660 n.) and
the sorrowing search of her mother Ceres for her.   There were two
degrees, the lesser and the greater.   The former was celebrated
in the early spring, and its initiates were known as *mystae* (847).
Only these were eligible to the final initiation, which occupied

ninc days, beginning about the middle of September. On the sixth
day of the celebration (the night of the equinox) the *mystae* in
countless numbers marched in procession to Eleusin, where the
final initiation took place in the succeeding nights.

845. **secretam Cererem**: *the mysteries of Ceres* (300 n.; *secreta
sacra*, 301). These mysteries were so sacred that one who divulged
them was accursed in the sight of gods and men.

847. **Attici**: Eleusin was in Attica, twelve miles from Athens. —
noctem . . . celebrare: *to throng the night*. We should expect
quot or *quam multi* with *mystae*, which, however, may be thought
of as a loosely connected elaboration of the collective noun *turba*
in 845.

848. **tanta . . . turba**: *so great a multitude;* the main clause,
to which all from 838 to this point is subordinate. Vergil (A. 6.
305–312) enumerates the same classes, old and young, youths and
maidens and the infant.

851. **melioris aevi**: gen. of quality — *youth* (cf. *bona aetas*, Cicero
de Senectute, 14). Note also the verbs used, *graditur* for old age,
currit for youth.

853. **comis nondum positis**: Seneca is writing with Roman
customs in mind. At an age not rigidly fixed the Roman boy
exchanged his boyish garments for the *toga virilis*, and at the same
time the hair, which till then had been worn long, was trimmed
short. These words therefore characterize those who were still
boys. — **ephebi**: the Greek ἔφηβοι, here corresponding nearly to the
Latin *pueri*.

854. *The infant, just taught to lisp the name of mother.*

855. *To these alone, that they may be less afraid, it is permitted to
temper the darkness with a torch, borne before them.* In early times
it was customary at Rome to bury the dead at night, and the
practice was continued in the case of poor persons and children.

857. **ceteri**: *the rest*, excepting the children.

858. The chorus suddenly apostrophizes the dead.

862. **color malus**: *black*.

863. **otium**: *lethargy of the silent world* (cf. 550–554, 699, 702–
705).

865. Even the latest hour comes too soon for such a journey.

867. *Why does it please us to hasten our cruel fate ?* i.e. by rushing into needless dangers, or even by suicide.

868. vaga: equivalent to *vagans*. — **omnis . . . turba:** *all that live must die.*

870. Cocyto: abl. Here is more geographical confusion (see 777 n.). — **tibi:** *mors* (872). — **crescit:** for *accrescit* — *is added to your possessions.*

871. The ends of the earth (cf. 883).

874. *The hour of birth, which gave us life, also plucks it away* (cf. Oed. 988: *primusque dies dedit extremum* — *the first day has given the last;* de Prov. 5. 5: *quantum cuique temporis restat, prima nascentium hora disposuit* — *our first hour at birth has determined how much time remains for each*). This is the Stoic doctrine of causation.

875. The lighter glyconic verse corresponds to the change in thought.

876. supplices: nom.

881. *The tillers of the fertile field.*

882. *By Hercules' might there is peace from the rising to the setting of the sun, and (in the south) where the sun overhead refuses the body a shadow.*

887. Tethyos: Greek gen. sing. of *Tethys*, whose name here stands for sea (cf. *Tethys*, 1328).

889. vada Tartari: the Styx.

892. An unconscious answer to 614.

893. sacrificus: used, for the sake of quantity, in place of the ordinary vocative form *sacrifice*. *Stantes comas* represents the priest's frenzy of inspiration.

894. pōpulo: the poplar was sacred to Hercules (cf. 912; *populus Alcidae gratissima*, Vergil, E. 7. 61).

ACT IV

SCENE 1 (vv. 895–1053). — Hercules returns in triumph from his slaying of the usurper Lycus, and is on the point of offering sacrifice himself to Jupiter when he is seized with madness, shoots to death his wife and children, and finally falls into a deep sleep.

896. cecidit: from *caedo*, lit. *has smitten the earth.*

o

897. et poenae: *a sharer of his punishment as well.*

902. saxifico: the *aegis*, or round shield of Pallas (Minerva), had at its center the face of Medusa the Gorgon, which Perseus had given her.

903. Lycurgi domitor: Bacchus. Lycurgus, son of Dryas, was a king of the Thracian Edoni, who expelled Bacchus from his kingdom and in consequence was stricken with madness and afterward slain. — **rubri maris:** not what we call the Red Sea, but that part of the Indian Ocean lying west of Hindostan, including the Persian Gulf (cf. *rubenti freto*, Tro. 11; *pelagi rubentis*, Oed. 120). Bacchus is said to have made a triumphal progress along its coasts.

904. Cf. 474 n.

905. geminum numen: see 15 n. Med. 700 has the plural, *gemina numina*.

907. frater: *whatever son of Jove* (cf. Juno's wrathful declaration, 5–18).

908. non ex noverca: a child of Juno's might be expected to share her hatred of the hero. For the word *noverca* see 112. — **appellite:** he orders that victims and incense be brought for a sacrifice.

909. quidquid . . . seges: *whatever the fields of the Hindus* (*yield*), cinnamon, cassia and other spices. Note the literal meaning of *seges* here, *grain field*. The reading here is doubtful; if it be correct a verb such as *dat* or *reddit* must be supplied.

910. odoris quidquid: *tus*, frankincense. — **arboribus:** frankincense is a kind of gum resin that oozes from certain trees in Arabia (cf. *cinnami silvis Arabes beatos*, Oed. 117 — *the Arabs, fortunate in their forests of cinnamon*).

912. populea . . . arbor: see 894 n.

913. te: Theseus. — **gentili:** the olive was the national tree of Athens, the home of Theseus, and was sacred to Pallas Athené.

915. conditores urbis: Cadmus, who founded the city, and Amphion and Zethus, who reared its walls (262 n.).

916. trucis . . . Zethi: of the twin brothers, Amphion devoted himself to the art of music, Zethus to the care of cattle, living in the wilds (*silvestria antra*), and from his uncouthness is called *trucis*. — **nobilis Dircen aquae:** *Dirce, of the far-famed water.* Queen Dirce had been killed by Amphion and Zethus on account of her cruelty to their mother, and at death was converted into a great spring, the pride of Thebes. *Dircen* is a Greek form, acc. sing.

917. advenae: Cadmus was a Phoenician by birth, but came to Boeotia in the course of his search for his sister Europa, and there under direction of the gods built the city Thebes (Ovid, M. 3. 1–130).

919. expia: purification before performing sacrifice was regarded as essential (cf. Vergil, A. 2. 717–720; Livy 1. 45. 6).

921. libare: it was customary to make a preliminary offering of some liquid, usually wine; here Hercules wishes he could make a libation of his enemy's blood. — **capitis invisi:** Lycus.

924. finiat: sc. *ut*, omitted after *opta.* — **genitor:** Jupiter *pray that your father may put an end to your labors.*

927. Iove . . . dignas: instead of the purely personal petition suggested by Amphitryon, Hercules offers a prayer for universal peace — *may heaven, earth and sea abide each in its own place, i.e.* not invade one another's rights.

928. inoffensos: *unobstructed.*

930. Cf. Isaiah 2 : 4, repeated in Micah 4 : 3: " They shall beat their swords into plowshares, and their spears into pruning hooks."

934. nutritus: *swollen.* — **trahat:** *lay waste.*

938. *If earth is to produce any wickedness, may she hasten to do it while I am living; and if she is creating any monster, may it be mine to meet and kill.*

939. quid hoc: sc. *est.* In the midst of his haughty challenge he is overtaken by madness. The passage that follows gives in bold strokes the visions of his distorted imagination.

941. quis . . . fugat: he sees the sun darkened, though there is no cloud, and moving back toward its rising as if it saw some unnatural sight on earth (cf. 60 n.).

944. primus . . . labor: the Nemean lion (225 n.), now the constellation Leo, which in Thy. 855 is called *Leo Herculeus.*

945. *Shines in no small part of the sky.* It is one of the twelve signs of the zodiac.

949–952. *At one bound will spring over all that fruitful autumn and chill winter yield, and will attack and crush the neck of the Bull of spring.* The sun enters Leo in July and Taurus in April (*verni;* cf. 8 n.). Hercules imagines that the starry lion is crouching for

a leap which will carry it over all the intervening constellations
and enable it to attack the Bull.

954. acieque turbida: *with eye confused.* — **falsum:** *unreal.*

955. Perdomita: sc. *est.* — **cesserunt freta:** in the affair of
Geryon and several of the *parerga*.

957. *Earth has been subdued, two of the three realms of the gods
have felt my prowess, and only the heavens remain* (cf. Juno's fear,
64–74).

958. sublimis: nom. — **ferar:** subjunctive (cf. *petatur*).

959. promittit: cf. *astra promissa*, 23. The story of Hercules'
choice between the two careers offered him in the wilderness by
Virtue and Pleasure respectively, and of the former's offer of immortality as a prize, is told by Prodicus, as quoted in Xenophon's
Memorabilia, 2. 21–34.

960. capit: *contain.*

963. una vetante: Juno, who is addressed in the question that
follows — a question which implies a threat — *Are you going
to admit me, or must I force my way?* In *recipis* and *reseras*, also
traho and *dubitatur*, the present is used where we should expect the
future.

965. Saturno: dat. of interest. Saturn had been dethroned
by his sons (53 n.), and according to one account confined in
Tartarus (Ovid, M. 1. 113). Hercules in his frenzy proposes to release the fallen god (*avum resolvam*) and aid him in recovering his
kingdom.

966. patris: Jupiter. — **impii:** *unfilial* toward his own father,
Saturn. — **impotens:** best taken with *regnum*, in the sense of
violently won.

967. avum: Saturn. — **Titanes:** these had dethroned Uranus,
or Caelus, in favor of Saturn (79 n.). Hyginus (Fab. 150) represents Juno as trying to incite the Titans against her husband, as
Hercules here speaks of doing.

969. *With my right hand I will catch up the mountains full
of centaurs,* i.e. the mountains of Thessaly, where the centaurs
dwelt.

970. monte gemino: Ossa and Pelion, which with Olympus
(972 n.) were piled one on the other to make a ladder whereby the
Titans might reach heaven.

971. Chiron: nom. — **suum:** the centaur Chiron dwelt in a cave near the summit of Mt. Pelion (Tro. 830 ff.; Statius, Ach. 1. 106–108; Ovid, F. 5. 383 ff.), where he received as pupils such heroes as Jason, Hercules, Aesculapius and Achilles, teaching them the arts of music and of healing and giving them the fruits of his long experience in life and war.

972. Cf. Tro. 829: *Pelion . . . tertius caelo gradus;* Vergil, G. 1. 281: *Ter sunt conati imponere Pelio Ossam | scilicet atque Ossae frondosum involvere Olympum* — thrice they tried to place Ossa on *Pelion, you see, and to roll the leafy Olympus on Ossa.* As the mountains were piled one upon the other, Olympus was the third step ascending. Apollodorus (1. 7. 4. 2–4), in telling of the attempt of the Aloidae (Otos and Ephialtes), has the mountains piled in inverse order.

974. averte: a prayer — *avert these dread imaginings.* — **parum:** modifies *sani* — *not sane, yet great.*

976. quid hoc: a continuation of the vision (939 n.). In the following verses the attack of the Giants on heaven is described (cf. Thy. 805–812).

977. profūgit: perfect. The madman imagines that Tityos has escaped from Tartarus. For his torment there see 756 n. and Vergil, A. 6. 595–600.

978. inane: *empty,* the liver gone. — **quam . . . caelo:** *how near to heaven* his giant stature has raised him. Vergil makes him cover nine *iugera.*

979. Pellene: perhaps better written *Pallene,* the peninsula also known as Phlegra (444 n.), where the conflict of the gods and Titans took place. It *shakes* here with the shock of battle.

980. Macetûm: *Macetarum,* the Macedonians. Though the Vale of Tempe was in Thessaly, not Macedon, it was so near the border as to make the expression easy. — **rapuit:** *one (giant) has caught up the range of Pindus, another Oeta,* with intent to pile them up as a ladder to the sky (971 n.).

981. Mimans: *Mimas,* mentioned by Horace (C. 3. 4. 53) as one of the Giants. — **horrendum:** a cognate acc. with *saevit* (cf. *belua Lernae horrendum stridens,* Vergil, A. 6. 288).

982. Erinys: the Fury. With this and the next verse cf. 102, 103.

984. in ora tendit: *holds up the torches* (sudes) *in my face* (cf. *fige luminibus faces,* Med. 965). — **Tisiphone:** *since Cerberus has been stolen away cruel Tisiphone, her head wreathed with serpents, has guarded the vacant portal, with torch presented.*

987. ecce: he catches sight of his children and thinks they are his enemy's.

989. reddet: see 639 n.

990. sic: he draws his bow and aims an arrow at one of the little children (cf. same scene in Euripides, H.F. 962–1010).

992. coactis cornibus: *the tips drawn forcibly together in stringing the bow* (for this sense of *cornu* see Ovid, M. 1. 455). Translate: *He has strung his mighty bow, he opens the quiver, the speeding shaft whizzes in its rush — the point flees from the child's mid neck, leaving the wound behind it.* This is Amphitryon's description of the first child's fate. It is not quite certain whether we should think of this tragic scene as actually occurring on the stage as does the killing of Medea's two sons (Med. 970, 1017), or whether the action itself took place behind the scenes. In favor of the latter view is the fact that it all is described by Amphitryon as *facundia praesens,* but on the other hand Hercules himself speaks repeatedly, and in 1015 we hear his wife's appeal. The best Roman critics condemned the presentation of such horribly unnatural scenes, *e.g.* Horace, A.P. 183–188: "Remove from the sight of the audience many incidents which a messenger (*facundia praesens*) may later narrate. Don't have Medea kill her boys in the people's presence, nor the wicked Atreus publicly prepare human flesh for the banquet. . . . Whatever you present to me so I reject with loathing incredulity." In Thy. 970–1034 and Med. 970, 1017, our author does precisely what Horace declares he ought not to do. Euripides (H.F. 870–1010) leaves it to chorus and messenger to tell the tale.

994. harundo, spiculum: the shaft (lit. *reed*) and tip of the arrow respectively. — **fugit:** present — has passed through the neck and is coming out, as if fleeing from its horrid work.

995. eruam: this verb has two related meanings here, one with each object (a case of zeugma): *I will unearth the rest of my enemy's offspring, and will overturn their every hiding place.* Megara and

her two remaining children had fled for refuge into the temple,
whither Hercules now follows.

997. bellum: against Eurystheus, whose mastery now is ended
(830 n.). His home was at Mycenae. — **Cyclopia . . . saxa:** the
massive masonry of the ancient buildings at Mycenae and Tiryns
is described by Schliemann (chapters 1 and 2 of his *Mycenae*), and
mentioned by Pausanias (2. 16) and Euripides (H.F. 939, 940).

999. eat . . . valva: *let one of the double doors fly this way and
the other that.* He is attacking the doors of the temple in order to
come at his victims. — **obice:** the same noun is used in 237 of
natural mountain barriers.

1000. rumpat: the subject is *valva* — it is to be flung open with
such violence as to carry away its supports and even cause the roof
to totter. This is accomplished when in the next line he exclaims,
The whole temple (regia) is exposed to the light.

1002. patris: Lycus. He sees one of his own little boys, but
still supposes it the child of his enemy. — **blandas:** *coaxing,
caressing.*

1003. manus . . . tendens: cf. Med. 247 n. and Tro. 691 n. —
rogat: *entreats.*

1006. bis . . . misit: *has swung it twice or thrice about his head
and hurled it from him.* The object, of course, is the child, who is
referred to also in *illi . . . sonuit — his head crashed* against the
stones.

1010. Tonantis: Jupiter's very bosom instead of his temple. —
condaris: middle voice — *though you hide yourself.*

1012. misera: Amphitryon here, as Hercules in 1010, addresses
Megara.

1017. habitusque reddit: *reflects your image.* She holds the
child up to his father in the hope of arousing some recognition
in the madman's mind. — **ut manus:** *how he holds out his little
hands to you.*

1018. Teneo novercam: he fancies it is Juno who is before him,
and proposes by destroying her to relieve the king of the gods
from her espionage. The next instant, however, he imagines that
the woman before him is the mother of his enemy's (Lycus') children, and in 1036 he speaks, perhaps ironically, of the whole
massacre as a sacrifice to Juno.

1020. hoc monstrum: the infant, which Megara had been guarding in her bosom (1008).

1021. tuum: *your own blood,* flowing in the veins of your child.

1026. nec usquam est: her head is utterly annihilated by the blow.

1027. vivax senectus: addressing himself (cf. same phrase in Tro. 42 n.). — **luctus:** gen.; sc. *te,* acc.

1028. pectus in tela: *courage against those deadly weapons.*

1029. istuc: *turn upon yourself that club, stained with the blood of our children. Istuc* is used instead of *huc* because the speaker is addressing himself in the second person. Note the inconsistency of *nostrorum* in connection with *istuc.*

1031. remove parentem: *do away with your false and earthborn (turpem) father, lest he sound a discord in the chorus of your praises.* This is said to Hercules.

1033. quo: *whither?* In 1032 it rather meant *to what purpose?* — **latē:** imperative.

1034. unum . . . scelus: *save him the one sin yet possible —* parricide.

1035. bene habet: *it is well.* — **regis:** Lycus, whose children the hero still thinks he has slain (987 n.).

1038. te digna: *vows worthy of thee.* — **Argos:** For Mycenae, the home of Eurystheus, who was to be the next victim.

1040. hostia: the speaker himself (cf. 1027–1031).

1041. praebeo: *I offer myself, I hasten to meet my slayer, I even follow him up in my eager desire to be sacrificed.*

1042. The frenzy leaves Hercules and with it his strength and his consciousness. Euripides (H.F. 997–1001) makes Pallas appear and cast the hero down senseless.

1047. The fall of Hercules is compared with that of a tree in the forest (cf. Vergil, A. 2. 626–631), or of a mass of rock slipping from a cliff into the sea in such a way as to form a breakwater and create a harbor. Vergil's more elaborate simile for the fall of Bitias (A. 9. 710–714: "So falls sometimes a pier of rock which, reared beforehand in mighty mass, men cast into the sea," etc.) evidently refers to an artificial structure, and Seneca here may have had the same idea in mind.

1048. **vīvis**: the verb, as appears from the quantities. — **dedit**: sc. *te*.   The subject, of course, is *idem furor*.

1049. **tuos**: object of *misit*.   Hercules' wife and children are meant.

1050. **reciprocos . . . agit**: the breath causes the breast to rise and fall.   *Spiritus* is subject and *motus* object.

SCENE 2 (vv. 1054–1137). — The chorus, gazing on the sleeping Hercules, prays for his release from the evil spell that has befallen him, anticipates the agonies of his remorse, and closes with an apostrophe to the slain children.   The meter is the anapestic dimeter.

1054. **aether**: heaven, and so the gods. — **parens**: Jupiter. Heaven, earth and sea are called upon to mourn this tragedy.

1056. **unda**: nom.   It is a rare thing for a dimeter in these tragedies to close with a trochee, except in the *Octavia*, whose authorship is doubtful.

1058. **tractus**: acc. plu.

1060. **Titan**: here as often for Phoebus or Sol.

1062. **utrasque domos**: *both the rising and the setting*, as above.

1068. **matris . . . Astraeae**: Somnus, as well as Mors (*frater*, 1069), is represented usually as the son of Erebus and Nox.   Farnabius suggests that Astraea is here called his mother *because it is by the favor of justice that we sleep in safety and security*.

1069. **frater . . . Mortis**: cf. Vergil, A. 6. 278: *Consanguineus Leti Sopor*.

1070. **veris . . . falsa**: in dreams. — **futuri certus**: in all ages belief in the prophetic character of dreams has been prevalent. Often, too, they have so impressed the dreamer's mind as to lead him into the act suggested, hence *idem pessimus auctor*, 1071.

1073. **lucis**: objective gen. with *requies*.   In 1066 the same noun is followed by *animi*, subjective.   The genitives in this sentence are worthy of study.

1075. **pavidum leti**: *the human race, so fearful of death* (cf. *lucis pavidos*, 293).

1076. **longam . . . noctem**: death, as if our sleep were but a preparation (*prolusio*) for the longer sleep which it so nearly resembles.

1077. fessum: sc. *Herculem;* so with *devinctum.*

1085. clavae: *as a pillow.*

1086. vacua: abl., with *dextra.*

1089. aestus: the hot surgings of fever and madness.

1091. vento cessante: abl. abs. of concession.

1092. To complete the sentence, whose conclusion evidently is wanting, Leo has suggested *sic pristina adhuc quatit ira virum — so does his late frenzy still shake the hero. Pelle* then will begin a new sentence.

1094. vel sit potius: a new thought occurs to the chorus, that such a crime could be venial only if the criminal were insane (1097, 1098); with the additional idea that *the next best thing to innocence is ignorance of one's guilt* (1098, 1099). Therefore the petition is changed, *may the madness continue.*

1100. percussa . . . palmis: for this mode of expressing deepest grief or despair see Tro. 64, 79, 93, etc. Note the alliteration here and in Tro. 64.

1101. mundum . . . lacertos: see 70 n., 528.

1105. atri regina poli: Proserpina (cf. *inferni Iovis,* 47 n.). Translate, *let his mighty moans be heard in heaven and hell.* The subjects of *audiat* are *aether, regina* and *Cerberus.*

1114. tria regna: heaven, sea and hell (53 n.).

1115. collo: after *suspensa. —* **decus, telum:** appositive to *harundo.* The arrows and their quiver are exhorted to lash their master and aid in the expression of his boundless despair.

1119. robora, stipes: the club (cf. *robur,* 800; *trunco,* 625).

1135. Ite: the chorus apostrophizes the dead sons of Hercules. Leo's arrangement of the verses is retained in spite of its apparent violence.

1136. noti: with *laboris — along the gloomy path of your father's far-famed labor* (the taking of Cerberus), *i.e.* the road to Pluto's realm.

1123. As Hercules had done in many cases, most recently in that of Lycus (895).

1126. Between the two halves of this verse Leo has inserted 1130 entire (*nondumque . . . iubatae*), and has assumed a further lacuna whose sense he attempts to supply as follows: *vulnere gaesi frangere torti.* Accepting this we shall have as the general sense of 1124–1128: *You who have not been trained in the heavier exercises of the arena nor taught to hunt the lion, still have ventured already to aim with sure hand the light arrow such as boys can use,* *i.e.* though not yet able for manly sports they have indulged in such as their years and strength permitted (cf. Andromache's lament over her son in Tro. 775–782). — **fortes:** with *vos* (1122), as are *ulti, docti* and *ausi.*   The infinitive *frangere,* supplied by Leo, depends on *docti,* while the two that follow (*librare* and *figere*) depend on *ausi.*

1131. *Go to the haven of the Styx, ye shades, go as innocent spirits, whom a father's sin and madness have overwhelmed on the very threshold of life.*

1137. **iratos . . . reges:** Pluto and Proserpina, angered at Hercules' invasion of their world.   Farnabius suggests as an alternative meaning that *iratos* here may be equivalent to *tristes* in 611 (but cf. *Iovis, sed fulminantis,* 724).   It is possible, too, that *reges* may refer to the shades of the many tyrants (*reges,* 1123) whom Hercules had slain.

ACT V

SCENE 1 (vv. 1138–1343). — Hercules awakes in his right mind, learns what he has done, and in his despair proposes self-destruction, but finally is induced to seek purification instead.

1138. This whole passage, depicting the hero's awakening from his trance, is admirably done.   With it cf. Euripides, H.F. 1079–1099.

1139. **cardine:** the pole star.

1140. **Hesperii:** *western — am I in the far east, the north, or the west?*

1142. **fesso:** sc. *mihi.*

1143. **redimus:** perfect — *surely I returned from Hades.*   The plural may be "editorial," or it may include Theseus with the speaker.

1144. **an . . . inferna:** *am I still dreaming of what I saw there?*

1146. **turba feralis:** the countless throng of the dead (838–849).

1149. **grege animosa:** *proud of her brood* (cf. *vobis animosa creatis,* Ovid, M. 6. 206).

1151. spolio leonis: the lion's skin, which he had worn on his left shoulder and arm as a shield (*tegimen;* cf. 797 ff.). — **abit:** perfect, for *abiit.*

1152. torus: the lion's skin was his shield by day (45) and his couch by night; so his club was his weapon of offense (45 n.) and also his pillow (1085).

1154. spolia: properly the arms of an enemy slain in battle (cf. *opima,* 48 n.).

1157. exurge: for *exsurge.* — **virtus:** *brave hero,* abstract for concrete, and in that sense followed by a masculine relative, *quem.* — **novum:** *later born than I.*

1159. nox longior: cf. 24 n. Hercules imagines he has been mastered in his sleep by some hero, still unseen, who can be the son of none other than Jupiter, and whose generation must have cost more than the day involved in that of Alcmena's son. — **quod cerno:** he begins to recognize the scene, which before had seemed to him but a horrid nightmare or a lingering impression of what he had witnessed in the world of the dead (cf. 1143–1146).

1161. Lycus had usurped the throne of Thebes in Hercules' absence; what greater Lycus had now done the same after his return?

1163–1166. He appeals for aid to the men of Thebes, of Athens (*Actaea arva*), and of Corinth. — **gemino mari:** the Aegean Sea and the Corinthian Gulf, separated near Corinth by a narrow isthmus (cf. *gemino litore,* Med. 35 n.).

1169–1171. He fancies he has been despoiled of his weapons by the successor and avenger of some one of his victims. — **Thracis cruenti:** Diomede (226 n.). — **Geryonae:** see 231 n. This name is more usually of the third declension (487). — **Libyae:** Africa in general. — **dominos:** Atlas, Antaeus, Busiris, etc.

1172. nudus: *unarmored and unarmed.* — **meis armis:** which had been taken from him as he slept.

1175. He has noticed the averted faces of his father and his friend, and now appeals to them to postpone their lamentations and tell who has done the bloody deed.

1177. tua . . . fide: *on your honor* (cf. *mea fide spondeo ego,* Pliny, Epist. 1. 14 fin.).

1181. dominator: Eurystheus.

1183. per: with *laudem* and *numen — by the glory of my deeds. —* **te:** object of *precor.*

1185. numen secundum: *next after that of Jove;* yet the phrase may well mean *favoring divinity.*

1186. cui . . . iacui: *to whom have I fallen prey? Iacere* often means *lie slain,* and here the figure is carried a step further.

1187. ut . . . sim: indignant question (cf. 372 n.).

1191. quota: *how small* (cf. Med. 896).

1193. refūgit: perfect — *he shrunk from my touch.*

1194. hic cruor: he sees a blood stain on his own hand.

1195. Lernaea nece: the hydra's deadly poison (45 n.).

1196. The terrible truth begins to dawn upon him.

1198. vix recedentem: *which hardly yields to my own strength.*

1199. nostrum: *my.*

1200. luctus: emphatic — *non scelus sed luctus.* It is contrasted also with *crimen — the sorrow is yours, the guilt is Juno's. —* **istic:** *in that act to which you point.*

1202. genitor: Jupiter. In 1176, 1184, 1192, 1199, Amphitryon is so addressed.

1203. oblite: the participle often implies a concession — *though thou hast forgotten me, at least avenge with tardy hand thy grandsons.* In leaving him to Juno's persecution the king of the gods had seemed to forget his great son.

1204 ff. Let all the forces of nature conspire to punish this crime.

1206. rupes Caspiae: the rock in the Caucasus (*scopuli, vertice,* 1208; *latus,* 1209) to which Prometheus had been bound while a vulture (*ales avida, feras volucres*) preyed upon his liver. He had been released by Hercules.

1207. For the aposiopesis cf. Vergil, A. 1. 135: *quos ego —*

1208. vertice immenso: abl. of quality with *latus.*

1210. The Symplegades, two islands in the Euxine, identified by Pliny (N.H. 4. 13. 27) with the *insulae Cyaneae,* just north of the entrance to the Bosporus. Whenever any object passed between them they dashed violently together (cf. Med. 342 n.). In his agony Hercules demands that he be bound with one hand fast to each of these islands, that he may be alternately racked and crushed by their oscillation.

1214. mare: object of *expriment*. For the sense cf. Med. 345 n.

1215. mora: an obstacle to be crushed between them.

1216. quin: in its literal sense, *why not?* — **nemore:** *forest* (cf. *congerite silvas*, 506). He here forecasts the fate that finally did befall him.

1218. reddam: *restore* him who had braved the infernal gods and escaped.

1220. quod: the antecedent is the clause *in se ipse saevit* (cf. *in se semper armatus Furor*, 98).

1228. hic . . . nescit: *this countenance of mine, hardened by ill fortune, knows not how to weep.*

1231–1234. tibi, tibi, tuis, tuos: addressing in turn each of his victims — the three children and their mother (see 990, 1004, 1022, 1025). For one he would sacrifice the arrows, for another the bow, for a third the club, and for the last the quiver.

1233. umbris: *for thy shade my club shall burn.* — **frequens:** *full.*

1236. novercales manus: his own hands, which had done this deed at Juno's instance (cf. 1297). — **cremabo:** cf. 1216, 1217.

1239. Amphitryon appeals to Hercules' pride by reminding him of how he had relieved Atlas and borne the heavens on his shoulders (see 70 n.).

1240. *My sense of shame has not been so far quenched by madness as to let me shock and repel all men by the sight of my unnatural self.* He fears that all would shrink from him as his own father had done.

1245. Cf. 1218, and Juno's purpose as stated in 116.

1246. per . . . nostri: *by the rights implied in either name,* father or foster father.

1249. senectae parce: not *spare my life* (see 1039–1041), but *spare yourself to me* (cf. 1252, 1256, 1257, 1303).

1250. unicum: all the rest of his line were gone.

1251. afflicto: sc. *mihi.*

1255. aris: alluding to Busiris (483 n.).

1257. fructum: *enjoyment;* so in 1253.

1258. cur . . . est: *there is no reason why I should live longer.*

1261. etiam furorem: *I have lost all . . . even the madness which alone could render me innocent* (cf. 1097). Note the asyndeton in 1260. — **polluto . . . mederi:** *minister to a mind diseased.*

1263. In reply to Amphitryon's cry, *you will destroy your father* (by destroying yourself), Hercules answers, *I will die that I may not be able to destroy you* (in some new fit of madness).

1265. *Rather consider your great deeds, which are worthy to be sung by all men, and seek from yourself forgiveness of your one sin.*

1268. iussus: by Eurystheus and Juno. — **hoc est:** cf. 477–480.

1271: vincatur . . . dextra: *let my ill fortune be overcome by my own hand.*

1272. patriae: an adjective.

1274. movere: imperative.

1275. tuum . . . malo: *a match for any misfortune.*

1278. tuli: sc. *scelera.*

1280. que, et, ac: the force of these conjunctions was practically leveled in the Silver Age.

1282. To destroy the hero of the twelve labors would be a labor greater than all the twelve.

1283. ignava: feminine because it is *dextra* that is addressed. — **fortis . . . matres:** *brave only against women and children* (cf. *fortis in pueri necem*, Tro. 755).

1285–1287. Cf. 506–508, 1216, 1217. — **domibus:** *households.* — **suis:** *their,* referring not as is usual to the grammatical subject, but to the nearest substantive for its antecedent.

1290–1294. *And if the falling walls shall come as a trifling weight upon my mighty shoulders, and if I shall not be crushed sufficiently when covered by the seven gates, I will overturn upon my head the whole mass which rests at the center of the universe and separates sky from sky.* — **condar:** *be buried.* — **septem:** Boeotian Thebes had seven gates; Thebes in Egypt a hundred.

1297. manibus: abl. of means; *'Twas Juno's deed, not thine* (cf. 118).

1299. pectus: acc., object of *ferit, smites.*

1300. Aptata . . . est: sc. *nervo.* — **iam:** emphatic; now *you will commit a crime willingly and knowingly.*

1301. Pande . . . iubes: Parataxis, in place of the more commonplace indirect question, *quid iubeas.*

1302. *Sorrow is assured for me in any case.*

1304. **nec tu:** sc. *potes* — *not even you can take him from me, i.e.*
I will share your lot, be it life or death.

1306. *Make your decision, knowing that your cause and your
fame are at stake.*

1308. **aut . . . occidis:** sc. *me; either you live, or you slay me.*

1310. **in ore primo:** *on my very lips,* ready to let it go (cf. Tro.
952 n.). The aged man has declared that Hercules' death would
involve his own, and now, seeing him hesitate, asks, *Does any one
grant life so reluctantly to his own father?*

1312. *I will deck my breast, resolved on death, with the steel
pressed home* (cf. *induere se hastis,* Livy 44. 41. 9, and with a
different sense *pectus in tela indue,* 1028). Amphitryon here
threatens to kill himself with one of Hercules' arrows.

1313. *Here, here will rest the crime of Hercules sane,* a deadlier
sin because committed without the excuse of madness (cf. 1094–
1099, 1300).

1316. **eat:** *be added.* — **hic . . . labor:** in a kind of loose
apposition to *vivamus.*

1318. **dextra . . . refugit:** cf. 1193, 1241, though there the
others shrunk from him and here the relation is reversed. In
1319 Amphitryon clasps the hand of his son and gives utterance
to his joy.

1323 ff. The rivers named are at the ends of the earth — in
Scythia, Egypt, Armenia, Germany, Spain.

1325. **Hibera . . . gaza:** the golden sands which were thought
to abound in the bed of the Tagus.

1326. **abluere:** purify with flowing water (cf. 919 n.).

1330. **recedes:** said to himself.

1333. **obliqua:** *askant.* A poetical fancy based on the fact that
the apparent motion of the stars is not directly over our heads
but includes a swerve toward the south. In his guilty self-con-
sciousness Hercules imagines that the very stars are turning out
of their way to avoid passing near him. — **Titan . . . vidit:**
cf. 60, 61.

1336. **semper . . . arbiter:** Theseus had been witness of
Pirithous' impious attempt upon Proserpina, and now of Hercules' fearful crime.

1337. *Show gratitude and make return for my service to you, by delivering me to Pluto in your stead.*   Hercules had rescued Theseus from his imprisonment by Pluto (806 n.).

1341. ille: sc. *locus.   Even Hades knows me.* — **nostra . . . tellus:** Attica (cf. 913).

1342. **solutam caede:** *acquitted of the charge of murder.* — **Gradivus:** Mars, who was tried before the gods, sitting as a court in the Areopagus at Athens, for the murder of Halirrothius, a son of Neptune, and was acquitted. Reading *restituit* (perfect) we must take *manum* as the hand of Mars and read, " There Mars restored to the sword his hand, acquitted of murder; and that land, which is wont to prove gods innocent, is calling you." This is better than to read *restituet* and understand the sense to be that Mars will acquit Hercules.

1343. **superos:** in using this word Theseus delicately flatters his friend, implying that he is entitled already to rank as a god (cf. 121, 122, 959).

THE STORY OF THE TROADES

Paris, the Trojan prince, had decided that the beauty of Venus surpassed that of her rivals, Juno and Minerva, and was to receive as his reward the most beautiful woman in the world. This was Helen, who already was the wife of the Spartan Menelaus. Under the guidance of Venus Paris visited Sparta and persuaded Helen to elope with him. All Greece united to avenge the wrong, and "the thousand ships" assembled at the Boeotian port of Aulis. There they were detained by opposing winds until the commander-in-chief, Agamemnon, sacrificed his daughter Iphigenia to the offended divinity, when they sailed and presently landed on the Trojan coast.

The siege lasted for ten years, with many deeds of valor on both sides. Achilles being the strongest champion of the Greeks and Hector of the Trojans, at length these two met in single combat. Hector was slain and his body dragged away behind the victor's chariot. The corpse was ransomed by King Priam and given decent burial.

Without its chief defender the city could not long hold out. It was taken by a stratagem at night and sacked and burnt. Most of its men were slain and its women made captive. It is at this point that the play begins.

NOTES ON THE TROADES

ACT I

SCENE 1 (vv. 1–66). — Queen Hecuba mourns the misfortunes of her house and kingdom, showing from what a height to what a depth they have fallen.

1. *Whoever puts his trust in royal power and lords it mightily in his proud palace, and has not feared the fickleness of the gods but has committed his trustful soul to prosperity, should look upon me and thee, O Troy.* A similar thought is elaborated in Oct. 34 ff.

5. **documenta:** *warnings.* — **quam . . . loco:** *in what perilous position.*

6. **columen:** Troy, here thought of as the bulwark of the Orient against aggression from the west.

7. **caelitum . . . labor:** the walls of Troy were built by Neptune and Apollo. The perfidy of King Laomedon, who after the work was finished refused to pay the promised price, provoked Neptune to send a sea monster which ravaged the Trojan coast. The exposure of his daughter Hesione as an expiatory victim, her rescue by Hercules, Laomedon's second breach of faith and Hercules' destruction of the city in revenge (133 n., 718 n.), are familiar myths, for which see articles Laomedon, Hesione, etc., in Classical Dictionary.

8. **ad . . . venit:** as auxiliaries. Those most commonly named of the allies who came to the aid of Troy are Rhesus, Memnon and the Amazons. Leo's retention of *quae*, with his deletion of vv. 12, 13, results in the entire omission of any mention of the first, and therefore I follow Richter and the older editors in this place. — **qui . . . bibit:** Rhesus, king of Thrace (cf. Vergil, A. 1. 469–473). It is true the king of Thrace can hardly be said to "drink the waters of the Don," which river is far to the east and was regarded as the boundary between Asia and Europe. It happens, however, that Seneca in another place (N.Q. 6. 7. 1) has made the same mistake of confusing the Don with the Danube, which did border upon Thrace. He speaks of "the Danube, which checks the inroads of the Sarmatians and separates Europe and Asia." — **frigidum Tanain**: this river, now known as the Don, empties into the Palus Maeotis (Sea of Azov) by two principal mouths (Pliny, N.H. 6. 7). The number given in the text, *septena*, is traditional, being the number of branches ascribed to the delta of the Nile and thence transferred to other rivers as if it were a standard (Med. 763 n.).

10. **qui . . . immiscet**: Memnon, son of Tithonus and Aurora (cf. 239), who is said to have led the Persians to the aid of Priam, his father's brother (*patrui*, 239 n.). Memnon often is described as black (Ag. 212; Vergil, A. 1. 489), and sometimes as king of the Ethiopians. — **renatum**: yesterday's sun, *reborn* to-day (cf. Horace's address to the sun god, *Aliusque et idem nasceris*, C.S. 10: *Thou art born another and yet the same*).

11. **rubenti . . . freto**: the Mare Rubrum, Greek 'Ερυθρόν, Ερυθραῖον, not the modern Red Sea, but the Indian Ocean west of Hindostan, and especially the Persian Gulf. Pliny (N.H. 6. 28) quotes four theories as to the origin of the name: (1) From a mythical King Erythras; (2) from the color caused by a peculiar reflection of the sun's rays; (3) from the reddish tint of the sandy bottom; (4) from some peculiarity of the water itself. The Tigris does not fall directly into the sea, as suggested by the text, but into the Euphrates. Noticing the absurdity of saying that Memnon "mingles the Tigris with the sea," Leo suggests *mero* in place of *freto*.

12. **quae . . . ferit**: *the Amazon leader, who, looking forth as a neighbor upon the nomadic Scythians, scourges the Pontic shore with her unwedded troops*. The Amazons were generally assigned to a region on the southern shore of the Black Sea, along the Thermodon River (H.F. 246; Med. 215; Vergil, A. 11. 659). They came to the aid of the Trojans (673; Ag. 218; Vergil, A. 1. 490–493), and their queen Penthesilea was slain by Achilles.

14. **excisa est**: sc. *Troia*, implied antecedent of *cuius* (8). The same thought is repeated in *Pergamum incubuit sibi*, with which cf. Vergil's description in A. 2. 624–631.

15. congestis . . . tectis: *heaped together,* as if to form a funeral pyre for the city and its people (cf. *congerite silvas,* H.F. 506; *nemore congesto,* H.F. 1216).

17. Assaraci: Assaracus, an early king of Troy.

19. diripitur . . . Troia: the inversion adds emphasis to the thought — *Troy is being pillaged even while burning.* — **nec . . . patet:** *is enshrouded.*

22. avidus irae: *greedy of (the gratification of) his wrath.* — **lentum:** *slow to yield* (cf. the ideas in *decem annis* and *haud credit* below).

24. ignoscit annis: *forgives the long delay,* because of what it has brought him at last. — **horret:** the victor shudders with fear at sight of Troy, even though she is prostrate. — **afflictam:** sc. *Troiam;* so with *victam,* and as subject of *potuisse* (26).

27. mille: not to be taken too literally, but as a round number often used by the poets in speaking of the Grecian fleet before Troy (*e.g. mille carinis,* 708; *mille velis,* 370; *mille carinae,* Vergil, A. 2, 198, etc.). Homer's catalogue of the ships (Il. 2. 484–759) gives a total of 1186, and the numbers stated by Hyginus and others vary considerably. — **non capiunt:** *the thousand ships do not (cannot) contain the booty.*

28. testor: *I call to witness the divinity of the gods, ever hostile to me, I call to witness Priam and Hector and all my children . . . that I foresaw and foretold all this* (36). *Testor* takes one or more personal objects and a secondary object which here is the independent clause beginning with *prior.*

29. te: Priam.

30. toto conditum regno: *buried beneath a whole kingdom* (cf. the idea in 158).

31. quo . . . stante: abl. abs.; *during whose lifetime Troy lived, i.e.* while he stood Troy stood, and at his fall the city fell. Hector, of course, is meant (cf. 204–206).

32. magni greges: cf. *turba,* 958. Priam was the father of many children. In the Iliad (24. 495 ff.) he is made to say: —

"Fifty were with me when the men of Greece
    Arrived upon our coast; nineteen of these
    Owned the same mother." — (Bryant's translation.)

"The same mother," of course, was Hecuba. Hyginus (Fab. 90) gives a list of fifty-four sons and daughters of Priam, and other Greek and Roman writers give various numbers (*e.g.* Vergil, A. 2. 501–503). In the Hecuba of Euripides (v. 421) the aged queen is made to speak of herself as "bereft of fifty children."

33. umbrae minores: *shades less than those of Priam and Hector (manes,* 31).

34. Phoebas: nom. sing. Cassandra, who had rejected the suit of Phoebus after having received from him the gift of prophecy, and as punishment was doomed to see all her predictions disbelieved and disregarded (*credi deo vetante,* 35; *vana vates ante Cassandram,* 37; *falsa vates,* Ag. 725; Vergil, A. 2. 247, etc.). She is called *Phoebas, priestess of Phoebus,* by Ovid also (Am. 2. 8. 12; Trist. 2. 400), and in Ag. 588, 710. Prophetic inspiration was regarded as akin to madness, hence *ore lymphato furens.*

35. credi: dependent on *vetante.* — **deo:** Phoebus.

36. prior: before Cassandra (see next line). — **gravida:** nom. sing. — **nec tacui metus:** *nor did I keep my fears to myself.* Before the birth of Paris his mother dreamed that she had borne a firebrand which was destined to be the destruction of Troy (see 40). She told her fears, and on the advice of prophet Aesacus the child was exposed on Mt. Ida as soon as it was born; but like Romulus and Remus of Roman legend he was found and brought up by a shepherd (see note on 66).

38–40. *It was not Ulysses nor Diomede nor Sinon that kindled this fire; it is mine.* — **cautus . . . Ithacus:** Ulysses, the type of craft as opposed to brute force in war. His Homeric epithet is πολύμητις, while his enemies, of course, employed terms less complimentary. In all, however, was the same general idea (see notes on 613, 614, 750 ff., 857, etc., and cf. *fallacem,* 149, and Vergil's *pellax,* A. 2. 90). — **Ithaci comes:** Diomede, who was Ulysses' comrade in several notable exploits, such as the capture of the spy Dolon and of the Palladium, the attack upon Rhesus and the adventure of the wooden horse. As a rule these adventures occurred in the night (*nocturnus*); hence Ovid (Met. 13. 100) makes Ajax say of Ulysses, *Luce nihil gestum, nihil est Diomede remoto* — *no deed was done by day, none apart from Diomede.*

39. For the story of Sinon and the wooden horse see Vergil, A. 2. 57 ff.

42. vivax senectus: an abstract noun for concrete, *old age* for *aged woman* (cf. *nimis vivax senectus*, H.F. 1027). She is addressing herself. — **respice:** not literally *look back* but *have regard to.*

43. Troia . . . vetus . . . malum: the downfall of Troy was now an old story, because of the more personal sorrows that had crowded upon her since.

44 ff. For the death of Priam see Vergil, A. 2. 533–558, where many of the same details are given.

46. Aeacidis: Pyrrhus (Neoptolemus), son of Achilles and descended from Aeacus. The reading is doubtful, and is accepted merely as a makeshift. *Aeacidis* properly is a feminine patronymic. The proper masculine form occurs in 253, *Aeacidae*, but would be impossible metrically here. — **scaeva . . . torta:** *the hair twined about his left hand.*

47. reflectens: here in its literal sense, *bending back.*

48. vulneri: the poetical dative with *abdidit* (cf. Vergil's *lateri abdidit ensem*, A. 2. 553, in describing the same scene).

50. siccus: *bloodless, unstained* (cf. Ag. 656–658: *Vidi | senis in iugulo telum Pyrrhi| vix exiguo sanguine tingui — I saw that Pyrrhus' sword in the old king's throat was hardly stained with his scanty blood*). This is an exaggeration based on the well-known fact that in old age the blood flows more sluggishly than in youth. Seneca's own death supplies an illustration (Tac. Ann. 15. 63, 64). The reading of one MS., *tinctus*, gives a very different sense.

51–54. *Whom could such a sight not appease and hold back from cruel murder?* The subjects of *potuit* are *Priamus* (implied with *premens*), *superi* and *quoddam sacrum*, in the sense of "a kind of inner sanctuary of the fallen kingdom." The altar at which the aged king had sought refuge, and the sight of his grief and his humiliation should have given his murderer pause.

54. regum: *princes* (see 32 n. and cf. Med. 56).

55. flamma: the flame of the funeral pyre. The king's body could not be burned as it should, though the city was blazing all about him. *Ardente Troia* is abl. abs. concessive.

56. superis: the gods, not satisfied with the destruction of the city and the death of its king, are permitting the reduction of its noble women to the rank of slaves and concubines. For the agency of the gods see Vergil, A. 2. 604–623.

57, 58. The captives are being apportioned by lot among the victors (cf. 974 ff.).

58. praeda: appositive to the subject of *sequar — I shall follow my new master as an unprized captive.* — **vilis:** *cheap, unprized,* in comparison with the younger women (cf. 62, 980).

59. hic, hic, hic: *one of the victors, another and a third.* — **Hectoris coniugia:** Andromache. In *coniugia* is met another instance of the use of an abstract for a concrete noun (cf. *senectus,* 42; and *coniugio,* Vergil, A. 3. 296, where it is said of this same Andromache). Hector's wife fell into the hands of Pyrrhus (976), and after his death became the wife of her brother-in-law Helenus (Vergil, A. 3. 294–297). — **despondet sibi:** in Roman phrase the father betrothed (*spopondit*) his daughter to her husband. Here the victors ask the consent of none but themselves.

60. Helenus and Antenor are named here simply as representative Trojans. The name of Helenus' wife is not known; Antenor's was Theano (Il. 6. 298).

61. dest: a common contraction for *deest* (cf. *derat,* Med. 992; *derit,* Med. 403). — **tuos . . . petat:** Agamemnon (see 978; Ag. 191).

62. Each fears that the lot may assign to him the old and feeble Hecuba; she alone remains a terror to the Greeks (cf. *vilis,* 58; *Ithaco nolenti,* 980).

63. turba captivae mea: a favorite arrangement of appositives in Seneca (cf. *alta muri decora,* 15; *maesta Phrygiae turba,* 409; *fortis armiferi cohors,* Med. 980). The queen here addresses the chorus of Trojan women.

64. planctus: the beating of the breasts in utter abandonment of grief (cf. 79, 93, etc.; H.F. 1100–1103). The alliteration here is noticeable.

65. iusta Troiae: the service, here the formal lamentation, due the fallen city and its dead (cf. *iusta functis,* Med. 999; *iusta patri,* Oed. 998). — **sonet:** *let Mt. Ida reëcho our wailing.*

66. Ide: the Greek form corresponding to the Latin *Ida*, used when a long ultima is desired. — **iudicis diri**: Paris, who when exposed (see 36 n.) had been found and reared as a shepherd on Mt. Ida and there had given the verdict upon the relative beauty of Juno, Minerva and Venus which had proved so fatal to his country (hence *fatalis Ide;* cf. *fatalis pastor*, Ag. 730). In *Ide* the Greek form is used for the sake of its long ultima (cf. 74; *Polyxene*, 367; *Alcmene*, H.F. 22, etc.).

SCENE 2 (vv. 67–164). — The chorus of Trojan women, responding to Hecuba's direction, laments the fate of Troy, of Hector and of Priam. The meter is the anapestic dimeter, with several monometers interspersed.

67. non rude: *not wanting in experience* (cf. *non indocilis lugere*, 81; *non rudem*, Med. 915). — **vulgus**: a company of people sharing a common lot (cf. *vulgus vile*, 80).

69. ex quo: sc. *anno* or *tempore*.

70. Phrygius . . . hospes: Paris, who employed his opportunities as Menelaus' guest to alienate his wife's affections. — **Amyclas**: a Laconian town near Sparta, here named in place of the latter.

72. Cybebae: a form used for Cybele when the meter requires a long penult. This goddess was worshiped extensively in Asia Minor and especially among the Phrygians (see Lucretius, R.N. 2. 600–643, where an extended account is given; cf. Vergil, A. 9. 80; Catullus, 63). High places were sacred to her, and here the timber (*pinus*) which had stood on Mt. Ida also is called *sacra Cybebae*. Here, as often, *pinus* stands by metonymy for ship.

74. nudata rogis: *denuded of its woods for our funeral pyres.*

76. decumas . . . aristas: *his tenth harvest.* The form *decumas* for *decimas* illustrates the interchangeability of the two close vowels when they are short — seen also in the dative and ablative plural of the fourth declension, *e.g. artubus* or *artibus*.

77. ut: temporal, *while.*

79. levā . . . manum: *lift your hand* to lead the chorus (cf. the handling of his baton by the conductor of a modern orchestra).

84–89. Common manifestations of grief or despair (cf. our familiar "sackcloth and ashes").

218 THREE PLAYS OF SENECA

85. tepido: still warm from the burning of the city.

102 b. complete manus: sc. *pulvere* or *pulveris*.

103. *Ashes we may take, though the enemy claim all else.*

87. paret: *let the chorus make ready their bared shoulders,* for the *planctus* detailed in 93 ff. Scansion will determine mood and meaning of *paret*. — **exertos:** for *exsertos*.

88. *Having loosed the robe (from its position about the shoulders) bind its folds (to prevent its falling too far) and let the body be uncovered as far as the waist.*

90. coniugio: *husband* (see note on *coniugia*, 59) — *what call for modesty now, when our husbands are slain and all is lost?*

92. *Let the palla bind the loosened tunic.* This is a more particular form of the instruction given in 88. The tunic was a long, loose, sleeveless gown worn under the more formal articles of dress. The palla, instead of being employed as usual for ornament, here is to be bound around the waist as a girdle to keep the loose tunic in place and leave the hand, which otherwise must hold it up, free (*vacet*) to beat the breast.

94. placet . . . turbam: *this guise meets my approval; I recognize now the Trojan chorus,* in its appropriate garb of mourning. — **Troada:** acc. sing., used as an adjective modifier of *turbam*.

96, 97. veteres, solitum: *old and habitual,* from the ten years of terror and woe (cf. *solitus ex longo est metus,* 632). — **vincite:** *outdo.*

99. solvimus: perfect, as is seen from the following coördinate verbs — *we have loosed our hair and sprinkled it with ashes as bidden* (in 83–95).

101. cinis fervidus: cf. *tepido pulvere,* 85.

104, 105. *Our raiment falls away from our shoulders, thus uncovered, and hangs about the waist* (cf. 92 n.). — **suffulta:** *girt up* by the palla.

106–115. The *planctus* mentioned in 93, 108, 114, etc. — **vocant:** *invite.*

109. Echo: originally a beautiful nymph, but changed by Juno into a stationary echo, unable to speak of itself or to remain silent when another spoke (Ovid, M. 3. 339–401). This is a good example of the personification which lies back of most of our mythology. *Let Echo not, as she is wont to do, briefly repeat the last words only,* *but let her give back Troy's whole dirge* (cf. the very similar passage in H.F. 1100 ff.).

115. The chorus's response (antistrophe) closes in nearly the same terms as Hecuba's invitation (strophe) in 97, 98.

117. tibi: Hector is apostrophized. — **ferit**: not from *fero.*

121, 122. *Whatever scar I made on my body at your burial, let it break open anew and flow and well with plenteous blood.* — **fluat, manet**: the subject is *cicatrix*, 123. Mood and meaning of *manet* are determined by scansion.

124. mora fatorum: Hector's heroism could only delay, not avert, the fall of Troy.

125. praesidium: followed here by the dat., like its primitive *praesideo.*

127. illa: sc. *patria*, found in 124 and 129.

128. tecum cecidit: cf. 31 n.

130. Hecuba now suggests a new theme, which the chorus takes up in 132.

133. bis capte: first by Hercules (7 n.), when Priam alone was spared of the royal family (cf. 718, 729), and now by the Greeks.

134. nil . . . semel: *there is no ill that Troy has suffered but once in your reign, having twice endured the battering of its walls by Grecian steel and twice felt the arrows of Hercules.*

137. Herculeas: the Greeks learned from the oracle that they could hope to take Troy only with the aid of Hercules' arrows, which then were in possession of Philoctetes. He therefore was sent for and contributed materially to the final result (see 824, 825). — **post . . . partus**: *after the burial of Hecuba's sons.*

138. regum: cf. 54 n. — **gregem**: cf. *magni greges*, 32 n. *Gregem* is to be read with *elatos*, like *partus.*

139. pater: voc., or appositive to subject of *cludis* and *premis.*

140 Priam was slain near the altar of Zeus (Jupiter).

141. truncus: appositive to the subject of *premis;* for the same word, used in the same connection, cf. Vergil, A. 2. 557.

144. felix Priamus: the phrase as a whole is the thought object of *dicite*, as of *dicimus* in 157. For a similar construction see Horace, C. 3. 24. 27: *Si quaeret "pater urbium" subscribi statuis — if he desire the inscription "father of cities" carved beneath his bust.*

148. duos . . . **Atridas:** Agamemnon, commander-in-chief of the Greek forces, and Menelaus, the husband of Helen, both naturally mentioned as foremost enemies of Troy.

149. fallacem . . . **Ulixen:** cf. 38 n., 568, 613, etc.

150. praeda: appositive to *Priamus,* easily understood as subject of *feret.*

152. manus . . . dabit: *submit to be bound.*

153–156. Suggested by the Roman *triumphus.*

155. fiet pompa: *be made a spectacle.*

158. Cf. 30 n.

162–164. Cf. Vergil, A. 1. 94–101.

ACT II

Scene 1 (vv. 164–202). — Talthybius, the Greek herald, in response to a request of the chorus, tells of the apparition of Achilles' ghost and his demand for the sacrifice of Polyxena.

Talthybius: the herald plays a much more conspicuous part in the plays of Euripides than in those of Seneca. This is his only appearance here, while in the *Troades* of Euripides he appears repeatedly and in the *Hecuba* describes to the aged queen the death of her daughter Polyxena — a task assigned in the present piece to an unnamed *nuntius.* In the *Medea* of the two poets we note the same difference in the importance of the herald.

164, 165. As the Greeks had been detained at Aulis in setting out for Troy (*petere bellum*) till the offended Diana had been appeased by the sacrifice of Iphigenia, so now they were delayed in beginning their homeward voyage (*petere patriam*) by the necessity of appeasing the angry shade of Achilles (see 191–196, 360–370; Euripides, Hec. 35–44; Ovid, M. 13. 441 ff.).

167. reduces: *homeward,* in agreement with *vias.*

168. This verse opens with the rare proceleusmatic, never found in Seneca except in the first place. The same words are found at the beginning of Med. 670.

170. vidi ipse, vidi: *seeing is believing,* and it is thus that the herald solves the doubt expressed in the preceding verse. This apparition is described as having occurred at dawn instead of midnight, when ghosts are commonly supposed to walk (cf. Andromache's vision of her dead husband, 438).

171. caeco: *whose source was unseen.*

172. The precise meaning of this verse is open to question Perhaps the most satisfactory solution is that offered by Grono‹ vius, who explains *totos . . . sinus* as meaning *earth uncovered and brought to light her inmost recesses.*

173. mōvēre: perfect. — **nemus:** on Mt. Ida; so *lucus,* 174.

176. suum Achillen: as the son of Thetis, who was one of the daughters of the sea-god Nereus (cf. *te . . . tot pelagi deae . . . suam vocabunt,* 879).

177. stravit: *stilled* (cf. *stravere ventos,* Horace, C. 1. 9. 10; and for the sense cf. *immoti iacent tranquilla pelagi,* 199).

178. immensos specus: *caverns measureless to man* (cf. *immensi specus,* H.F. 679).

179. superos: *living men,* as in H.F. 48, and often.

180. tumulum: the tomb of Achilles (Euripides, Hec. 37).

181. Thessalici ducis: Achilles, whose home was at Larisa in Thessaly. The following verses mention his principal exploits.

182. proludens . . . fatis: *practicing for thy destruction* (cf. *prolusit hydrae,* H.F. 222; Med. 907). — **Threicia arma:** referring to Cisseus, father of Hecuba, who came with his Thracian forces to the relief of Troy and was defeated by Achilles.

183. Neptunium iuvenem: Cycnus (Ovid, M. 12. 72–145), who on his death at the hands of Achilles became a swan; hence *cana . . . coma* (cf. *nivea proles Cycnus aequorea dei,* Ag. 215).

185. Marte: *war, battle* (so in 1058).

186. In the *Iliad* (21. 7 ff.) we read that "The roaring stream of Xanthus thus was filled before Achilles with a mingled crowd of steeds and men."

187. tardus: because its usually swift current was checked by the bodies.

189. Hectorem et Troiam: the story of Hector's having been dragged behind his conqueror's chariot is familiar (Il. 22. 395 ff.; 24. 14–21; Vergil, A. 1. 483; 2. 272). The coupling here of his name with that of the city implies that his fate necessarily involved the like destruction of his country (cf. 31, 124).

190. irati: sc. *Achillis.* In the *Hecuba* of Euripides (37) he appears above his tomb (ὑπὲρ τύμβου) with the same demand.

191. manibus: the quantity of *a* determines the meaning. — **meis:** monosyllabic by synizesis.

192. honores: the spoils that should have been his (cf. 292–294, 360–370).

193. nostra maria: cf. *suum,* 176 n. — **luit:** perfect; *Greece has paid for the wrath of Achilles at no small price, and shall atone for it now at great cost.* The allusion is to the hero's withdrawal from the Greek camp before Troy (Il. 1 init.) and its disastrous consequences to the besiegers, and it is threatened that their present neglect of his rights shall prove as costly. — **non parvo, magno:** abl. of price.

195. Polyxene: a daughter of Priam and Hecuba. Achilles had been attracted by her beauty and made repeated proposals for her hand, but the terms offered him were too hard. Finally, according to one account, he was invited to a conference on the subject, led into an ambush, and slain by Paris (347). His shade now demands that the maiden be offered by Pyrrhus as an expiatory sacrifice to his *manes* (Ovid, M. 13. 441 ff.), which demand is reën-forced by the decision of the seer Calchas (360–370). The name appears throughout this play in its Greek form *Polyxene* for the sake of the long ultima (cf. *Ide,* 66 n.). *Andromache,* on the other hand, is met in both forms, with final *e* in 968, and with final *a* in 533, where see note.

196. riget: from *rigare.*

197. Text and sense are doubtful. We have retained the reading of the Florentine MS. *(codex Etruscus),* whose authority in most cases is decisive. The explanation has been offered that the apparition, occurring after dawn and accompanied by a darkness of its own, *divided the day with its deep night.* Another version has *voce dimisit — with deep voice he bade farewell to the day.*

198. specum iunxit: *closed the cavern,* by bringing its walls to-gether. This is the converse of *aperit . . . specus,* 178.

199. immoti: gen. with *pelagi.* It would be more natural, if it were possible metrically, to read *immota,* with *tranquilla — the tranquil deeps lie motionless.* Such hypallage is common, how-ever, and does not alter the sense.

202. hymenaeum: the wedding song of Achilles and Polyxena. The last three lines of the scene, with their smooth movement and abounding liquids, echo the change of spirit from the fierce wrath of the hero to the peace that followed his departure.

SCENE 2 (vv. 203–359). — Pyrrhus recounts the deeds of his father Achilles, and when his declared purpose to sacrifice Polyxena is opposed by Agamemnon a violent quarrel ensues. The matter at last is referred to Calchas the seer.

204. excidit: *was forgotten*, lit., *fell from the memory* (cf. 714; Med. 561 n.). In this sense *excidere* may be followed by an abl. with *de* or *ex*, or by a simple abl., or may be used absolutely as here. In Med. 561 a dative of the person forgetting occurs. — **cuius . . . stetit:** Troy received her death blow when Hector fell before Achilles, and though her final destruction was delayed a little by the removal of her greatest foe (*quidquid . . . remoto*) the issue never was in doubt.

206. dubia quo caderet: like a tree, which stands tottering after its stem is cut through, as if hesitating in what direction it should fall. Vergil (A. 2. 624–631) compares the downfall of Troy with that of a great tree.

207. dare: with *velis* as well as *properes*. — **quod petitur:** what the shade of Achilles demands.

208. iam . . . pretium: the living leaders have made their choice of the spoils and left little for Achilles.

211 ff. Thetis, the mother of Achilles, did all in her power to prevent his going to the Trojan war (see 214 n.). Among other things she foretold that if he went his life would be short and glorious, while if he remained at home he would enjoy a long and peaceful old age (Il. 9. 410–416).

212. Pylii senis: Nestor, whose great age and wisdom were proverbial (Il. 1. 247–252).

214. falsasque vestes: his feminine disguise (*sumptae fallacia vestis — the trick of a dress put on*, Ovid, M. 13. 164). Placed by his mother at the age of nine in the court of Lycomedes, king of Scyros, the future hero grew up there as a maid among maids until he was detected by an artifice of Ulysses (570 n.). The latter brought

gifts of laces and jewels for the girls, and also some pieces of
armor.   While they were examining their gifts a trumpet suddenly
sounded, and Achilles, forgetting his assumed character, seized
the armor and hastily put it on (*fassus est armis virum*).   The
whole story is told briefly by Hyginus (Fab. 96), and in greater
detail by Statius (Achilleis 1. 207 ff.; 670–674).

215–218.   Telephus, king of Mysia, opposed the landing of the
Greeks and was wounded by Achilles.   When at the point of
death he was told by an oracle that the wound could be healed
only with the weapon that had inflicted it.   In answer to his
appeal Achilles applied some rust from the spear point and the
patient recovered (Ovid, M. 12. 112: *opusque meae bis sensit Telephus hastae — Telephus twice felt the power of my spear.*)

217.   rudem: cf. 67 n. and Med. 908.   This was Achilles' first
warlike exploit. — **rēgio:** an adjective. — **dextram:** sc. *Achillis;
Telephus stained the hero's unpracticed hand with the blood of a
king (his own), and found the same hand strong (in battle) and gentle
(in healing).*

219.   Thebae: Thebe, a city of Mysia, ruled by Andromache's
father, Eetion (Il. 1. 366).   Achilles took the town and slew its
king (Il. 6. 414–419; Ovid, M. 12. 110).

221.   Lyrnesos: a town of the Troas, the home of Mines, who
was the husband of Briseis.   The latter was a native of Pedasus,
a neighboring village, referred to in 222 as *the land renowned
for the captive Briseis*.   This was the captive over whom Agamemnon and Achilles quarreled (Il. 1).

223.   Chryse: the home of the priest Chryses, whose repulse by
Agamemnon when he came to reclaim his daughter provoked
Apollo to send a pestilence upon the Greeks and led finally to the
rupture between the two leaders (*causa litis regibus*). — **iacet:**
lies prostrate by Achilles' hand.

224.   Tenedos: Taken by Achilles (Il. 11. 624). — **quae . . .
nutrit:** It seems that our poet here carelessly ascribes to Scyros
the characteristics assigned by Homer (Od. 15. 515 ff.) to Syros,
another island in the Aegean: —

> " It is not large,
> But fruitful, fit for pasturage, and rich
> In flocks, abounding both in wheat and wine."

The taking of Scyros by Achilles is referred to by Homer (Il. 9. 668), and possibly by Ovid (M. 13. 175), though the common reading there is Syron.   It is not unlikely that the present passage was suggested by the one just referred to in Ovid, as the latter names many of the same places — Thebae, Tenedos, Lesbos, Chryse, Cilla, Scyros (?), Lyrnesos — and mentions the fate of Telephus.

226. Lesbos: Achilles' capture of this island is referred to by Agamemnon (Il. 9. 129).

227. Cilla: a town in the Troas, sacred like Chryse to Apollo Smintheus (*Chrysenquo ot Cillam, Apollinis urbes*, Ovid, M. 13. 174). — **quid:** sc. *memorem terras* (or *urbes*) — *why should I tell of the lands that the Caycus laves ?*

228. vernis . . . aquis: the river Caycus (in the Troas) swollen by the rains and the melted snows of spring.

230. sparsae: *the wrecks of so many cities, scattered by him as by a tornado.*

232. iter est Achillis: what would have constituted another's full claim to renown (231) is but the preparation of Achilles for greater achievements (see next verse, and cf. *proludens*, 182 n.).

235. *Would not his defeat of Hector alone have been sufficient ? Yet my father conquered all Troy — and you have plundered it.*

237. sequi: *pursue (the subject of) my father's deeds.   Sequi* is the subject of the impersonal *iuvat.*

239. patrui: sc. *ante oculos.*   Both *patris* (238) and *patrui* here refer to Priam — Hector lay slain before his father's eyes, Memnon before his uncle's.   Both Tithonus, the father of Memnon, and Priam were sons of Laomedon, hence either would be *patruus* to the other's children. — **parens:** Aurora, goddess of the dawn. With her manifestation of grief on this occasion cf. that of Phoebus the sun-god over the fate of Phaethon (Ovid, M. 2. 329–331): "The father, pitiable in his sickening sorrow, had covered and hidden his face; and, if we believe the tale, they say that one day passed without the sunlight."

242. et: *even.* — **dea natos mori:** *that even the sons of a goddess may die.*   As the son of Aurora had fallen, so might his slayer, the son of another divinity.

243. Amazon: see 12 n. — **ultimus . . . metus:** appositive to *Amazon.*   These female warriors came to the aid of the Trojans in the last year of the war, and with their defeat disappeared all hope of relief from without.

244. debes: sc. *eam* from *virginem*, 245 — *even if he should demand (the sacrifice of) a Grecian maiden instead of a Trojan, you owe it to him to grant his desire.*   This, like *iam placita* below, may contain an allusion to the sacrifice of Agamemnon's daughter Iphigenia at Aulis (cf. 164 n.).

246. improbas: the verb.   Pyrrhus here addresses Agamemnon, who though he had not yet spoken may be supposed to have given some token of dissent — *Do you disapprove now, all at once, such an act as met your favor awhile ago at Aulis?*

247. ferum . . . credis: *deem it cruel.*

249. Helenae: *for Helen's sake,* because the sacrifice of Iphigenia was made in order that the fleet might be permitted to sail to Troy for the recovery of Helen. — **solita . . . expeto:** *I am asking (no new thing, but) what is customary with you and has been done before.*

251. aetatis . . . fervor: *the glow of youth* (cf. *iuvenile,* 250; and Horace's *pectoris in dulci iuventa fervor,* C. 1. 16. 22).   The stately Agamemnon assumes an attitude of contemptuous tolerance toward the youthful Pyrrhus, whose natural ardor as a young man was intensified by his inheritance of his father's fiery spirit (*paternus,* 252).   Agamemnon could speak from experience of Achilles' wrath.

253. lentus . . . tuli: *I bore unmoved,* on occasion of the famous quarrel.

254. possis, feras: the "general" second person — *the greater your power the more should you patiently bear.*   Sc. *eo* correlative to *quo.*

255. caede dira: of Polyxena.

256 ff.   *We should consider first the rights of victor and vanquished.* These, however, were not carefully defined in ancient times (see 333, 335).   The tone of this speech is not quite consistent with the spirit displayed by "the king of men" in the first *Iliad,* and we cannot help suspecting that he is indulging in a bit of special pleading against his old foe.

259. quo: correlative to *hoc,* 261.   *The higher fortune has raised him the more does it befit a man to hold himself in check.*

262. **casūs tremere:** this transitive use of *tremere* is poetic and
ate (cf. *hostem tremens,* 317).

263. **nimium faventes:** *too indulgent* (cf. *vento nimium secundo,*
Horace, C. 2. 10. 23).

264. **vincendo:** the final *o* in the ablative is naturally long, and
unless we regard it here as shortened *in arsi,* having neither word
accent nor metrical *ictus,* this is a notable exception to the rule
that the second foot of a dipody must begin with a short syllable
(cf. *Sigeon,* 932 n.).

265. **hoc . . . loco:** *at the zenith of power and warlike renown.*

266. **illa:** *Troia* (from 264). — **impotens regni:** *carried away
by the possession of power,* not self-controlled (as if *impotens sui*).

267. **altius memet tuli:** *have borne myself too loftily, e.g.* in
dealing with Achilles.

268. *My pride has been humbled by this cause — the favor of
fortune — which might have been a source of pride to other men.*

270. **superbum, timidum:** in antithesis, to emphasize the lesson
of Priam's fall — *proud at once, and fearful.*

271. **nisi:** with *vano,* not with *putem — am I to consider kingly
power aught but an empty name, a brow adorned with a coronet whose
promise of happiness is delusive?*

274. *My power perhaps may vanish in less time and for less cause
than Priam's.* For *mille* see 27 n.

277. **affligi . . . volui:** *I would have had Troy humbled but not
destroyed.*

279. **sed . . . ira:** cf. H.F. 404, 405; Med. 591–594, where
the subject is *love spurred on by wrath.* — **regi:** the infinitive; note
the quantity of *e.*

281. **commissa nocti:** the sack of a city by night, when the darkness conceals and encourages excesses (cf. *tenebrae* below).

284. **felix:** *victorious.* — **infecti:** sc. *sanguine.* Observe the
personification—*the sword, the lust of which, once stained with blood,
is frantic.*

289. **thalamos:** predicate — *call the foul deed marriage.*

291. A fine expression of the responsibility that goes with power.
— **cum . . . possit:** to be connected with *vetat.*

295. **levatur . . . infuso:** *appeased by the shedding of blood*

296. opima: may be taken literally, *rich, fat* (cf. *greges opimos*, H.F. 909), or may mean *rich spoils of battle* (cf. H.F. 48 n.). Agamemnon proposes to release Polyxena and substitute a sacrifice of cattle. — **colla:** appositive to *greges*.

297. matri: *no human mother.*

298. iste: *that which you propose.* — **quando . . . hominis:** *when was a human victim ever offered to the shades of a man?*

301, 302. Note the antithesis between the two vocatives *tumide, timide.*

303. tyranne: used here in its original Greek sense of *usurper,* as if Agamemnon had no valid claim to the title he boasted, " king of kings " (cf. *regum rector,* 978; *rex regum, ductor ducum,* Ag. 39). — **iamne . . . novae:** *do you now wear a heart fired with a sudden love, and love of a new object?* Pyrrhus intimates that the true reason for Agamemnon's opposition may be a newly kindled desire to possess Polyxena himself — as formerly he had taken Briseis from Achilles (cf. 305).

308. dignam: sc. *victimam* (also with *maiorem,* 307). This is a veiled threat against Agamemnon himself. He would be a *victima digna quam det Pyrrhus* and *par Priamo* (310). The same menace is implied in *nimium . . . manus — 'tis long since I have slain a king,* the allusion of course being to the death of Priam at his hands (44–56; Vergil, A. 2. 550 ff.).

310 ff. haud . . . paternus: intensely sarcastic — *yes, it is true that your greatest warlike achievement was the slaughter of a helpless old man; one, furthermore, who had knelt at your father's feet, i.e.* in seeking to recover the body of his son Hector (Il. 24. 571–601; Vergil, A. 1. 483–487).

313. supplices . . . novimus: *I recognize my father's suppliant (spared because he was a suppliant), and the same man as an enemy (whom I slew because he was an enemy in arms).* Though plural. *supplices* and *hostes* refer to Priam.

315. praesens: *yet Priam came in person to Achilles,* a thing you dared not do (see next note).

316. nec: emphatic, *not even.* — **Aiaci . . . clausus:** when disaster to the Grecian fleet had followed Achilles' withdrawal Agamemnon sought a reconciliation; but instead of venturing himself into the offended hero's presence he sent an embassy com-

posed of Ulysses, Ajax and Phoenix (Il. 9. 165 ff.). — **hostem:**
Achilles. For the construction with *tremens* cf. *casus tremere,*
262 n.

318. tunc: at the time of the embassy. — **fateor:** ironical, as
is the whole sentence — *of course your father was not afraid. . . .*
He lay idle, forgetful of war and arms, thrumming the tuneful lyre
with polished plectrum.

321. levi: note the long *e*. For the sense cf. Il. 9. 150 ff.:
Achilles there drew solace from the music of a harp, sweet-toned and
shapely, in a silver frame. . . . To soothe his mood he sang the
deeds of heroes.

322 ff. *Though Hector despised your warlike efforts, he feared this*
very music (because it indicated the presence of Achilles, whom alone
he dreaded), and, secure in this fear of his, my father's Thessalian
naval camp enjoyed deep peace.

325, 326. Agamemnon retorts that in that same Thessalian
camp an enemy (Priam) was permitted to go and come in safety.

327. spiritum: *life* (so in 328, 379). Pyrrhus maintains that it
was a kingly act to spare a king's life, and so lays himself open to
his opponent's next thrust, *why then did you not spare him too?*

330. *Is it in mercy now that you seek to sacrifice this maiden?*

331. Iamne: emphatic, as in 303 — *have you come* now *to believe?*
The allusion is to the offering of Iphigenia to Diana (see 249 n.).
The father's defense is given in 332.

336. libere: infinitive of the impersonal *libet;* lit. *it should please*
him to do least (in the way of cruelty to the vanquished) to whom much
is permitted, i.e. the more power one has the less should he use it
wantonly (cf. Seneca's words to Nero, Oct. 450: *Hoc plus verere*
quod licet tantum tibi — you should fear the gods all the more because
so much is committed to you).

337. *Do you make these boasts to the Greeks, whom I (by my part*
in ending the war, and now by my defiance of you) have just released
from your ten years' tyranny? The implication is that Agamemnon's actions and the lofty sentiments just uttered are not in har-
mony.

339. hos . . . animos: *Does tiny Scyros assume such airs?*
The reference, of course, is to Pyrrhus' native place (342, 343 n.;
Scyrius iuvenis, 976). — **Scelere . . . caret:** in allusion to the

tragic feast of Thyestes (Ag. 26. 27; Thy. 970–1034, etc.), prepared by Agamemnon's father, Atreus.   The antecedent of *quae* is *Scyrus*—*it is clear of such sins of brothers as has stained your house* (cf. 341).

340. inclusa: in agreement with *Scyrus*.   Pyrrhus interrupts. — **maris:** dependent on *fluctu*.   It is called *cognati* as being the home of Achilles' mother (Pyrrhus' grandmother), Thetis (cf. *suum*, 176 n.).

341. Cf. 339 n. — **nobilem:** ironical (cf. the like double meaning of *famosus*).

342, 343. Pyrrhus was the son of Achilles and Deidamia, one of his associates in the court of Lycomedes, where he lived disguised as a girl (see 214 n. and the references there given); hence *nondum viro*.

345. omne . . . regnum: each of the three realms into which the universe (*mundum*, 344) was divided on the fall of Saturn (see H.F. 53 n.).   These are mentioned in the following verse, where the ground of Achilles' claim to recognition in each is given — the sea through his mother Thetis (176 n.), the underworld through his paternal grandfather Aeacus, who was a judge there (Ovid, M. 13. 25; Horace, C. 2. 13. 22), and the heavens through Jupiter, the father of Aeacus.

347. Illo ex Achille: sc. *nate* from 343. — **manu Paridis:** according to the usual account Achilles was wounded in his vulnerable heel by Paris, the arrow being guided by Apollo (cf. Il. 22. 359 ff., where the dying Hector foretells his conqueror's fate; Ovid, M. 12. 597–606; Vergil, A. 6. 56: "Phoebus, who didst guide the arrows of Paris into the body of Achilles ").   The speaker says contemptuously, *That Achilles whom the effeminate Paris slew.*

348. Though the gods often baffled Achilles by rescuing his intended victims (*e.g.* Aeneas, rescued by Neptune, Il. 20. 318–329; Hector by Apollo, Il. 20. 443–446), they did not meet him in direct conflict. — **petit:** perfect.

349. malo: cf. the familiar *malum* and *mala res* of the comedy — *I could check your speech and tame your bold self with punishment.*

350. captis quoque: *even captives,* another allusion to Pyrrhus' cruel proposal regarding Polyxena (cf. 333).

352. Calchas: the chief diviner of the Greeks, to whom all important questions regarding the will of the gods were referred (Il. 1. 68; Vergil, A. 2. 122 ff.). — **poscent:** sc. *Polyxenam;* also with *dabo.*

353. Tu: Calchas. — **qui . . . solvisti:** by arranging for the sacrifice of Iphigenia at Aulis and so appeasing the angry Diana.

355. viscerum: the entrails of animals offered in sacrifice, a common method of divination. — **mundi fragor:** thunder.

356. Cf. Vergil, A. 2. 693–698. — **longa:** abl.

358. mercede: abl. of price — *whose responses are of great cost to me.* The allusion probably is to the requirement through Calchas of the sacrifice of Agamemnon's daughter (249 n.), and perhaps to the enforced return of Chryse to her father (Il. 1. 92–100). In Il. 1. 106 Agamemnon protests to Calchas, *Prophet of evil, never hadst thou yet a cheerful word for me.* — **ora:** for *oracula.*

SCENE 3 (vv. 360–370). — The seer's response.

360. Cf. Vergil, A. 2. 116–119 — *with blood and a maiden's death you appeased the winds when first you came to Trojan shores; with blood your return must be sought, and atonement must be made with a Grecian life.*

362. *Let her be clad in Grecian marriage robes* (cf. 865, 1132).

369. nepos Hectoreus: Astyanax (461–474, 503–512; *Hectorea suboles,* 528). In the *Iliad* (6. 400) he is described as an infant in arms.

SCENE 4 (vv. 371–408). — The chorus speculates concerning a future life, and concludes that there is none. The measure is the minor asclepiadean, the last verse incomplete.

372. corporibus conditis: abl. abs. of concession — *is it true that the souls live on though the bodies are buried, or does a myth beguile us ?*

374. *When the last day of life has stood in the way of the sun,* and prevented its rising again for us. — **solibus:** plural, as if a new one rose each day (cf. Horace's *aliusque et idem nasceris* — *art born another, yet the same,* C.S. 10).

377. miseris: dat. — **longius:** *i.e.* after death. In their despair immortality seems to the Trojan women a curse instead of a blessing.

378. Cf. Horace's declaration, in a somewhat different sense, *non omnis moriar, multaque pars mei vitabit Libitinam,* C. 3. 30. 6.

379. spiritus: *life,* as in 327 — *when with the fleeting breath the life has fled into the air, mingling with the vapors.*

381. subdita fax: the torch applied to the funeral pyre.

382–385. Cf. Epig. 7: *Devouring time feasts upon all things, grasps all things, removes all things from their place, lets nothing long exist. . . . Death claims all things. . . . Sometime this universe will be nothing.*

384. bis . . . fugiens: in the ebb and flow of the tides.

385. Pegaseo . . . gradu: *with the swift pace of Pegasus,* the flying horse.

386. bis sena . . . sidera: the twelve signs of the zodiac. — **turbine:** the apparent revolution of the heavens about the earth.

388. astrorum dominus: the sun (cf. *dux astrorum,* Thy. 836), whose apparent motions give us the day and the year, and so the *saecula* (387).

389. Hecate: *Luna* (Med. 7 n.). — **obliquis . . . flexibus:** *in the sidelong curve of her orbit.* The moon does not pass westward directly overhead at this latitude, but apparently swerves to the southward (cf. H.F. 1333 n.).

390. hoc: sc. *modo* from 388. — **nec amplius . . . usquam est:** *nevermore does he exist.* For the phrase cf. H.F. 1025: *caput abest nec usquam est.*

391. iuratos superis . . . lacus: the Styx, by which the gods of heaven swore and were bound inviolably (Vergil, A. 6. 324: *di cuius iurare timent et fallere numen — the Styx, by whose divinity the gods fear to swear and prove false.* **tetigit:** *has died and been ferried over the Styx.*

395. dissicit: for *disicit* (cf. Lucretius, R.N. 3. 639).

397. Cf. Lucretius, R.N. 3. 830: *nil igitur mors est, ad nos neque pertinet hilum — therefore death is nothing, and concerns us not at all;* Seneca, Epist. 54. 3: *Mors est non esse.*

398. *The final goal of a swift race.*

401. individua: explained by *noxia . . . nec parcens—Death is indivisible; it is fatal to the body and does not spare the soul.* The idea, consistent with the thought of the whole passage, is that death cannot attack the body and leave the soul alive. In his third book Lucretius gives an elaborate argument, based in part on the soul's nature as conceived by the Epicureans, and in part on analogy drawn from physical existence, to prove the soul's mortality.

402. Taenara: the Greeks (H.F. 662 ff.) located the entrance to the lower world near Spartan Taenarus (here in the neuter plural form), as Vergil did in the volcanic region about Cumae. — **aspero domino:** Pluto. *Taenara, regnum, Cerberus* (with *custos* in apposition) are the subjects and *rumores, verba* and *fabula* predicate nouns with *sunt,* suggested by *est* in 401. *Limen* is object of *obsidens,* and itself is modified by the descriptive ablative *non facili ostio, of no easy passage.*

405, 406. *Idle tales, empty words, a myth of no more weight than a troubled dream.*

408. quo: sc. *loco.* — **non nata:** *the unborn,* things not created.

ACT III

SCENE 1 (vv. 409–425). — Andromache, the widow of Hector, declares that the woes of Troy are too deep for tears, and that only her duty to her son induces her to live on.

409. maesta Phrygiae turba: addressing the chorus. *Maesta turba* is appositive to *Phrygiae* (cf. *turba captivae mea,* 63 n.). *Phrygiae,* meaning Trojan women, is found in Vergil, A. 6. 518.

411. levia . . . patimur: *we have suffered light evils if we suffer what can be expressed with tears.*

413. olim: *for me Troy fell long ago, when Hector fell.* One of the finest passages in the *Iliad* contains Andromache's lament over the death of her husband (22. 437–515).

414. mea membra: in the person of Hector.

415. Peliacus: *i.e.* of Achilles, son of Peleus. For the dragging of Hector's body see 189 n. — **pondere . . . tremens:** cf. *gravi gemeret sono,* 414. It was a common thing to represent the heroes of the epic as gigantic in size and strength.

416. tunc . . . fero: *since then I have borne.*

418. erepta Danais: *rescued from the Greeks* by death. The sense of *erepta* is proleptic.— **sequerer:** *I would have followed him to the tomb.*

419. hic: pointing to her child, Astyanax, who now constituted the only tie holding her to life (*mori prohibet,* 420).

422. *He has stolen from me the greatest good of misfortune — the ability to fear nothing* (cf. 632, 633; *fructus est scelerum tibi nullum scelus putare,* Med. 563).

424. qua veniant: *but sorrow has a place where (a side on which) it may assail me* — in the person of my son.

425. A general statement, but with special reference to her own position.

SCENE 2 (vv. 426–523). — Andromache expresses her fears for the safety of her son, and on consultation with an aged man hides the boy in his father's tomb.

428. stetit: *paused* — it has not yet attained its full measure.

429. *What new calamity will the god find for us even if he desire it ?*

430 ff. From this it would appear that the apparition of Achilles, described by Talthybius in 170 ff., was known to Andromache and the other Trojans, though not its precise object (927 ff.).

432. hostes . . . conditi: *the enemy, though dead and buried.* As but one is meant, *hostes* perhaps is the "plural of preëminence" (cf. *supplices, hostes,* 313), though it is not unlike the plural of proper names often used in English in general statements.

433. retro: *Back from the land of the dead* (cf. H.F. 55 for a similar expression). The thought is, *Could not Hector have returned as well as his enemy ?* (cf. *redit Achilles,* 806 n.).

434. *Surely death is impartial!* — **turbat . . . terror:** *that terror (Achilles' appearance), common to Greeks and Trojans alike, troubles and disturbs us.*

435. hic . . . sopor: *this dream terrifies* my *soul in particular.*

438. It is not always certain whether Seneca's phrases refer to Greek or to Roman customs: if to the latter, here the time would be midnight; if to the former, it would be near dawn, when two of the three watches had elapsed. This would correspond to the time of the apparition of Achilles (170 n.). — **alma:** a common epithet of *sol, dies, lux,* and words of kindred meaning, here applied to *nox,* as in Med. 876.

439. septem . . . stellae: in the constellation Ursa Major. — **iugum:** *wagon, cart* (cf. *curtum temone iugum,* Juvenal, Sat. 10. 135). The same constellation is called *plaustra* by the Latin writers (*e.g.* in Med. 315), and in England is still known as "Charles' wain."

440. ignota: *unfamiliar.* — **afflictae:** sc. *mihi,* or take in a general sense, *unfamiliar to one stricken with grief.*

442. somnus: a predicate noun. Compare the account of this vision with that given of another apparition of Hector by Vergil (A. 2. 268 ff.), which is similar in several details and may have been Seneca's model.

445. *E.g.* in Il. 15. 704 to end (cf. *Danaum Phrygios iaculatus puppibus ignes,* Vergil, A. 2. 276).

447. While still unwilling to aid the Greeks in person, Achilles was persuaded at a critical point in the siege to lend his armor (*vera spolia*) to his friend Patroclus (*Achille simulato*), who, after creating dismay among the Trojans by his appearance, finally was encountered and slain by Hector (Il. 16. 783 to end). Hector's triumphant donning of Achilles' armor is described in Il. 17. 188 ff. (cf. Vergil, A. 2. 275: *he returned clad in the spoils of Achilles*).

448. *His eye flashing fire. Vultus* is nom. sing.

450. nostro: sc. *vultui; like my own.* — **squalida:** Vergil (A. 2. 277) has *squalentem barbam et concretos sanguine crines.*

455. utinam . . . tota: there was a tower still standing, and from this the boy was to be cast (368, 621, 1068).

456. quocumque: as if *quocumque possis.*

458. The feminine adjectives, of course, modify *ego,* subject of *quaesivi*— *Trembling, turning my eyes this way and that, forgetful of my son, I sought, unhappy woman that I am, to clasp Hector in my arms.*

460. fallax: *elusive* (cf. Aeneas' experience, A. 2. 792–794; 6. 700–702: *Thrice I tried to cast my arms about her neck ; thrice the apparition, vainly clasped, fled through my hands like the light winds and very like a fleeting dream*).

461. Here for the first time Andromache addresses her son, Astyanax, who of course has been with her throughout the scene. — **certa progenies**: note the points of resemblance enumerated below: *vultus*, 464; *incessu*, 465; *habitu, manus*, 466; *umeris, fronte*, 467; *cervice, comam*, 468.

462. Observe the two different constructions with *spes*, dative in *Phrygibus*, genitive in *domus*.

464. similis: what case? — **hos . . . Hector**: *my Hector had these features*, *i.e.* the same which are now to be seen in his son.

467. celsus, minax: sc. *fuit*.

468. iacta: *thrown proudly back*.

469. *Born too late to save Troy, too soon for your mother's good*, *i.e.* so soon as to share these perils and add to her anxieties (cf. 418-425).

472. rediviva . . . Pergama: *restore the towers of Troy*.

474. sed . . . vivamus: *remembering my condition, I fear to cherish such high hopes — life is all a captive can expect* (cf. 732-735).

478. deum: gen. Apollo and Neptune are meant (see 7 n.).

479. invidiae gravis: this may be a genitive of quality, *characterized by the burden of envy it bore;* or *gravis* may be nom. and *invidiae* a kind of specifying genitive, which was used so freely in the Silver Age.

481. ne . . . infans: *not even so much as will serve to conceal a child.*

482. quo lateat: result. — **fraudi**: *stratagem*, the concealment of the boy.

483. coniugis: Hector. The genitive with *sacer* is the classical usage.

484. verendus hosti: *which the enemy should reverence.* — **quem**: the antecedent is *tumulus*. — **parens**: Priam.

485. in luctus . . . non avarus: *liberal in spending money upon the objects of his grief.* Another illustration is found in his ransoming of Hector's body (Il. 24. 571-601; Vergil, A. 1. 484).

486. credam patri: *intrust the boy to his father.*

488. To hide the child in a tomb was too suggestive and ominous.

497 ff. Verse numbers here represent their arrangement in the oldest MS., but the sense was so obscure that modern editors have rearranged them.

497. The sense is general —*Let the unfortunate take what refuge he can; let him choose who is safe.* In this case, of course, there was no choice.

492. doli: same idea as *fraudi,* 482 — *exclude all witnesses of the act.*

493. perit: Perfect. The sense is, *If an enemy seek him, give it out that he lost his life in the sack of the city.* This is the course the mother actually attempted (556 ff.).

489. causa: explained by its appositive, *credi perisse—that they were believed to have perished.*

490. est super: for *superest* (cf. 507, 960, 1068).

491. pondus: appositive to *nobilitas.*

494. redituro: conditional in force; *what will it avail him to have hidden, if he is to fall again into their hands ?*

495. His safety lies in the cooling of the victor's rage after its first flush.

498. te: again addressing the boy. — **invia:** *inaccessible.*

500. qui semper: sc. *tuitus es.*

501. furtum: abstract for concrete, like *senectus,* 42; *coniugia,* 59, etc. It here stands for the boy himself, stolen from the enemy and hidden (cf. the same word in 706). The sense is, *Guard our son, thus stealthily intrusted to thy keeping.*

502. victurum : from *vivo ;* note its antithesis to *cinere.*

505. fugā: imperative.

506. quos: sc. *animos— assume the spirit fate has permitted.*

507. *See what a company of us remain* — explained by *tumulus, puer, captiva — dead father, infant son, and captive mother.* — **simus super:** see 490 n.

512. claustra . . . tegunt: the boy has been hidden and the entrance to the tomb closed. — **commissum:** sc. *eum tumulo;* or *commissum* may be regarded as a neuter substantive, *your trust* (cf. *depositum,* 521; *furtum,* 501).

513. The old man fears that the mother's agitation may arouse suspicion if she is seen lingering near the tomb. — **quem:** antecedent is *eum,* implied in *commissum.*

517. cohibe . . . ora: *be silent, do not speak.*

518. dux Cephallanum: Ulysses, who enters at 524. Cephallania was a large island near Ithaca, and its inhabitants are spoken of by Homer (Il. 2. 631) as subjects of Ulysses.

519. tuque: she appeals to her dead husband, as in 500 — *Cleave asunder the earth, riven from its deepest abyss.* In 684 she fancies he has come.

521. depositum: a technical term in Roman law denoting an object of value intrusted to another for safe-keeping. Here, of course, it is said of Astyanax (cf. *commissum*, 512).

522. dubio: the hesitating step of one approaching a difficult task and debating within himself the manner of its performances.

523. astus callidos: the characteristic of Ulysses at all times (cf. 38, 568, 613, 750, 857, 927).

SCENE 3 (vv. 524–813). — On Ulysses' demand for the surrender of her son Andromache pretends, almost successfully, that he is dead; but finally, when he proposes to demolish the tomb of Hector, she yields and gives up the child.

524. sortis: the response given by Calchas, 360–370.

527. seras: cf. 164. *Quos* is subject and *domos* object of *petere.*

528. hanc: sc. *subolem, i.e.* Astyanax. — **fata:** speaking through Calchas.

531. arma . . . sinet: *and will not permit their weapons to be laid aside.*

533. Andromacha: the Latin form of the name, used for the sake of the short ultima. In other cases (*e.g.* 968), where a long syllable is required, the Greek form *Andromache* is written. For accusatives in *-am* and *-en* see 576 and 804.

535. dicebat Hector: An instance is found in Il. 6. 476-481: —

> "O Jupiter and all ye deities,
> Vouchsafe that this my son may yet become
> Among the Trojans eminent like me,
> And nobly rule in Ilium. May they say,
> ' This man is greater than his father was!'

When they behold him from the battlefield
Bring back the bloody spoil of the slain foe —
That so his mother may be glad at heart." — (Bryant.)

et: intensive; *even.*

536. generosa . . . semina: the children of those nobly born. —
exurgunt: *exsurgunt.*

537. ille . . . parvus comes: the calf following its dam.

539. subito: *speedily.* As the young bullock soon reaches maturity, so will Hector's son.

541. The figure is changed, and an illustration taken from the
vegetable world — the sprout that shoots up from a fallen tree
or its stump soon grows into a great tree, the nucleus of a
forest.

544. A third illustration, from the rekindling of a smoldering
fire. The sense of the whole passage is this: as a young bullock
soon develops into the strength and spirit of his sire; as a tiny
shoot quickly grows to be a tree; as the coals of a fire apparently
dead may be fanned into new life, so may this infant become
another Hector, and be the scourge of Greece.

545. iniustus: with *aestimator.* — **dolor:** your present grief unfits
you to weigh considerations fairly. In the *Hecuba* of Euripides
(299–331) Ulysses makes a very similar plea to Hecuba.

546. exigas: *consider.*

547. bella: object of *timet*, next line.

549. numquam bene . . . iacentem: Troy had been prostrate
before (718–731), but had recovered.

551. futurus Hector: see 461–474; here appositive to *magna
res.*

552. deductas: *launched*, ready to sail. During the war they
had been drawn on up the beach.

553. hac: sc. *causa.* — **crudelem:** sc. *me.* — **neve . . . putes:**
prohibitive.

554. sorte: as in 524.

555. petissem Oresten: sc. *si sors iussisset.* Orestes was the
son of Agamemnon, and Ulysses says in substance, *Had the fates
demanded, I should have sought for sacrifice the son of the Greek
instead of the Trojan leader.* The idea was suggested, of course,

by the fact that Agamemnon had offered up his daughter at Aulis (249 n.), and there is the same allusion in *quod victor tulit.* — **patere:** imperative.

556. Andromache attempts to deceive Ulysses, as had been advised in 493.

559. **confossa:** in agreement with the subject of *exuissem,* 562; so *praestricta* and *cincta.* *Pectus* and *latus* are adverbial accusatives.

560. **secantibus:** *that cut into the flesh.*

564. **patriae vapor:** the heat of the burning city.

566. **numquid:** *can it be that — ?*

570. **etiam dearum:** alluding to Thetis, the mother of Achilles, whose attempt to save her son from his fate at Troy by concealing him at the court of Lycomedes had been defeated by the cunning of Ulysses (see 214 n., and cf. Statius, Ach. 2. 166 ff.).

573. **coacta:** nom. sing.; *you shall tell under compulsion what you will not of your own accord.*

574. **perire:** complement of the three verbs that follow.

576. **Andromacham:** see note on 533.

577. *Threaten me with life, not death.*

579. **invitam:** sc. *te.*

585. **istis:** *this body which you threaten.* *Istis* is used in preference to *his* because the speaker is addressing the man who had threatened the torture, and in a sense is repeating his thought. — **caeci:** *as black as blindness.*

586. **iratus timens:** *the victor, enraged at the resistance he has met, and still fearful of its renewal* (530, 548, 551).

590. Because Astyanax grown up may avenge the woes of his parents upon the Greeks of the coming generation (cf. *Telemacho bella paras,* 593).

595. **premis:** *are concealing* (cf. *curam premebat,* Vergil, A. 4. 332).

596. **gaudete Atridae:** apostrophe. — **laetifica:** *glad tidings,* object of *refer.* — **ut soles:** Ulysses had been a conspicuous actor in nearly all the spectacular exploits of the Greeks — the repulse of Sarpedon, the capture of Rhesus, the taking of the palladium, etc. (38 n.).

597. **obit:** for *obiit* (cf. *perit,* 493).

599. *So may the greatest ill the conqueror can threaten (i.e.* death, which to her would seem a blessing, 418 ff., 577) *befall me . . . as he lies among the dead.* This imprecation is constructed very ingeniously so that while the speaker is telling the literal truth she conveys a false impression.

604. debita exanimis: *what is due the dead, i.e.* the funeral rites (cf. *iusta Troiae*, 65; *iusta functis*, Med. 999). — **exanimis:** dat. plur., though usually of the consonant declension.

605. *I'll gladly bear word to the Greeks that the oracle has been fulfilled by the removal of Hector's offspring.* For the moment Ulysses is convinced, but doubt returns immediately (607).

607–618. Spoken aside.

608. tu cui: sc. *credis.* — **fingit . . . pavet:** to the Greeks and Romans the thought of death was so abhorrent that periphrases were commonly used in order to avoid direct mention of it (*e.g. Si quid mihi humanitus accidisset,* Cicero, Phil. 1. 4). Here Ulysses can hardly believe that Andromache would dare pretend so horrible a thing as the death of her own son, as if the very pretense might prove an omen (*auspicium*) of its reality (cf. the mother's own fears, 488).

610. Ulysses answers his own question — *They fear omens who have nothing worse to fear.*

614. totum Ulixen: as the incarnation of craft.

615. maeret: she does show signs of grief, as might a mother bereft of her child, but her gait and anxious listening to every sound suggest another emotion.

618. *It is more fear of something still to come than grief for the past.*

619. alloqui in luctu: *commiserate.*

621, 622. He states for the first time his precise purpose, and watches the effect. For *sola . . . manet* cf. 1068. Andromache's speech which follows and the first two lines of Ulysses' next speech (625, 626) are aside.

627. ite celeres: to his attendants.

630. Aside. **bene est; tenetur:** *she is caught!* (cf. Med. 550).

631. Tauntingly to Andromache. **iam certe perit:** in mocking allusion to her attempted deceit (556–567). — **perit:** perfect.

R

632. *Would my son were living, that I might fear for him. What you take for signs of terror are but the result of long habit.*

633. Long familiarity with any emotion often begets insensibility to it (cf. 422 n.).

634–641. We need not suppose that Ulysses had any suspicion as to where the boy was hidden, but merely that he seizes on this idea as a means of torturing his victim into some expression that may supply a clew. It is ingeniously conceived. — **lustrale sacrum**: *rites of purification.*

638. **plăcet**: from *placare*. — **sparsi**: in agreement with *Hectoris* by hypallage (cf. 643). The real idea of course is "the scattering of Hector's ashes."

640. **ille**: Astyanax. — **effūgit**: perfect.

642–662. Aside. **quid agimus**: *what am I to do?* We should expect the subjunctive in such a question, but the connection shows clearly enough what is meant.

644. **pars utra vincet**: by giving up her son she might save her husband's ashes from profanation; by remaining silent she might possibly find opportunity to spirit away the boy and leave the tomb to its fate. A modern mother would not hesitate long between the living and the dead; but to Andromache, believing that burial was essential to the happiness of the dead, it was a fearful dilemma. Hence it is not strange that she wavered, inclining now to save the child (647, 651, 655, 659, 662), and now to guard the father's ashes (648, 653, 658), finally deciding upon the latter (691 ff.). — **immites deos**: the gods who have permitted all the woes that have befallen her.

645. **manes**: appositive to *deos veros.*

646. **non aliud . . . quam te**: *'tis his likeness to you that most endears my son to me* (cf. 461–468). This infinitive clause is object of the "witness" idea in *testor.*

649. **mergetur**: *shall his ashes be sunk in the sea?* — as proposed in 638.

650. **hic**: Astyanax (so in 655, 659).

652. **poteris**: sc. *videre*. **fastigia**: cf. *turre*, 368, 622, 1068.

654. **fata**: *death.*

656. **illum**: Hector; he is beyond their reach.

659. **sensus**: gen. with *potens* (cf. *mentis potenti*, Ovid, Tr. 2. 139).

660. Cf. 470–474, 550, 551.

663. responsa peragam: *I will fulfill the oracle* (639).

664. quae vendidistis: alluding to the ransom of Hector's body by his father (485 n.). Note the number of *vendidistis — destroy the tomb which ye Greeks have sold?* *Quae,* of course, is relative, with *busta* for its antecedent.

665. Caelitum fidem: *the protection of the gods; fidem Achillis,* on the other hand, may mean the good faith of Achilles as pledged in restoring Hector's body for burial.

667. munus tuere: *protect your father's gift,* do not desecrate the body which he gave up for burial.

669. deos . . . faventes: In Il. 20. 38–40 Mars, Apollo, Diana, Latona, Xanthus and Venus are named as taking the side of the Trojans; while Juno, Minerva, Neptune, Mercury and Vulcan favored the Greeks. In the sack of the city the temples of all suffered alike (Vergil, A. 2. 763, 764), and in particular was Minerva insulted by the attempt of Ajax Oileus to drag Cassandra from her shrine. Up to this time, however, the resting-places of the dead had been respected (*busta transierat furor*). Note the force of the tense in *fuerat* and *transierat.*

673. Amazon: see 12 n. In Phaed. 399–403 the Amazons are spoken of as having invaded Attica. The reference here may be to that or to their attempt to relieve Troy, in the course of which they may be said to have "laid low many of the Grecian (*Argolicas*) troops." The gentle Andromache threatens to play the Amazon.

674. maenas: the *maenades* were female devotees of Bacchus, famous for their wild orgies. With *deo percussa* cf. *recepto maenas insanit deo,* Med. 383; and with *entheo gradu* cf. *entheos gressus,* Med. 382.

675. armata thyrso: cf. H.F. 474 n. — **expers sui:** *beside herself.*

676. *Talis* is understood with the subject of *ruam,* correlative to *qualis,* 672, 673.

678. To his attendants.

681. repellor: Andromache is thrust aside, and her outburst of martial energy gives way to despair.

682. molire terras: *heave up the earth.*

683. vel umbra: *even as a shade (ghost) you are equal to the task* — arma . . . ignes: in her frenzy she imagines that her desire is realized and that Hector is coming.

686–691. Spoken aside, to herself.

688. conditum: sc. *natum* — *the enormous weight of the falling tomb will straightway crush him, buried there.*

690. ubicumque: *anywhere-soever.*

691. ad genua: she prostrates herself at the feet of Ulysses, clasping them, or his knees, with *the hand that no one's knees have ever known before* (for this mode of expressing submission and appeal see Med. 247 n.).

696. mitius: sc. *eo,* correlative to *quo* in 695. For the sentiment cf. 336 n.

697. " He that hath pity upon the poor lendeth to the Lord," Proverbs 19: 17.

698. coniugis sanctae: *chaste wife* — Penelope.

700. Laerta: Latin form of the Greek *Laertes,* which latter is found in Thy. 587 (cf. *Andromacha,* 533 n.). — iuvenis tuus: Telemachus (cf. 593).

702. avum, patrem: Laertes, famous for his great age, Ulysses for his unrivaled craft and wisdom. Her adjuration is, *according as you pity me, so may you see wife and father and son again.*

704. hic: the child; so in 707. — exhibe . . . roga: *produce the boy, then ask your boon.*

705. The change of measure indicates the speaker's agitation, and the passage, in anapests, has almost the effect of a chorus. — procede: *come forth* — addressed to Astyanax.

706. furtum: as in 501.

707. *This, Ulysses, this helpless babe, is that source of terror to the thousand ships!* (cf. 550).

708. submitte: to Astyanax — *lower your hands, and with appealing touch entreat your master's feet* (691 n.).

712. *Put away from your thoughts your royal ancestry* (Horace has *atavis regibus,* C. 1. 1. 1).

713. senis: Priam.

714. excidat: *be forgotten* (cf. 204 n.).

715. gere captivum: *play the captive* (cf. *dedisce captam,* 884).

718 ff. Troy was taken and its king Laomedon slain on account
of his breach of faith with Hercules (7 n., 133 n.). Priam, then a
child (*pueri regis*), known as Podarces, was spared by the victor
(or, according to Apollodorus, was ransomed by his sister Hesione
and hence called Priam from πρίασθαι, *to ransom*), and ascended
the throne.

721, 722.   Cf. H.F. 30–42, and the enumeration of Hercules'
labors in H.F. 215–248 and Ovid, M. 9. 182–199.

723, 724. In quest of Cerberus (H.F. 46–56, 807–827).

725 hostis parvi: Priam (*pueri regis*, 718).

727. sedē: imperative.

728. fide meliore: the treachery of Laomedon was proverbial,
and his name was applied as a term of reproach to his descendants
(*e.g. Laomedontiadae*, Vergil, A. 3. 248; *Laomedonteae periuria
gentis*, 4. 542).

729. *This it was to be taken by such a conqueror.*

731. *Will you emulate only his prowess (and not his
mercy)?*

732. non minor . . . supplex: *a suppliant (Astyanax) not inferior to that suppliant (Priam)* whom Hercules spared.

737, 738. Cf. 529–535, 550–553. — **crescit:** see 534–545.

739. *Shall this child fan to life these ruins of the city, now reduced
to ashes?* (cf. Ulysses' figure of the supposedly dead fire in 545). —
excitabit: cf. *vires resumit*, 545.

742. non sic: *we Trojans do not yield while we have any strength
left to harm our foes.*

743. spiritus: *pride* (so *animos*, 745). — **genitor:** Hector — *does
the thought of his father give him pride?   But surely he was dragged
behind his chariot by Achilles.*

747. *Let the yoke of a slave be placed upon his highborn neck;
let the privilege of being a slave be granted him — does any refuse
this to a prince?*   Note the antithesis between *famulare* and *nobili,
servire* and *regi.*

751. Andromache is unfair to Ulysses here, for he had courage
as well as cunning (see 757).

753. etiam Pelasgi: *e.g.* Iphigenia (249 n.), Palamedes (Vergil, A.
2. 82), and Ajax, who killed himself in a fit of insanity after being
defeated by Ulysses in the contest for the arms of Achilles (Ovid,

M. 13. 382–398). — **vatem praetendis:** *do you screen yourself behind a seer and the blameless gods ?*

754. *This is the deed of your own heart, i.e.* you have controlled the response you quote. Vergil (A. 2. 122 ff.) makes Sinon ascribe to Ulysses a similar mastery over Calchas.

755. nocturne miles: *brave only in secret attack* (cf. Ovid, M. 13. 100, quoted in note on 38).

756. *No other would dare* (i.e. *be shameless enough) to attack an infant in the light of day;* or, *This is one deed you dare do alone, without Diomede's help* (see 38 n.).

758. non vacat: *there is not leisure.*

759. ancoras . . . legit: *is weighing anchor* (cf. *naves deductas,* 552 n.).

762. misereri: so far as to spare the child.

765. implere: used as a middle.

767. summum: *last* (see 418–425).

768–770. Cf. 700–702.

770. demens: a doubtful reading, repeated from 768; MSS. have *medios,* while Leo suggests *toties.*

774. caedes: the verb. — **terga:** implying their cowardly flight. — **non Pyrrhum trahes:** in retaliation for his father's treatment of your father's body.

775. tenera, parva: agreement may be determined by scansion. For the thought cf. H.F. 1126 n.

777. sequeris: tense is shown by scansion. — **lustri:** a Roman word and idea (cf. 782 n.).

778. referens: *reproducing.* — **sollemne . . . sacrum:** the *Lusus Troicus* or *Ludus Troiae* was very popular in the time of the early Empire at Rome. It consisted of an exhibition of skillful riding by boys or youths of the noblest families (see Vergil's description, A. 5. 545–603).

780. The reference is to the wild worship of Cybele, which had its origin and chief seat near Troy, and in later times was introduced at Rome. The spirit of it is well reproduced in the *Attis* of Catullus (C. 63).

781. flexo . . . cornu: *while the curving trumpet echoes back the stirring measures.*

782. barbarica: *Phrygian.* To the Greeks, and to the Romans who copied their literature, *barbarus, barbaricus,* etc., meant simply *not Grecian.* Of course the word is hardly appropriate in the mouth of a Trojan woman.

783. So inglorious a form of death was worse than the cruelties of war.

785. muri videbunt: the towers on the walls of Troy had been a favorite vantage point for those who would watch the combats in the plain beneath (Il. 3. 145–153; Ovid, M. 13. 415–417 — "Those towers from which Astyanax used often to see his father, pointed out by his mother, as he fought for himself and his ancestral kingdom"). It was from the wall that Hector's parents had seen his fall, and there Andromache had fainted at sight of his body dragged away by his victorious enemy (Il. 22. 462 ff.). Here, by an easy figure, the walls themselves are said to see. — **rumpe . . . fletus:** Ulysses forgets the promise implied in his words *arbitrio tuo implere lacrimis,* 764.

788. paucas: sc. *lacrimas.* — **condam:** *close.*

789. viventis: sc. *pueri.* — **occidis:** said to her son.

790. expectat: *awaits you in the land of the dead.* — **tua:** the Troy that is worthy of you; all who survive are slaves (cf. *liberos Troas*).

792. The only speech of Astyanax. His fellow-victim, Polyxena, does not speak at all.

793. cassa praesidia: appositive to *manus.*

802. perfer: *carry to your father.* — **si . . . priores:** in Oct. 138 it is declared that "To the dead, among the spirits, remains no care of their offspring." — **flammis:** the funeral fire, which consumed the body.

804. Andromachen: see 533 n. and cf. *Andromacham,* 576.

806. redit Achilles: *i.e.* his ghost (181–186). The thought is, *If Achilles has been able to return, why may not Hector?* (cf. 433 n., 434 n.). — **redit:** for *rediit.* — **sume . . . comas:** cf. *laceros crines excipe,* 800. The reference is to the tearing of the hair in grief (99, 100). — **iterum:** *now, over our son, as formerly at your death.*

807. viri: *my husband.*

809. parenti: Hector. — **hanc . . . vestem:** as a memento.

810. tumulus . . . meus: cf. *mea membra,* 414.

811. siquid . . . ore: *if any of his ashes remain in this garment, I will search it out with my kisses.*

813. abripite: to his attendants. — moram: with a double reference — to the actual delay, which he is impatient to see ended, and to Astyanax as the cause of the delay (552).

SCENE 4 (vv. 814–860). — The chorus wonders to what part of Greece each of the captive women will be dragged, and prays that the lot may not send any to Sparta, Mycenae or Ithaca. the homes of Troy's worst foes.   The measure is an irregular arrangement of sapphic and adonic verses.

814. vocat: the subject is not only *sedes*, but each nominative place-name in 815–843.   The whole is little more than a list of names, taken with the exception of four — Tempe, Peparethos, Eleusin and Pisae — from the Homeric catalogue of the ships (Il. 2. 484–789).   A similar choral passage, much less extended, is met in the *Hecuba* of Euripides (444–481). — captas: sc. *Troadas.*

817. Phthiē: Ionic Greek form of *Phthia*, the birthplace of Achilles — hence *viros tellus dare militares aptior.*

818. lapidosa Trachin: cf. *aspera Trachin*, H.O. 195; a village near the most rugged portion of Mt. Oeta, said to have been founded by Hercules.

819. maris . . . domitrix: it was from Iolcos that the Argo sailed, the first Greek vessel to attempt a long sea voyage (cf. Med. 596, where Jason, its captain, is characterized as *mare qui subegit*).

820. Crete, early settled and thickly populated, is often called "the land of a hundred cities" (see H.F. 230 n.).   This, of course, as well as "the thousand ships" (27 n.), is merely a round number, like the *trecenti* so often used by the Romans.   In the *Odyssey* the number of cities is given as ninety.

821. Gortynis: Gortyn, Gortyna, Gortyne (all these forms are met) was a Cretan town.   As its introduction here after the whole island has been characterized seems awkward, it has been conjectured that Gyrtone was meant, which, like Tricce in the same line, was a Thessalian town.   Both are mentioned by Pliny (N.H. 4) in his account of their respective regions.

822. Mothone: this is hard to explain. There was a Mothone in Messenia, but it was not the home of Philoctetes (137 n.) and so did not *send the bow twice for the ruin of Troy* (824). Another reading is Methone, described in Il. 2. 715–719 as the home of Philoctetes, but in the first place its initial syllable is long and will not fit the measure, and in the second place it was nowhere near Mt. Oeta. Gronovius suggested making the question end with this line and a new one begin with *quae*.

826, 827. Olenos, Pleuron: towns in Aetolia. — **virgini . . . divae**: Diana. Oeneus, king of Calydon, the portion of Aetolia in which these towns stood, neglected this goddess while offering sacrifice to all the others, and in punishment his lands were ravaged by a monstrous boar (845), whose capture was the object of the famous Calydonian hunt, described at length by Ovid (M. 8. 260–439).

828. Troezen: situated on a fine bay of the Aegean, hence *maris lati sinuosa*.

829, 830. regnum . . . superbum: Prothous was leader of the Magnesians, in whose territory Pelion stood, against Troy. — **tertius . . . gradus**: *the third step* in passing from earth to heaven. The Titans of the line of Iapetus attempted to dethrone Jupiter, who had succeeded his father Saturn, and in order to scale the heavens piled one mountain upon another to make a ladder (see note on H.F. 972).

830–835. A digression suggested by the fact that on Mt. Pelion the terrible Achilles had received his early training (see H.F. 971 n.).

831. antro: in Statius, Ach. 1. 106, we read that "A lofty hall penetrates the mountain and supports Pelion on a long arch. Part was excavated by hand and part was the work of time." In this cave dwelt the centaur Chiron, who was tutor of both Hercules and Achilles. *Iam trucis pueri* refers to the latter.

836. Carystos: a town of Euboea, noted for its marble (*varii lapidis*).

838. Chalcis: also in Euboea, at the narrowest part of the channel Euripus, whose current, flowing swiftly and changing direction repeatedly under the influence of wind and tide, was believed to ebb and flow seven times each day (see note on H.F. 378 for fuller explanation).

839. **Calydnae:** a group of islands near the coast of Caria, especially exposed to winds from all directions.

840. **Gonoessa:** called by Homer αἰπεινή, *lofty*, and so assailed by every wind that blows.

841. **Enispe:** a town of Arcadia, called by Homer "wind-swept."

842. **Peparethos:** there is an island of this name off the coast not of Attica but of Thessaly. Some have explained the name here as that of an Attic deme instead of the island.

843. **Eleusin:** not in the Homeric catalogue, but probably selected in place of its old and successful rival, Athens, as representative of Attica. It was the seat of the celebration of the mysteries of Ceres (cf. notes on H.F. 300, 844). To reveal the Eleusinian mysteries to any but a regular initiate was an offense against gods and men (hence *sacris tacitis*).

844. The abrupt change of construction here suggests the possible loss of one or more verses. Hitherto the geographical names have been nominative, but from here on are accusative. Scaliger attempted to supply the thought-connection thus: *Quove iactatae pelago feremur exules ? ad quae loca, quas ad urbes ? — Tossed on what sea shall we be borne as exiles — to what places, to what cities ?* This will make *Salamina*, etc., appositives to *urbes*. — **Salamina:** the island near Athens, as the Cyprian city was not founded till after the Trojan war. — **veri:** a doubtful reading. As printed *Aiacis veri* would mean the greater as distinguished from the lesser Ajax, son of Oileus. *Veram*, which has been suggested, would agree with *Salamina* and mean the original as contrasted with the later Salamis, in Cyprus. This would involve an anachronism in the speech of the Trojan chorus.

845. **fera:** the great boar (see note on *divae*, 827). — **Calydona:** acc. sing.

846. **quas . . . terras:** Thessaly. — **Titaressos:** an affluent of the Peneus. Its current was less rapid than that of the larger stream (*segnibus undis*). — **subiturus aequor:** as the Titaressos entered the Peneus but a short distance from its mouth this may be understood as meaning *soon to enter the sea*, which is sufficiently commonplace. A more satisfactory sense is suggested by the old belief that it had its source in the infernal world (Lucan, Phars. 6. 378: *Hunc fama est Stygiis manare paludibus amnem,*

The story is that this stream flows forth from the Stygian waters), and is *destined to plunge beneath the sea* in returning.

848. Bessan et Scarphen: towns in Locris. — **senilem:** belonging to Nestor, who was noted for his great age.

849. Pharin: in Laconia. — **Pisas:** Pisae or Pisa, situated near Elis and an old rival of that city for the honor of celebrating the Olympian games. It is mentioned often in that connection, either with Elis as here, or as a substitute for it (*e.g.* Thy. 123; Juvenal 13. 99). — **Iovis:** *belonging to Jupiter,* whose temple, containing the famous Phidian statue of the Olympian Zeus, stood near the athletic field. — **coronis:** the prizes took the form of wreaths.

850. Elida: Elis, the scene in classic times of the Olympic games (hence *coronis claram*). Of course all this reference by the chorus to the Olympic games is anachronistic.

851–857. *Let it be any land but Sparta (the home of Helen and source of all the woes of Troy), or Argolis (the realm of Agamemnon, who commanded the besiegers), or Ithaca (whence came the cunning Ulysses, most dreaded and hated of all).* — **procella mittat:** *let the wind bear us where it will.*

853. dum . . . absit: conditional. — **luem:** either *destruction* in the abstract, or Helen as the concrete cause (cf. *lues,* 892, applied to the same Helen; *luem,* Med. 18%, applied to Medea).

854. Sparte: Sparta, in its Greek form.

855. saevi Pelopis: father of Atreus and so ancestor of the two Greek leaders, Agamemnon and Menelaus. His particular act of perfidy and cruelty was the killing of Myrtilus, son of Mercury, who had helped him win his bride, Hippodamia.

856. Neritos, Zacyntho: two islands near Ithaca and employed to suggest it and its king, as was Cephallania in 518. — **brevior:** *smaller.*

857. dolosis: the stock epithet of Ulysses, here and often applied to places and things associated with him.

859. Hecuba: the ultima is long, either arbitrarily so *in thesi* or from retaining the quantity of its Greek form Ἑκαβή.

ACT IV

Scene 1 (vv. 861–887). — Helen comes to lead Polyxena away on pretense of marriage to Pyrrhus.

Helena: according to Euripides (Hec. 218) it is Ulysses who brings the news to Hecuba.

861–863. *Whatever marriage, fatal and joyless, involves mourning and bloodshed, deserves Helen for its priestess.* — **eversis quoque:** *even when overthrown.*

864. Pyrrhi toros: for Polyxena (see 871–887).

865. cultus, habitus: *dress, costume* (cf. *cultu*, 362 n.; 1132). For the bride of a Greek general this naturally would be Grecian (*Graios*).

868. fallatur: *let her be lured to death under pretext of marriage.* — **ipsi:** Polyxena. — **levius:** *a less evil* than otherwise she would suffer. In 967, 968, her sisters, doomed to live, are represented as envying her.

869. mors, mori: predicate and subject respectively with *est.* Note the alliteration.

870. iussa: nom. sing. — *why, when bidden, do you hesitate to act? The fault of a crime that is forced recoils upon its author.* This is a comfortable evasion of responsibility, with which may be compared the chorus' prayer for Jason in Med. 669: *Parcite iusso — Spare him; he acted under orders.* In *cessas* the speaker addresses herself.

872. virgo: Polyxena, who here is addressed. Euripides (Hec. 175–437) assigns her a spirited part in the dialogue between herself and her mother on the one side, and Ulysses, who has come to lead her away, on the other; in this play she does not speak at all.

875. sospes: *Troy in her best days* (lit. *when safe*) *could not give you such a match, nor could Priam.*

876. decus: Achilles had been and Pyrrhus now was *the glory of the Greeks.* There is a double sense running through this passage. On the surface Helen's proposition appears to be that Polyxena shall be wedded to Pyrrhus; yet all she says is equally true on the supposition that the captive is to become the bride of the dead Achilles.

879. deae: the Nereides, sisters of Thetis, the mother of Achilles.

882. Peleus, Nereus: the fathers respectively of Achilles and Thetis.

883. *Put off your mourning, don your festal garb.*

884. dedisce captam: *unlearn the rôle of captive* (cf. *gere captivum*, 715 n.). — **deprime:** *smooth, arrange* the hair, disheveled in mourning.

885. crinem . . . distingui: in allusion to the Roman custom of parting the bride's hair into six locks (Festus, p. 339: *Senis crinibus nubentes ornantur — Brides are adorned with six locks of hair;* Ovid, F. 2. 560: *Comat virgineas hasta recurva comas — The hooked pike dresses her maiden locks;* cf. Browning, Sordello, Book II: —

> " A Roman bride, when they'd dispart
> Her unbound tresses with the Sabine dart,
> Holding the famous rape in mem'ry still,
> Felt creep into her curls the iron chill."

patere: imperative.

886. excelso magis: *more exalted* than that of Troy.

SCENE 2 (vv. 888–954). — To Andromache's reproaches and laments Helen replies that her own lot, hated by all and forced to mourn in secret, is the hardest. The former then renews her lamentation.

888. Though Helen had addressed Polyxena it is Andromache who replies.

889. gaudere: a marriage was regarded as an occasion essentially festive and joyous, with which death and mourning were utterly incongruous. Hence a wedding amid the ruins of Troy would be out of place, an aggravation of their misery, and might fittingly be characterized as *a new kind of marriage* (*novis thalamis*, 900; cf. Med. 743, and *nuptias novas*, Med. 894).

890–892. Note the keen irony.

892. lues utriusque populi: *the bane of both Greece and Troy* (cf. *Troiae et patriae communis Erinys,* applied to the same Helen by Aeneas, Vergil, A. 2. 573).

895. The ancients believed that if the body were not buried the soul must stray about in outer darkness for a hundred years before it could be admitted to its proper place in the other world (Vergil, A. 6. 327–330), and so *inhumata* suggested a greater horror to them than it would to us. — **haec . . . tuus:** *your own marriage (to Paris) has sown these bones broadcast* (cf. Helen's own expression in 861–863).

897. dimicantes . . . viros: *you joyfully beheld your two husbands fighting.* The reference is to the combat between Menelaus and Paris, described in Il. 3. — **prospiceres:** Helen viewed the combat from the city wall near the Scaean gate (see 785 n.; cf. Il. 3. 145–153, 383, 384).

898. incerta voti: *undecided as to your desire, i.e.* for whose victory she should wish.

900. igne: in post-Augustan Latin this form prevailed over the earlier *igni.* It here depends on *opus.* — **thalamis novis:** see 889 n. — **Troia praelucet:** no need of specially prepared torches (*taedis, face, igne*) when the whole city, burning, lights up the bride's path.

902. planctus . . . sonet: these expressions of grief would celebrate fittingly (*digne*) the marriage proposed. Distinguish the sense of *planctus* and *gemitus.*

903–905. Cf. Ulysses' words, 545, 546.

906–926. A fine bit of special pleading, in which Helen makes out that her own lot is the hardest of all and that she herself is wholly innocent (cf. Euripides, Tro. 920 ff.).

906. *I can maintain my cause, even before a hostile judge.* — **iudice infesto:** concessive abl. abs. The *iudex,* of course, is Andromache, who had received Helen's proposal with such sarcasm.

907. graviora passa: cf. Aeneas' address to his men, *O passi graviora,* Vergil, A. 1. 199.

908. occulte: *you can mourn your dead; I dare not mourn my Paris* (cf. Octavia's lament that she dares not show her grief for father and brother, Oct. 65–69; Tac. Ann. 13. 16. 7).

910. patior . . . captiva: *I have borne this yoke (of slavery)* *long, a captive for ten years.* *Annis* is abl. of time within which.

913. **gravius timere:** *bad as it is to lose one's native land, it is worse to fear it as I do.* — **levat tanti mali comitatus:** cf. our proverb, "Misery loves company," in a slightly different sense (cf. 1009 ff.).

916. **me ... dominus:** Helen complains that she was deprived of the pleasant suspense (*incerto ... pependit*) of being assigned to a husband by lot, which the Trojan captives had enjoyed (57, 974), but had been fated from the first to return to Menelaus.

919. **Spartana puppis:** of course it was in Paris' ship, not Spartan but Trojan, that Helen had been brought to Troy; and she had come undeniably as *praeda* (920, 922; cf. *captiva*, 911), though certainly as the willing prize of her lover.

921. **donum:** appositive to *me*, understood as the object of *dedit*. — **iudici:** Paris, whose award of the prize of beauty to Venus (*victrix dea*) and her gift to him of Helen had led to the war and the downfall of Troy (cf. 66 n.).

922. **ignosce praedae:** sc. *mihi* — *forgive me, the passive prize.* — **iudicem iratum:** Menelaus. Euripides (Tro. 862 ff.) represents Menelaus as seeking Helen after the capture of the city with the avowed intention of giving her up to death as the cause of all the sufferings of the Greek besiegers — and as relenting when he came under the influence of her charm.

924. **hanc ... flecte:** *leave off your mourning for a little and persuade this maiden (Polyxena) to accede to my proposal;* I can scarce restrain my tears at the thought of my own misfortunes, and so cannot argue the matter with her myself.

927. **fare ... nectat:** Andromache sees through Helen's assumption of sympathy and bluntly demands that she tell her errand and reveal what new mischief Ulysses has devised.

929. *Is the maiden to share the fate of my Astyanax?* (see 368–370, 621, 1068–1117).

931. **latere scisso:** *of sheer side — the sheer-faced cliffs which Sigeon rears, as he looks forth from his shallow bay upon the deep.*

932. **Sigeon:** the penult of this Greek name is properly long (cf. *Sīgēīs*, 75), which gives us a spondee in the fourth foot, in violation of all the laws of the iambic trimeter (cf. *vincendo*, 264)

In pure Latin words a vowel before another is usually short, and it may be that the poet "felt" the *e* to be so here. As a rule Seneca's verse is very accurate.

934. quam . . . Pyrrhus: *than that Pyrrhus should be,* etc.

937. falli: appositive to *hoc unum.* — **paratas:** sc. *nos.*

938. Helen here throws off the mask and with real or pretended feeling reveals the plot of which she is the agent (861–867). — **interpres:** Calchas.

939. lucis invisae: *hated life* (cf. Vergil's *lucem perosi,* 6. 435).

941. occidere: the *i* is short. — **comitantem:** agrees with *me,* 938.

945. animus: of Polyxena (cf. 1146–1152, where her courage in death is described). — **necem:** *doom.*

946. cultus decoros: *the becoming garb.* With 946, 947, cf. 883–885 n.

948. illud, hoc: the marriage with Pyrrhus, and actual death. Note the accurate use of the demonstratives.

949. Andromache's attention is attracted to the aged Hecuba, who now approaches. — **luctu . . . audito:** abl. abs. — *at word of this new grief.*

952. quam: best taken with *levi* — *on how slight a thread hangs the frail life.*

953. minimum: *a very little thing,* i.e. the snapping of the thread.

954. prima . . . fugit: *death is the first to flee.*

Scene 3 (vv. 955–1008). — Hecuba and Andromache lament the hapless fate imposed upon them by the fall of Troy and the issue of the lot. Pyrrhus enters and drags away Polyxena, followed by her mother's cry of despair.

956. rebellat: *does he still renew the war?* — **o . . . levem:** *too light the hand that smote Achilles,* if he still return to plague us (347 n.).

957. cinis, tumulus: cf. Hecuba's words in Ovid, M. 13. 503: *Cinis ipse sepulti* | *in genus hoc saevit; tumulo quoque sensimus hostem* — *The very ashes of the buried foe are fierce against our race; from the tomb itself we have felt our enemy.*

958. turba: see 32 n., and cf. *gregem,* next line.

960. matrem: *motherly care and affection.* — **haec:** Polyxena, as in 924, 962, 971. — **est super:** for *superest*, as in 490, 507, 1068.

963 ff. She calls upon her soul to flee away by the gate of death and spare her (*remitte*) the sight of this last cruel deed — the murder of her daughter.

970. huc et huc: with *sparsas* (cf. the chorus, 814–860).

972. invidebis: sc. *huic.* — **si:** almost temporal in its force.

974. urna: see 57, 58, and cf. *sorte*, 917. In the Troades of Euripides (230 ff.) it is the herald Talthybius who announces the issue of the lot to the captives.

976. Scyrius iuvenis: Pyrrhus (339 n.).

977. furor . . . Phoebusque: in reference to her well-known inspiration and supposed madness (34 n.), which it is assumed will exempt her from the common fate.

978. regum . . . rector: Agamemnon (cf. Pyrrhus' phrase, *regum tyranne*, 303). In all accounts Cassandra is represented as having fallen into Agamemnon's hands on this occasion, and having shared his fate at Mycenae.

967. nata: Polyxena. — **quam vellet:** *how Cassandra and Andromache would choose your marriage (to the dead) in preference to that assigned them by the lot!* (cf. Vergil, A. 3. 321–323: "O maiden, happy above all others, who wast bidden to die at the enemy's tomb, not subject to the outcome of the lot!").

980. nolenti brevis: two words which give a peculiarly brutal tone to the speech, as the one implies that Hecuba had been forced upon her future master and the other reminds her of her worn-out life. — **brevis:** *short-lived.*

982. regibus reges: *has made princes the slaves of princes.* Of course the word means royal personages in general, women as well as men (Med. 56).

985. matrem . . . miscet: *gives Hecuba to the man who had won the arms of Achilles, her son's slayer.* After Achilles' death Ulysses and Ajax argued their respective claims to his armor, and the former won (Ovid, M. 13. 1–383).

991. sterilis . . . meos: *barren Ithaca does not contain my tomb,* i.e. I am not to be buried in Ithaca. The common story of her fate is that she was transformed into a dog before the Grecian fleet left the Chersonesus, leaped into the sea, and was drowned ncar a point of land which from that circumstance was known thereafter as Cynossema, "the sign of the dog" (Ovid, M. 13. 567).

994. me . . . sequentur: *my ill fortune* (cf. *mea . . . mala,* 996) *shall follow me* and involve all those about me (cf. 1006–1008). **non . . . mare:** a prophecy of the disastrous storm that befell the Greek fleet on its homeward way (Ag. 460–578).

After 995 there appears to be a break in the sense, due probably to the loss of one or more lines. Leo attempts to restore the general meaning by supplying the line, *sociosque merget, obruent reducem quoque.* If this be adopted we must make *reducem* agree with *te* (Ulysses) supplied, and take the nouns in 996 as subjects of *obruent.* The whole then will read, *The sea shall rage and overwhelm your comrades, and war and fire and my fate and Priam's shall overtake you, even when restored to your home.*

997. ista: sc. *mala.* — **hoc:** explained by its appositive, the sentence in 998: *Meantime* this *serves instead of vengeance: that* I *have fallen to you in the drawing of lots, and so prevented your securing a more desirable prize* (cf. *praeda vilis,* 58; *praeda brevis,* 980).

999. Pyrrhus enters in quest of Polyxena, to complete the sacrifice.

1001. reclude . . . pectus: cf. Vergil's *pectus mucrone recludit,* A. 10. 601; *reserat . . . pectora,* Oct. 367). With *pectus* sc. *meum.*

1002. coniunge soceros: *reunite Achilles' parents-in-law,* i.e., *As you have slain this maiden's father* (310–312; Vergil, A. 2. 550–558), *so slay her mother now.* The word *soceros* is used of the same persons, Priam and Hecuba, by Vergil (A. 2. 457; cf. Med. 106). — **mactator senum:** the same taunt is uttered by Agamemnon, 310–312.

1003. hic: *this blood of mine.* — **decet:** the very rare personal use of this verb. — **abreptam:** sc. *Polyxenam.* The change of thought is abrupt, but may be explained by the intense emotion of the speaker.

1005. vobis: *you Greeks.*

1006. his . . . aequora: *a sea cruel enough and treacherous enough to match your cowardly murder of this maiden.*

1008. meae . . . rati: sc. *accidat — whatever befalls my ship, when I am carried away as a captive, may the same befall the whole* *fleet.* The allusion is to her prophecy (992) that she would not live to see Greece, and amounts to a prayer for destruction upon her foes.

Scene 4 (vv. 1009–1055). — The chorus finds comfort in the thought that the calamity of the Trojans is universal, none faring better than his neighbor. The measure is sapphic, with one adonic.

1009. For the sentiment cf. 913, 1016 and notes — *To a mourner the sight of a nation of mourners is pleasant,* that is, *misery loves company.*

1011. *Tears which a multitude unite in shedding sting less sharply.*

1016. ferre: depends on *recusat.* The younger Pliny, in describing his experience during the eruption of Vesuvius, A.D. 79, utters much the same sentiment: " I might boast that I uttered no groan, no cowardly word, amid such perils, if I had not believed that all things were perishing with me — a pitiful but powerful solace in mortal peril" (Epist. 6. 20 fin.).

1018. The imperatives in this and the following verses suggest a conditional idea, with *credet* and *surgent* as apodoses.

1020. centum: with *bubus.* Supply *eos* as object of *removete* and antecedent of *qui.*

1022. iacentes: *downcast.*

1024. posito: dat.

1027. singulari: one alone as compared with the thousand vessels of 1030.

1029. aequior: *with greater equanimity.*

1032. terris: poetic dat. of place whither.

1034. Hellen: acc. sing. For the story see artt. Phrixus and Helle in Classical Dictionary.

1035. gregis ductor: the ram of the golden fleece.

1037. iactum fecit: like *iacturam fecit* — *threw overboard.*

1038. tenuit: *restrained.* Phrixus, having suffered bereavement which left him alone, had mourned; but the two survivors of the deluge, being together in misfortune, did not.

1039. Pyrrha: though nom., this word retains its long *a* from the Greek. — **vir:** Deucalion. The succession of two verses of

like ending here probably is imitated from Ovid's account of the
situation of Deucalion and Pyrrha in M. 1. 361, 362: —

> *Namque ego, crede mihi, si te quoque pontus haberet,*
> *te sequerer, coniunx, et me quoque pontus haberet.*

1042, 1043. *The fleet, driven hither and thither, will break up this
assemblage of mourners (questum), and scatter wide our tears.* —
huc, illuc: possibly with *sparget*, better with *agitata*.

1044. Some editors have regarded *nautae* as a second subject of
sparget. To avoid the awkwardness of the sense thus made, Leo
has suggested supplying some such line as this: *Caede cum pontus
fuerit piatus — When the sea has been appeased by the slaying*
of Astyanax and Polyxena. *Nautae* then becomes the subject of
prenderint. — **tuba:** case can be determined by scansion.

1045. simul: practically equivalent to *cum* (cf. *simul his*, Horace,
S. 1. 10. 86). — **properante remo:** abl. abs. The sense is, *When the
sailors shall steer out into the deep, with wind and oar both aiding,
and the shore slip away from our sight*, etc.

1047. miseris: sc. *captivis*.

1049. *When even lofty Ida shall sink beneath the horizon.*

ACT V

SCENE 1 (vv. 1056–1179). — A messenger announces that he
bears woeful tidings. In response to Andromache's command he
describes in detail the death of Astyanax and Polyxena; Hecuba
gives voice to her hopeless woe; and the captives are ordered to
embark for exile in Greece.

1058. quid: equivalent to *utrum, which of the two*, as is shown by
the degree of *prius*. — **referens:** *relating*.

1059. tuosne: sc. *luctus*. The first *tuos* is addressed to Andromache, the second to Hecuba (*anus*).

1061. sua: sc. *clades*. — **tantum:** *only*.

1062. miser: predicate with the first *est; whoever is unfortunate
is Hecuba's*.

1063. The double sacrifice (*duplex nefas*, 1065) commanded by
Calchas has been consummated. In this instance Seneca has
followed the Greek poets and complied with the law enunciated

by Horace forbidding the representation of such unnatural scenes on the stage (see note on H.F. 992).

1064. generosa: *with noble spirit,* such as befits one highly born.

1067. tractare: *to dwell upon.*

1068. una: cf. *turre sola quae manet,* 622. — **magna:** with *Troia.*

1069-1071. Cf. 785 n.

1070. pinnis: *pinnacles* or *battlements* (cf. Vergil, A. 7. 159). — **arbiter:** *sitting as witness of the war.*

1072. nepotem: Astyanax.

1073. face: *torch,* with which attempts were made to fire the fleet (cf. *facibus,* 445 n.).

1076. cautes: a precipitous mass of stones — a ruin.

1078-1087. A very natural picture of a crowd eager to see what is going on. — **his, his, hunc, illum, hunc, ille, ille, aliquis:** several groups or individuals in the crowd.

1079. aciem: *a view.*

1081. *Stood on tiptoe* (lit., *balanced tiptoes*). — **erecta:** either in its literal sense of *erect, stretched to their full height,* or, figuratively, *alert, attent.*

1085. imminens: with *saxum.*

1087. ferus: *unfeeling.*

1088. plena: *thronged with people.*

1090. trahens: *leading.*

1098. superbe: the reading is doubtful. One conjecture is *superbus,* another *superbit.* The latter has the advantage of completing the sentence and the formal, balanced comparison so characteristic of the Latin. Of course it is possible to retain the adverb and supply some such verb as *stetit* or *se tulit.* Translate, *bore himself proudly.*

1100. qui fletur: Astyanax; he alone of all the multitude refrains from tears. — **fatidici . . . vatis:** Calchas.

1103. in . . . regna: cf. 158: *Priam, passing away, bore his kingdom with him.* The verse is incomplete, as if interrupted by the exclamation of the victim's mother.

1104-1106. *What barbarian, in the uttermost parts of the earth!* — **sedis incertae:** gen. of quality, *nomadic* (cf. *Scythiae multivagas domos,* H.F. 533).

1106. gens: probably referring to the Hyrcani, who from their remoteness were often taken as typical barbarians (cf. *Hyrcanae tigres*, Vergil, A. 4. 367). — **Busiridis:** Busiris, the Egyptian king who offered human sacrifices to Jupiter and finally was slain at his own altar by Hercules (H.F. 484 n.). Yet not even he, cruel as he was, murdered young children as the Greeks were doing. The same is said of Diomede in 1108.

1108. parva . . . membra: *bodies of children.* For the tale of Diomede and his flesh-eating mares (*gregibus suis*) see H.F. 226; Ovid, M. 9. 194–196. This of course is not the Diomede mentioned in 38 n., but a mythical king of Thrace.

1109. tuos: apostrophizing Astyanax. For the supposed necessity of burial see 895 n.

1113. patris notas: see 461–468.

1117. sic . . . patri: *so, too, is he like his father!* The body of Hector had been disfigured by being dragged behind his conqueror's chariot (189 n.; 744), and now his son is crushed and mutilated too.

1118. ut: temporal.

1119. *Wept over the wrong themselves had done.*

1120. aliud facinus: the sacrifice of Polyxena. Euripides (Hec. 35) lays the scene of this event in the Thracian Chersonesus, where Achilles' ghost appears and demands it as the price of the fleet's freedom to proceed on the voyage already begun. With the narrative here given cf. that in Eur. Hec. 516–580, where Talthybius the herald relates it to Hecuba (cf. also Ovid, M. 13. 449–480, where Euripides is followed closely).

1123. adversa: neuter plural, object of *cingit* — *the parts facing toward the city are bounded by the plain and valley.* Another reading is *aversa*, meaning the opposite side from the sea.

1130. suum: *i.e.* of one of their own people (cf. *mea membra*, 414).

1132. thalami more: as ordered by Calchas (362–365, 865).

1133. pronuba: a matron of honor who walked with the bride in the marriage procession. — **Tyndaris:** Helen, as in Vergil, A. 2. 569 and often.

1134. Hermione: Helen's daughter. The prayer is that Helen's own return to her husband, and her daughter's marriage, may be as sad as this scene. Hermione was married to Pyrrhus, though betrothed to Orestes, son of Agamemnon. Pyrrhus was killed by his disappointed rival, who then married Hermione.

1135. viro: Menelaus (cf. *dominus*, 917).

1137. ipsa: Polyxena; for her behavior cf. Eur. Hec. 541–568; Ovid, M. 13. 453, where the scene is described at some length.

1138. pudore: *modesty.* — fulgent: *glow.*

1144. peritura: neuter plural. We should expect *perituram*, but the meter forbids. It may have a general sense, *Most men praise the things that are passing away, Blessings brighten as they take their flight* (cf. Horace, C. 3. 24. 30, " Alas, we hate virtue when it is with us, and mourn it when taken away").

1145. vagae . . . vices: *vicissitudes of fortune.*

1146. animus: of the victim (cf. 945; Eur. Hec. 342–382, 541–568). It may be, however, a general statement, *Such courage affects men always.*

1148. mirantur, miserantur: note the assonance.

1150. iuvenis: nom., Pyrrhus. — paterni: of Achilles.

1154. est: the subject is the composite idea *Pyrrhus ad caedem piger.*

1157. moriens: concessive, as is shown by *tamen.* — nec . . adhuc: *nondum.*

1160. uterque coetus: Greek and Trojan.

1161. mīsēre: *uttered.* clarius: more loudly. victor: with collective sense.

1164. saevus: not in absorbing the blood but in requiring the sacrifice.

1165–1168. Intense irony and sarcasm are seen in the reiteration of the idea in *tuti* and *secura*, and in the antithesis of *concidit virgo ac puer* and *bellum peractum est* (cf. 705 ff.).

1169. expuam: for *exspuam* — *put from me with loathing.*

1171. The Florentine MS. (*Etruscus*) has *solam*, which is good grammatically but metrically impossible (cf. *peritura*, 1144). Gronovius makes the question end with *me*, taking *sola* with *mors*. As it stands we may read, *Shall I mourn all, or, being left alone, bewail myself?* — votum: appositive to *mors*.

1172. infantibus, virginibus: she is thinking of Astyanax and Polyxena.

1175. **quaesita:** in agreement with *mors*, as are *violenta* and *saeva* above.

1177. **quam prope . . . steti:** *how near I stood to Priam,* when he was slain — yet death passed me by.

1179. **movet:** in its rare intransitive use (cf. Livy 35. 40. 7).

THE STORY OF MEDEA

The introduction of the sorceress Medea to the western world is traceable ultimately to the flight of Phrixus and his sister Helle from Orchomenus. They were carried on the back of a flying ram with fleece of gold. Helle fell off and was drowned in the strait now known as Hellespont, but Phrixus rode safely on to Colchis, at the eastern end of the Euxine (Black Sea), where the ram was sacrificed to Jupiter and its fleece nailed to a tree.

At the Theban city of Iolcos the aged king Aeson had been displaced by his brother Pelias, to the exclusion of his son Jason. The latter protested, and Pelias promised to restore the throne to the rightful heir if the latter would find and bring him the golden fleece. A vessel, the Argo, was built under the direction of Pallas, was manned by fifty heroes, and under the captaincy of Jason set out on its long voyage. After many perilous adventures they reached Colchis and demanded the fleece.

The Colchian king Aeetes did not refuse outright, but imposed certain conditions — that Jason should harness a team of fire-breathing bulls and with them plow a piece of land; should then sow a quantity of dragon's teeth and garner the crop that should result. The very first condition seemed impossible, for the fiery breath of the bulls was deadly to any mortal.

At this point the king's daughter Medea enters the story. She saw the young leader of the Argonauts and loved him at sight. Mistress of all magic, she made and gave him an ointment to protect him from the fiery exhalations, and then advised and aided him at every step till he had fulfilled all the conditions. It still remained to secure the fleece, which was guarded by a sleepless dragon. This was drugged by Medea, and the Argo sailed away with its prize and the princess as well. Her father followed, but Medea had taken her young brother along and now she killed him and cut his body into pieces, which she threw one after another into the water as the pursuers drew near.   They stopped to collect the fragments and thus the Argo escaped and finally reached Greece, where Jason and Medea were married.

At Iolcos Medea with her magic arts restored old Aeson to youth.   Pelias' daughters desired the same gift for their father, but when on her direction they had cut up his body Medea refused to do her part.   Before the vengeance of Pelias' children she fled with her husband to Corinth, where presently he saw opportunity to better his fortunes by wedding the daughter of King Creon. It is here, on the wedding day, that the play begins.

NOTES ON THE MEDEA

ACT I

SCENE 1 (vv. 1–55). — Medea invokes the vengeance of the gods above and beneath on King Creon and his daughter, who have won her husband from her, and at the close vows that her repudiation shall be marked by scenes as terrible as had attended her marriage with Jason.

2. Lucina: a name often applied to Juno and to Diana, here to the former. — **quaeque . . . docuisti:** sc. *tu* as antecedent of *quae;* Pallas (Minerva) is meant. It was under her direction that the materials of the Argo were chosen and the vessel built (cf. 365–367).

3. Tiphyn: the pilot of the Argo. For his fate see 616–624. — **novam:** the Argo was thought of as the first Grecian vessel to attempt a long sea voyage.

4. profundi . . . dominator maris: Neptune (cf. *dominus profundi,* 597).

5. Titan: Helios, the sun god. In 410 *Titan* refers to Enceladus. — **orbi:** sc. *terrarum. Orbi* is indirect object of *dividens* (cf. *feminis . . . carmina divides,* Horace, C. 1. 15. 14); tr. *apportioning clear light to the world.*

6. tacitus . . . iubar: *lending thy bright face as witness to the silent mysteries (of night).*

7. Hecate triformis: cf. *fronte non una,* 751; *triceps Hecate,* Ovid, M. 7. 194; *diva triformis,* Horace, C. 3. 22. 4. This goddess was thought of as having functions in heaven, on earth and in the infernal world, and accordingly was identified or confused with Selene or Phoebe (Luna), with Artemis (Diana) and with Persephone (Proserpina). — **quosque:** acc. after *iuravit:* tr. *by whom Jason swore.* The antecedent is *deos,* attracted from the vocative, in which it naturally would be, to the case of the relative.

10. manesque impios: ghosts of the wicked dead, invoked with their rulers, Pluto and Proserpina, named in next line.

11. dominum: Pluto. — **dominam . . . raptam:** Proserpina, who had been carried off by Pluto and made his bride (Ovid, M. 5. 359–424), but not deserted later, as Medea had been. Hence the phrase, *with better faith.* — **voce non fausta:** because invocation of the powers of darkness was of evil omen.

13. adeste: *be present to aid,* a common form of invocation (cf. *ades,* 703). — **deae:** the Furies (Alecto, Megaera and Tisiphone), whose function it was to torment men for their evil deeds (cf. 959–961; H.F. 100–106).

14. crinem: acc. of specification, defining *squalidae.* — **serpentibus:** the hair of the Furies, like that of the Gorgons, was composed of living serpents.

16. thalamis: *as once you stood for my marriage.*

17. coniugi . . . novae: the princess Glauce, or Creusa, whom Jason was about to marry.

18. socero: King Creon. — **regiae stirpi:** the whole royal house of Corinth.

19. mihi peius aliquid: having called down destruction upon her rival's family, she now prays that a fate still worse may befall her faithless husband (with 20–25 cf. Dido's curse on Aeneas, Vergil, A. 4. 612–620).

20, 21. Cf. frag. X of the Medea of Accius (found in Ribbeck, v. 415): *Exul inter hostes, exspes, expers, desertus, vagus — An exile amid enemies, hopeless and portionless, a lonely wanderer.* Note in 21 the asyndeton (or omission of conjunctions), which is very common in these tragedies. — **incerti laris:** gen. of quality — *of no certain home,* hence *homeless.*

22. *Known as an alien, may he seek another's door.*

23. quo: abl. after the comparative — *than which I can pray for nothing worse.*

24. liberos: object of *optet* and antecedent of *quo* (23). — **similes . . . matri:** *like their father in faithlessness, like their mother in wickedness.*

26. peperi: the mention of her children suggests the thought that in some way (not necessarily definite yet) she may punish their father through them; hence her exclamation, *Vengeance is* *born, I have borne it!* (cf. 40, 549, 550). — **querelas . . . hostes**. it is time for action, not for mere words.

27. manibus: dat., *from their hands.* — **faces:** torches, carried in the procession from the bride's home to that of her new husband.

28. caelo: same construction as *manibus.* Medea was credited (Ovid, M. 7. 207–209) with power to darken the heavens (see her own account of her control of natural phenomena in 754–769). — **spectat . . . poli:** *does the sun god, my ancestor, see this, and does he still show his face and glide on in his wonted course?* The allusion here and in 31 is to the sun's having hidden his face and retraced his course in horror at sight of the feast of Thyestes. **nostri sator generis:** Phoebus, who was the father of Aeetes and so Medea's grandfather.

32–34. An evident allusion to Phaethon's adventure (Ovid, M. 2. 1–328).

35. Corinthos: Greek form of nom. sing.; the Latin is *Corinthus.* — **gemino . . . litore:** abl. quality (cf. *gemino mari pulsata . . . regna,* H.F. 1164).— **opponens moras:** by compelling vessels to sail around the Peloponnesus (cf. *flectens moras,* 149). Many attempts were made in ancient times to pierce the Corinthian isthmus, but it was not till our own day (1894) that a canal was completed. It follows the line surveyed in A.D. 67 for Nero, who himself broke ground for it (Suetonius, Nero 19).

36. cremata: nom. with *Corinthos.* — **flammis . . . duo:** *unite the two seas with flame.*

37. pronubam . . . pinum: a torch (cf. *faces,* 27) borne in the marriage procession by a young matron. *Pronubam* here is adjective, and the same phrase occurs in the pseudo-Vergilian Ciris, v. 439.

39. *Slay the victims on the consecrated altar.* Such a sacrifice was an essential part of the Roman marriage ceremony.

40. per viscera ipsa: *in your very offspring.* The idea already hinted at in *peperi,* 26. Another rendering suggested by the connection is, *Through the very entrails of the victims* (39) *seek a way for your revenge, i.e.* divine the future by augury.

41. anime: apostrophizing her own spirit (cf. 895).

43. Caucasum: *i.e.* the coldness and hardness of the rugged range near whose base her childhood had been spent.

44. Pontus, Phasis: the Euxine (Black Sea) and the river Phasis, familiar features of her native land, Colchis.

45. Isthmos: nom. sing., like *Corinthos*, 35. — **effera, ignota,** etc.: neuter.

47. vulnera, caedem, funus: appositive to *mala.* — **vagum funus per artus:** *death (or burial) limb by limb,* in allusion to her treatment of her brother (130 n.).

49. haec . . . feci: *all this I did as a girl* (cf. 909). — **exurgat:** *exsurgat* (cf. *exerunt* for *exserunt,* H.F. 11).

51. accingere: the so-called "middle" use of the passive, *gird yourself.*

52. paria . . . thalamis: her marriage with Jason had involved her betrayal of country and father and the murder of her brother. She now proposes to celebrate her rejection with crimes as dreadful.

54. hoc: sc. *modo.*

SCENE 2 (vv. 56–115). — A chorus of Corinthian women approaches, chanting the epithalamion, or marriage song, of Jason and Creusa.   First the gods above are invoked (56–74), then the beauty of the bride (75–81, 93–101) and of the groom (82–89) is praised, the youth are challenged to make the most of the unusual license granted them by the occasion (107–114), and a parting taunt is flung at the rejected wife (114, 115).   The meter to 74 and again in 93–109 is the minor asclepiadean, 75–92 glyconic, 110–115 dactylic hexameter.

56. *May the gods above, who rule the sky, and they who rule the seas, attend with their divine favor this marriage of princes, together with their peoples, duly silent.*

58. faventibus: at Rome a solemn ceremony was opened with an exhortation to all present to refrain from any speech which might offend the gods and so invalidate the rites.   As the only sure way to effect this was not to speak at all, the formula *Ore favete omnes* (Vergil, A. 5. 71; cf. *Favete linguis,* Horace, C. 3. 1. 2) came to be understood as a call for silent attention.

59. Tonantibus: the proper epithet of Jupiter here is made plural to include his sister-wife Juno as well, though she is mentioned as Lucina in 61.   The white bull and white cow (*femina,* 61, is adjective with *bos* understood) were the appropriate victims for sacrifice to Jupiter and Juno respectively. Furthermore they must never have been used for draught or burden, hence *intemptata iugo*, 62. The victims to the infernal gods were black.

62. placet: from *placare*, not *placere*.

63. quae . . . retinet: Pax, the personification and goddess of peace. Lucretius, however (R.N. 1. 31), invoking *Venus* declares, "Thou alone canst bless mortals with peace, since Mars controls the functions of war, and he . . . feasts his eager eyes upon thee."

65. *Holds plenty in her bounteous horn.* There are still extant coins of Augustus and of Vespasian representing Pax with her *cornu copiae*. Ovid (M. 9. 86–88) makes the river-god Achelous conclude the story of his struggle with Hercules thus: "As he held my horn he broke it and tore it from my brow. The Naides filled it with fruits and sweet-scented flowers and consecrated it; and Bona Copia, the goddess of plenty, now is enriched by my full horn."

66. tenera . . . hostia: abl. The *tender victim* was a lamb. — **mitior:** agrees with the subject of *donetur*, implied in the relative *quae*, 63.

67. tu qui . . . ades: Hymen (see 110 n.). — **facibus legitimis:** dat. The phrase, of course, means *lawful marriage*. Catullus (61. 6–15) thus invokes Hymen: *Bind thy brows with the blossoms of the sweet smelling marjoram; take the bridal veil and hither come with rejoicing, wearing on snowy foot the saffron-colored sandal; and, inspired by this joyous day, chanting the wedding song with high, clear voice, beat the earth with thy feet and with thy hand wave (quate) the pine-torch.* So our author in 68: *Dashing aside the night with auspicious hand.*

69. *Hither come, reeling with drunken step* (cf. 110–112, where Hymen is called the son of Bacchus, the god of wine, and is exhorted to light his torch and brandish it *with languid fingers*).

71. tu quae . . . redis: Hesperus (*Vesper*), the evening star (cf. Catullus 62. 2: *Vesper . . . expectata diu vix tandem lumina tollit* — *The evening star at length tardily lifts up his long-expected rays*). — **gemini praevia temporis:** *forerunner of the twilight* (cf *dux noctis*, 878).

75–109. A passage arranged in strophe and antistrophe, as in a Greek chorus (cf. Catullus, 62; Horace, C.S.). One part of the company sings the strophes, 75–81 and 93–101, in praise of the bride, the other the antistrophes, 82–92 and 102–109, in honor of the groom.

76. Cecropias nurus: *daughters of Cecrops,* i.e. Athenian maidens.

77. *Those whom the city that lacks walls (Sparta) trains like young men on the slopes of Taygetus.* Sparta was famous for the vigor of her women as well as her men. — **Taygetus:** four syllables; a mountain range near Sparta.

80. Aonius: Boeotian or Theban.

81. Alphēos: an Arcadian stream. The bride is said to outshine the maidens of all these regions, the fairest of all Greece.

82. formā: abl. of respect.

83. Aesonio duci: Jason, so called as the son of Aeson.

84. proles fulminis improbi: Bacchus; the allusion is to the manner in which Jupiter visited Semele, with lightning flashes and thunder, before the birth of the wine-god (Ovid, M. 3. 253–315).

85. Bacchus is represented as driving a team of tigers with harness of vines (cf. Vergil, A. 6. 804: *Qui pampineis victor iuga flectit habenis | Liber, agens celso Nysae de vertice tigris — Liber, who victoriously guides his chariot with reins of vine, driving tigers, down from the high crest of Nysa*).

86. qui tripodas movet: Phoebus Apollo, the god of prophecy, who inspired especially the oracle at Delphi, where the priestess occupied a tripod, or three-legged seat, while uttering her responses. In 785 *tripodas* is used in a more general sense.

87. virginis asperae: Diana.

89. Of the Dioscuri or Gemini Homer (Il. 3. 237) calls "Castor the horse-tamer and Pollux good with the fist." Horace (Sat. 2. 1. 26) declares that "Castor rejoices in horses, his brother in boxing" (lit. "in fists").

90–92. Having lauded the beauty of Creusa and set Jason above the four gods most noted for youth and beauty, the chorus prays that this preëminence of both may continue. — **vincat, superet:** *surpass, excel.*

93. haec: the bride; her beauty is compared with the sun's brilliance. — **constitit:** *has taken her place.*

95. cum sole: *with (at) the coming of the sun.*

97. Phoebē: note the long *e* (cf. the words in 770 and 874 and distinguish them by quantities). *When Phoebe, with a light not her own, incloses a solid disk with her circling tips,* i.e. with the extended tips of the crescent. — **non suo:** *reflected.*

98. The sense here appears to be incomplete, and Leo suggests two lines to restore the probable connection: *Talem dum iuvenis conspicit, en rubor | perfudit subito purpureus genas — While the young husband regards her thus, lo, a glowing blush has suddenly suffused her cheeks. So does the snowy hue (of wool or linen) blush when drenched with the scarlet dye; such does the shepherd behold the rising sun.*

101. luce nova: *at dawn.* — **roscidus:** *moist with dew* after his night watch in the open air.

102–109. The new-made husband is exhorted to forget Medea and fearlessly receive his bride. — **Phasidis horridi:** gen. The river's name here represents the country, but the reference is to his marriage with Medea. *Ereptus, solitus* and *trepidus,* like *felix,* modify *tu,* the implied subject of *corripe,* 105.

105. Aeoliam virginem: Jason's bride, Creusa, was a descendant of Aeolus, the son of Hellen — not the ruler of the winds.

106. Medea's father had been hostile to Jason; this time his intended father-in-law is willing. The plural *soceris* may be meant to include both Creon and his wife, as *soceros* in Tro. 1002 and Vergil, A. 2. 457 refers to both Priam and his wife Hecuba.

107. iurgio: cf. *fescenninus,* 113 n

108. hinc illinc . . . mittite carmina: sing responsively.

110. *Fair and noble scion of Bacchus.* Hymen, the god of marriage, is sometimes called the son of Bacchus and Venus, wine and love, though other accounts are given of his parentage (see Classical Dictionary, art. Hymen).

111. multifidam . . . pinum: a stick of pine *frayed out* at the end so as to burn readily (cf. *multifidas faces,* Ovid, M. 7. 259).

113. dicax . . . fescenninus: cf. *procax fescenninus,* Catullus 61. 126, where an example is given. The *fescennine verses,* containing rude banter (*iurgio,* 107) and coarse jests, were used in very early times by the rustics of central Italy on various occasions of public merrymaking, but later were restricted to the wedding feast. To make a Corinthian chorus of Medea's time use the word of course involves an anachronism. V. 113 is spondaic.

114. tacitis . . . marito: *let her pass away in silent gloom who runs away and weds a foreign husband.* The reference, of course, is to Medea, but the indefinite *si qua* makes it more general than the relative *quae* would have been.

ACT II

SCENE 1 (vv. 116–178). — Medea, hearing the *hymenaeus*, realizes that she actually has been deserted, calls to mind her claims on Jason's gratitude and repeats her vow to seek revenge. Her old nurse cautions her against speaking too freely, but in vain.

116. hymenaeus: the chant of the marriage procession in the last scene.

118. hoc: explained by its appositive *deserere*, 120. — **erepto . . . regno:** *after having deprived me of father, native land and royal state.*

119. solam: sc. *me.*

121. scelere: a term which Medea does not hesitate to apply to her own acts, *e.g.* in 129, 135, 500, 1016 (cf. *nefas*, 122). — **flammas:** *the fiery breath of the bulls, igneos tauri halitus,* 466.

122. *Does he forsooth think all my resources of evil are spent?*

123. Scansion easily determines agreement of *incerta* and of *vaesana.*

125. *Would he had a brother, who might be slain in retaliation for my own* (see 130 n.). — **est coniunx:** sc. *illi.* — **in hanc ferrum exigatur:** *into her let the sword be plunged.* For the sense, cf. Seneca, Consolatio ad Marciam 16. 3: *Tela quae (Fortuna) in Scipiones . . . exegit — The weapons which fortune thrust into the Scipios;* also *ferrum exigam,* 1006.

128. tuae: addressing herself; so *tua,* next line.

130–134. The noun-participle phrases *decus raptum, comes divisus, funus ingestum, corpus sparsum* and *decocta membra* are appositive to *scelera,* 129. It is worthy of note that the Latin commonly uses a concrete noun with an adjective modifier, *glory stolen, companion cut to pieces,* etc., where our idiom would be an abstract noun with a prepositional phrase, *the theft of our kingdom's glory, the cutting to pieces of the maiden's companion,* etc. — **inclitum decus**: the golden fleece, the recovery of which was the purpose of the Argonautic expedition. — **parvus comes**: Medea's brother, not named in the play, but commonly called Absyrtus. Seneca follows the more common of several versions of his story, that while still a boy he was carried off by his sister in her flight from Colchis, and, when her father was about to overtake them, was cut to pieces and his limbs thrown one by one into the sea, that the pursuit might be delayed while they were gathered up (cf. 47 n., 473, 963). This was the crime which troubled her most.

132. funus ingestum patri: *his burial imposed upon my father.*

133. Peliae senis: Jason's uncle, who had deprived him of his father's throne and sent him in search of the golden fleece in hope he would not return (*qui iussit,* 664). On reaching Iolcos with her lover Medea had shown her magic power in restoring the aged Aeson to youth (Ovid, M. 7. 162–293), and the daughters of Pelias desired her to do the same for their father. Medea agreed, but when by her direction they had cut up his body and placed it in a caldron (*aeno*), she refused to do her part. It was in their flight from the wrath of Pelias' son Acastus (415, 475, 664–667) that Medea and Jason had come to Corinth.

134. funestum . . . sanguinem: *lifeblood.* — **nullum . . . amor**: not anger, but love, had prompted all her crimes.

136. movit: sc. *scelera* or *me.*

137. By a sudden turn of thought she is led to seek excuses for her husband. — **alieni . . . factus**: *brought under another's will and authority* (cf. the common phrase *sui iuris,* meaning independent of any other's authority). — **arbitri**: gen. of *arbitrium.*

139. a: the interjection *ah.*

142. nostri . . . meo: this confusion of number in the first personal pronoun is frequent, especially in colloquial Latin. — **muneri . . . meo**: *my gift, i.e.* his life.

143. impotens: *headstrong, insolent,* as if *impotens sui.*

144. genetricem . . . natis: according to Euripides (Med. 275) Medea is commanded to take her children with her into exile. Seneca (cf. 284, 541–546) represents her as desiring to do so, but forbidden by Jason. — **natis**: dat.

146. petatur: sc. *Creon*.

149. Malea: a promontory at the southeastern extremity of the Peloponnesus, a hundred miles from Corinth. — **flectens moras:** cf. *opponens moras*, 35.

153. referre: *repay, take vengeance.* — **nocet:** *does harm* to its object.

156. clepere: a rare verb meaning *steal*, here *withdraw* or *hide*. This is its only certain occurrence in the tragedies, though one MS. has *clepit* instead of *tegit* in H.F. 799.

157. ire contra: sc. *hostes* (cf. *non ibo in hostes*, 27).

159. Fortuna fortes metuit: a proverbial expression, quoted with unessential variations by Terence (Phormio 203, *fortes fortuna adiuvat*), Vergil (A. 10. 284: *audentes fortuna iuvat*), Ovid (M. 10. 586: *audentes deus ipse iuvat*) and Pliny (Epist. 6. 16: *fortes fortuna iuvat*).

160. est probanda: the subject is *virtus, courage.* — **locum**: *opportunity.*

166. hic: *here, in me.*

169. sint . . . edita: *no, though they spring from the earth* — in allusion to the *terrigenae* (469, 470), whom Jason had vanquished by her aid.

171. fiam: in the nurse's unfinished speech *Medea* doubtless is vocative, but her mistress interrupts and makes it predicate with *fiam — I shall become Medea* (cf. *Medea nunc sum*, 910). — **cui sim vides:** *you see whose mother I am, i.e.* no one's, since my sons have been taken from me.

173. Forsan . . . moras: alluding to the manner in which she had delayed her father's pursuit (see 130 n.).

175. animos: *spirit, pride.* — **aptari:** middle voice, *adapt one's self.*

177. cardo strepit: the door of a Greek house hung not on hinges but on upright pivots (*cardines*), usually of wood, whose turning in their stone sockets was far from noiseless. In Plautus and Terence the entrance of an actor often is heralded by some reference to the creaking of the pivot.

SCENE 2 (vv. 179–300). — King Creon appears, declaring that Medea must leave his realm at once. She boldly accuses him of having wronged her and claims Jason's guilt at least equals her own. The king asserts that his own power is endangered by her presence, and repeats his order to depart. Finally, in response to her entreaties, he grants a respite of one day.

179. **Aeetae genus:** for *Aeeta nata*, as often.

183. **luem:** *offscouring*, a term of contempt applied here to Medea and in H.F. 358 to Lycus.

184. **gener:** Jason. For the truth of the statement, cf. 490.

185. **liberet . . . metu:** cf. 270, 872.

186. **contra:** *to meet* me.

189. **iubete sileat:** a post-Augustan usage for the classical *iubete eam silere*.

192. **fuga:** *exile.*

193. Either *innocens* is ironical here, or it is said as a general truth — (only) *an innocent woman asks. Quae . . . pellat*, of course, is indirect question.

194. *If you are sitting as judge, hear the case; if you are acting the despot, issue your orders.*

197. **Colchis:** dat. — *complain to your countrymen.* — **qui avexit:** Jason. This demand is repeated in substance at 246, 272, and to Jason himself, 489.

199. **parte . . . altera:** *without having heard the other side.*

200. *Though he may have given a fair decision, he has not been fair.*

201. **Pelia:** the Latin form of the Greek *Pelius*. For the meaning, cf. 133 n. As a retort to Medea's last speech Creon asks, *Had Pelius a hearing?*

203-206. *I learned in my royal home how hard it is to bend from wrath a mind once roused, and how kingly one who has laid his proud hand upon the scepter considers it to persist in a course once entered upon.*

207. Read *miseranda* with *clade* and the next six adjectives, *obruta . . . afflicta*, with the subject of *sim*.

209. **fulsi:** from *fulgere;* so in 218.

211. **placidis flexibus:** somewhat inconsistently she speaks of its current in 762 as *violenta vada.*

212. **a tergo videt:** *sees astern.* There is a strong current from the Black Sea (Pontus) to the Aegean, and one sailing with the current would naturally leave Colchis, at the head of the Pontus, *a tergo*.

213. **maria dulcescunt:** the Black Sea, naturally saline, receives a considerable amount of fresh water from the numerous rivers that flow into it.   Pliny (N.H. 4. 24) asserts that the Danube, on account of its powerful current, sweetens the waters of the sea for forty miles out.   See also Polybius, 4. 41.

215. **vidua:** *unwedded.* — **Thermodontiis:** the Amazons, according to the usual accounts, dwelt near the Thermodon River, in Asia Minor (cf. *regina gentis vidua Thermodontiae*, H.F. 245).

218. *Then I was sought; now I myself am forced to woo my husband.*

219. **rapida:** this adjective contains the same root as *eripuit* (220) and *erepto* (118), and here suggests the same idea of *snatching away* (cf. *rapax fortuna*, Horace, C. 1. 34. 14). — **levis:** *fickle,* as often (cf. *levis casus*, 221).

220. **eripuit, dedit:** sc. *me.*

222. **hoc:** explained by its appositives *prodesse, protegere:* so in 225 *solum hoc* anticipates its appositive *servasse*, 228.

226. **decus, florem, praesidia, prolem:** the Argonauts — fifty heroes, the very *flower* of Greece, some of whom she proceeds to enumerate.

228. **memet:** subject of *servasse.* — **Orpheus:** for his story see 625 n.

231. **sati Borea:** Calais and Zetes (cf. *Aquilone natos*, 634). — **quique:** *and Lynceus, who with far-flung gaze beholds objects removed* (*summota*) *across the sea.*

233. **ducem . . . ducum:** Jason, who was commander of the Argo.

235. **vobis:** *for you Greeks.* — **unum mihi:** *him alone for myself.*

237. **obici . . . reversa:** *only this one crime can be charged against me* (*by you*) — *that the Argo came back.* — **Argo reversa:** appositive to *crimen.*

238. The tenses in 238–241 suggest the rhetorical figure of vision — she is dwelling upon the scene as if it were now before her eyes and the consequences were still in the future. — **placeat:** *suppose it should please.*

240. **gener:** Jason, as in 184.

242. *Let what fortune will, o'erwhelm my cause.* A parallel expression occurs in Seneca's Brev. Vit. 7. 5: *Fors fortuna ut volet ordinet.*

244. *All the reward of all my crimes is now within your power.*

245. damnā: an imperative.

246. redde crimen: *condemn the accused if you will, but restore the object for which the crime was committed* (cf. 197, 272, 489). Jason is meant.

247. genua attigi: in token of submission and appeal (cf. *ad genua accido . . . dextrumque pedibus admoveo,* Tro. 691; *genua tangentes,* Brev. Vit. 8. 2).

248. peti: *petii, petivi* (cf. *redit,* 984). Such contraction is frequent.

250. urbe . . . placet: sc. *me tibi—if it please you that I be driven out.*

252–255. *By choosing an exile as my son-in-law I seem to have shown clearly enough that I am not one to . . . spurn the unfortunate.*
— miserias: an abstract noun used concretely (cf. *senectus,* H.F. 1027; Tro. 42).

256. quippe: this word, in connection with a relative as here, or alone as in 438, regularly introduces a clause of cause or reason.

257. Acastus: son and successor of Pelias as king of Iolcos (133 n.). Jason's fear of him is expressed in 521, 526.

258. trementem: shaking with palsy— *Acastus complains that his father, palsied by feeble old age and heavy with years, was slain and his members cut asunder* (133 n., 475, 664–667).

261. piae: *affectionate* (see note on *pietas,* 438). Note the antithesis between *piae* and *impium,* and cf. Ovid (M. 7. 339) on the same scene: *His, ut quaeque pia est, hortatibus impia prima est — In these exhortations each is foremost — unnatural daughter! — in proportion as she is fond of her father.*

265. vestro: the plural idea in this possessive serves to identify Medea with the powers of evil she had invoked.

267. *You . . . who have a woman's recklessness, . . . a man's strength, and no regard for reputation, go!*

270. liberā: imperative. For the thought cf. 185, 872. — herbas: those employed in her magic rites (see 706 ff.).

271. sollicitā: imperative. For the thought cf. *invadam deos,* 424; *vidi aggressam deos,* 673.

276. *For him, not for me, was Pelias slain.* Medea argues that Jason, who had profited by her acts, was at least as guilty as herself, who had done them. She puts it still more strongly to Jason himself in 500 (cf. *sontes duos,* 275). The kindred idea that not the agent but the principal is responsible is implied in *parcite iusso,* 669, and distinctly stated in Tro. 870: *Ad auctorem redit sceleris coacti culpa* — *The guilt of a compulsory crime recoils upon its author.*

277. *To the murder of Pelias add my flight from home, my theft of the golden fleece,* etc.

279. *Whatever crime even now he is teaching his new wife,* as if any marriage of Jason's must involve the necessity for crime. The plural *coniuges* implies a reflection on his fickleness.

281. exisse: sc. *te.*

282. illud: explained by the appositive clause, *ne . . . trahat.*

284. ut genitor: *as a father.*

285. Per . . . status: *by this marriage, of happy omen,* etc. — **ego:** subject of *precor,* 288.

287. Fortuna dubia: both words are known to be nom. because their final syllables, in the arses of the second and fourth feet respectively, must be short. Final *a* in *varia,* in the arsis of the third foot, may be either quantity, here no doubt long, making it abl. in agreement with *vice.*

292. malis: masculine — *for wicked people.*

293. *Do you deny me a respite, even one which is too short for my tears (at parting with my children)?*

296. *'Tis more than enough, though you should strike off a portion.*

297. propero: of course hasty flight would be necessary after the deed she was planning. — **Capite . . Isthmo:** in a fragment of Ennius' tragedy, *Medea Exul* (Ribbeck, 226, 227), Creon says: *Si te secundo lumine hic offendero moriere* — *If I find you here at the coming dawn, you shall die.* — **lues:** a verb.

299. Isthmo: abl. of place whence. — **sacra thalami:** the marriage rites.

SCENE 3 (vv. 301–379). — The chorus sings of the daring of him who first sailed the seas, the bliss of the Golden Age, the perils of the Argo's voyage, and the final conquest of the ocean.   The meter is the anapestic dimeter.

308. *Having drawn too narrow a bound between the ways of life and death.* The old Latin note of Farnabius will bear translation here: "When Anacharsis had learned that the thickness of the ship's bottom was only four inches, he exclaimed, 'So far from death are they who sail the seas!'"

329–334. These lines seemed out of place in their MS. position, and modern editors usually, though not invariably, insert them after 308.

329. candida: *pure, unspotted.* — **patres:** *forefathers.* The Golden Age, of which some features are described in the following lines, was a favorite theme with the Latin poets of the Empire, who found pleasure in dwelling upon the simple life of primeval man by way of contrast and relief from the complex and corrupt society of their own day.

331. piger: *unambitious, content* (cf. H.F. 198).

333. parvo dives: the philosophy of contentment was much preached by the Latin poets, and by Seneca and Horace in particular. — **nisi . . . opes:** *knew no riches but those his native soil had yielded.*

309. sidera: the constellations, from whose positions the ancient sailor determined the points of the compass.

311. pluvias Hyadas: a constellation whose setting, when it came at the evening or morning twilight, in April or November, coincided with a rainy season.   Ovid (Fasti, 5. 166) says: *Navita quas Hyadas Graecus ab imbre vocat* — *The Greek sailor calls them Hyades, from rain,* the Greek verb rain being ὕειν (*hyein*).   The form *hyadas* is acc. plu. of the Greek third declension.

313. Oleniae . . . caprae: Amalthea, nurse of the infant Jupiter, described now as a beautiful woman (see Classical Dictionary, artt. Aega, Amalthea), now as a she-goat, in either case translated to the skies and made a constellation.

315. plaustra: the constellation Ursa Major (Greek *arctos*, 405), often called "wagon" by the ancients from its shape and still known in England as "Charles' wain." From its position near the pole it was an object of deep interest to the mariner. — **Attica.** one form of the myth makes Bootes identical with Icarius, an Athenian. This would justify the epithet *Attica*, transferred from Bootes to the wagon he seems to be driving. — **tardus:** because the constellation, close to the pole, appears almost motionless.

318. Tiphys: see v. 3, and for his fate 617 ff.

321. tendere: sc. *ausus est.* — **toto sinu:** with yards squared to catch the stern wind. Vv. 320–322 refer to the angle at which the yards and hence the sails are set to catch the breeze from astern or from either quarter, while 323–328 regard the extent to which the sail was unfurled by hoisting the yard to midmast or topmast. — **prolato . . . Notos:** *catch the breeze with yards trimmed,* tack, sail close to the wind.

322. pede: the *pedes* were "sheets" or ropes attached to the lower corners of the square sail and used in making them fast to the vessel's sides. In the position here indicated they were not fastened amidships, but the sheet on one side was carried aft and the other forward, holding the sail obliquely across the deck, so as *to catch the side wind.* — **captare:** infin. of purpose.

326. avidus nimium: *too eager* to reach his destination, and therefore reckless in carrying sail.

328. sipara: small topsails, thought by some to have been triangular and set with the apex below. They showed ruddy (*rubicunda*) in the sunlight.

335. bene: modifies *dissaepti*, not *traxit — the Thessalian vessel has drawn together lands well separated before* (cf. Horace, C. 1. 3. 22: *Deus abscidit | prudens oceano dissociabili | terras — God in his providence separated the lands by means of the estranging ocean*). *Foedera mundi* by association of ideas suggests the regions which under these *laws of the universe* had been separated from one another (cf. 606 n.).

336. Thessala pinus: the Argo, commanded by Jason, of Iolcos in Thessaly.

338. partem metus: nature had terrors enough for man before, but his conquest of the sea added new ones.

339. mare sepositum: (formerly) *an element apart.*

340. illa . . . improba: *that impious bark;* the Argo, of course.

342. duo montes: the Symplegades, floating islands of rock which dashed together and crushed whatever tried to pass between them. The Argo barely escaped, with the loss of her rudder (cf. 456; *scopulos vagantes,* 610; H.F. 1210 n.), and ever after the rocks remained fixed.

344. aetherio sonitu: *with thundering sound.*

345. mare: subject of *spargeret — when the sea, caught (between the moving rocks), splashed their tops and the very clouds* (cf. H.F. 1213, 1214).

347. *Let slip the tiller from his faltering hand.*

349. vocem perdidit: referring to the Argo's figurehead, hewn from the speaking oak of Dodona and itself possessed of the power of speech.

350. virgo: Scylla, once a beautiful maiden, transformed into a monster which dwelt in a cave on the shore of Sicily opposite the maelstrom Charybdis. Her story is told by Ovid (M. 14. 1–74). Vergil (A. 3. 426–428) thus describes her appearance: "First the face of a human being, a maiden, of beautiful form as far as the waist, but at last a sea monster of huge size, uniting the tails of dolphins with the bellies of wolves."

354. malo: *monster;* Scylla.

355. dirae pestes: the sirens.

357. resonans: *sounding back,* in rivalry with the sirens.

360. sirena: acc. sing. (Greek form). *Orpheus almost compelled the siren to follow him, though she was wont to hold ships captive with her song.* For the power of Orpheus see 626, 629, and Ovid, M. 10. 86 ff. — **huius cursus:** *this voyage.* The alliteration in 359–362 may be accidental, but it is by no means uncommon in these plays and doubtless is sometimes intended.

362. *Medea, an evil greater than the sea, a cargo worthy the first ship.* The sin of overstepping the bounds appointed by the Creator (335 n.) has brought its own punishment. The use of the word *merces* suggests that the myth of the Argo and the golden fleece may represent allegorically the beginning of foreign commerce for the Greeks.

364. Nunc iam: *now,* transferring the thought from the Argo's own time to that of the chorus.

365. Palladiã: *built by Pallas* (2 n.). Abl. in agreement with *manu* —*no far-famed Argo, wrought by the hand of Pallas and bearing the oars of princes, is required* — *any little boat now sails the deep.*

369. motus: sc. *est*, with *orbis* as subject.

372. pervius: *become traversable.* — **orbis:** like *orbi*, 5 n.

373. *The Hindu drinks of the cold Araxes, the Persian of the Elbe and Rhine.* The names are selected to show how the ends of the earth are brought together by commerce.

375–379. This passage would be still more remarkable if we could suppose that Seneca meant by it anything more than a vague reference to some ideal Atlantis, such as Plato had described. One fanciful critic long ago suggested that the Spaniard Seneca is here foretelling the discovery of America by his countrymen under Christopher Columbus! Still more interesting is a marginal note written by Ferdinand Columbus in his copy of the tragedies, opposite these lines: *Haec prophetia expleta ẽ per patrẽ meu͗ Cristoforũ Colõ almirantẽ, anno 1492* — *This prophecy was fulfilled by my father, the Admiral Christopher Columbus, in the year 1492.*

379. Thule: an island, not now positively identified, lying to the north and west of Britannia, and assumed to be the remotest fragment of land in the great ocean that rolled round the ancient world.

ACT III

SCENE 1 (vv. 380–430). — The nurse describes Medea's fierce passion as shown by her features and behavior. Medea expresses her contempt for Jason's cowardice, reiterates her purpose, and overrides the nurse's timid protest.

380. tectis: cf. *Isthmo*, 299 n.; *penatibus*, 450.

381. resiste: *pause.*

382. incerta: possibly to be taken with *Medea*, understood as subject of *recursat* (385), but better with *maenas* — *as the maenad guides her frenzied steps uncertainly when she raves on the coming of her god . . . so Medea runs this way and that with frantic motion.* — **entheos:** a Greek adjective meaning literally *God in*, and hence *inspired.* This form may be nom. sing. with the subject of *tulit*, but better acc. plu. with *gressus* (cf. *entheo gradu*, Tro. 674).

383. **recepto deo**: the poets appear to have thought of the in-spiration of the bacchantes, the pythoness, the sibyl, etc., as an actual indwelling of the god (cf. *pleno Bacchi pectore*, Horace, C. 2. 19. 6; *Quo me rapis, Bacche, tui plenum*, Horace, C. 3. 25. 1). — **maenas**: the *maenades* (*bacchantes, thyiades*) were the female devotees of Bacchus, noted for their wild orgies. In 806 Medea applies the term to herself, and in 849 it is given her by the chorus.

384. **Nysae**: a city in India, where according to one account Bacchus was reared. One of his Greek names (Dionysus) has been supposed to be a derivative of this.

385. One of the two fragments certainly preserved of Ovid's tragedy of *Medea*, which was highly praised by Quintilian and Tacitus, reads thus: *Feror húc illuc, vae, pléna deo* — *I am hurried this way and that, ah me, possessed by the god*. The speaker is a woman (*plena*). The meter is anapestic.

387. **facies**: though the plural of this noun when it denotes the human countenance is rare, the sense is much simpler if we take it as acc. of specification and supply *Medea* as the subject of *citat*, as we do with the verbs that follow. Tr. *her face aflame* (lit. *aflame as to her face*), *she fetches her breath from deep*, *i.e.* sighs, sobs.

389. **omnis . . . capit**: *every passion claims expression.*

391. **quo . . . haeret**: *she hesitates on which side to incline the weight of her wrath.* The figure is that of a balance whose opposing weights are so nearly equal that it is doubtful which will go down.

393. **facile**: adjective with *scelus*.

394. **vincet**: *outdo.* — **irae . . . veteris**: as displayed in the cases of Pelias and her brother Absyrtus.

397. **odio**: dat. — **misera**: voc., addressing herself. — **quem . . . modum**: *what limit you should set* — indirect question.

398. **imitare amorem**: *copy your love*, which knew no limits, but sacrificed all to itself. — **regias . . . faces**: the marriage of Jason and Creusa (cf. *regum thalamos*, 56).

399. *Shall this day pass idly, this day obtained by such solicitation and granted for such solicitation (ambitu)?* She means the day of respite she had obtained from Creon (288–295).

401. *As long as Earth at the center shall bear the heavens poised* (cf. Ovid, M. 1. 12: *Circumfuso pendebat in aëre tellus | ponderibus* *librata suis — Earth hung in the enveloping atmosphere, poised by her own weight).*

403. derit: *deerit* (cf. *derat*, 992). — **dies:** sc. *sequetur* (from *sequentur*).

404. siccas: *never setting* (lit. *dry*). In the latitude of Greece and Rome, as in our own, the Arctoe (Ursa Major and Ursa Minor) are always above the horizon — do not dip into the surrounding ocean as constellations farther from the pole were thought to do (cf. *vetitum mare*, 758).

407. quae: interrogative —*What ferocity of beasts, what Scylla, . . . what Aetna, shall burn with such threats as I ?*

410. Titana: a Greek acc. sing. (cf. *sirena*, 360). The reference is to Enceladus, who was confined under Mt. Aetna (Vergil, A. 3. 578–582; cf. H.F. 80 n.) after the attempt to capture the heavens and dethrone Jupiter. Ovid (M. 5. 348) follows Aeschylus in making it Typhoeus who was thus punished. The myths of the Titans and the Giants are greatly confused.

413. impetum irasque: *the sweep of my wrath*, a case of hendiadys.

415. timuit: sc. *Iason.* — **Thessalici ducis:** Acastus (257 n.), who was demanding that Medea be given up as guilty of the murder of his father.

417. cesserit . . . dederit: *suppose he has* (cf. *placeat*, 238).

418. certe: *at least.* — **coniugem:** Medea.

419. ferox: said in irony, and rendered very emphatic by its unusual position and its antithesis to *extimuit*.

420. certe: *surely a king's son-in-law might defer the time of my cruel exile.* For the meaning of *laxare* cf. Quintilian, 10. 5. 22: *laxare dicendi necessitatem — postpone the necessity of speaking.* There is a sneer implied in the use of *genero* here as in *regius gener*, 460.

422. non queror: note the sudden change of tone — *I do not complain that the time is (too) short; it will go far* (cf. Seneca, Brev.Vit. 15. 3: *Sapientis multum patet vita — A wise man's life goes far*).

424. nullus: sc. *dies.* — **invadam deos:** cf. 271, 673.

428. pereas: the " general " second person. With the thought cf. Tro. 1009–1041, especially 1016 n. — **trahere:** *to drag down* others (cf. Samson's death, Judges 16: 28–30).

SCENE 2 (vv. 431–578). — Jason enters, lamenting his hard fate, which has placed him in such a position that he must either desert Medea or lose his own life. Medea urges him to fly with her, recounts her services and sacrifices for him, declares him equally guilty with herself, and, when he confesses his fear of the king and leaves her, bursts forth into a torrent of passionate reproaches and at once begins preparation for the consummation of her revenge.

432. malam: with *sortem*, acc. in exclamation — *evil alike when it smites and when it spares.*

434. fidem praestare: *show fidelity*, i.c. *be faithful.*

437. misero: sc. *mihi;* apparent agent.

438. pietas: *reverent affection*, commonly that of a child for its parents, here of a father for his children. In 779 *piae* is said of Althaea's love for her brother; in Oct. 52 and 737 it stands for the nurse's love for her foster child; and in Oct. 844 for the prefect's devotion to his imperial master. See also vv. 545 and 943 of this play. — **quippe:** causal as in 256, but here without the relative. — **sequeretur:** lit. *follow*, hence *share.*

439. parentum: dependent on *necem.*

441. ipsam: sc. *Medeam;* so with *iratam*, 444.

443. *Would rather have regard for her children than for her marriage.*

445. viso memet: abl. abs. — *at sight of me.*

446. fert prae se: *displays, exhibits.* — **odia:** the plural of an abstract noun, where we should use the singular.

451. at quo: MSS. have *ad quos.* Sc. *me* as object of *remittis* — *You send me back, but whither ?* A fragment of Ennius' *Medea Exul* (Ribbeck, 231) reads: *Quo nunc me vortam ? quód iter incipiam ingredi ? | Domúm paternamne ánne ad Peliae fílias ? — Whither now can I turn ? What course shall I begin to pursue ? To my father's house or to Pelias' daughters ?*

453. quas peti terras iubes: cf. Euripides, Med. 502 ff. This question is quoted by Quintilian (I.O. 9. 2. 8) to illustrate one use of the rhetorical question, which he says is employed, *to cast odium on the person addressed, as Medea says in Seneca, Quas peti terras iubes ?*

454. fauces: object of *monstras.* She asks, *What lands* (453), *what seas* (454), and then in reverse order particularizes — *the narrows of the Pontic sea, the Symplegades, Iolcos, Tempe?*

457. *Shall I seek little Iolcos (where Pelias was slain), or Thessalian Tempe?* — **Tempe:** a Greek acc. plu., the name of a beautiful valley in Thessaly.

459. exuli: *you impose exile on one already an exile — and give no place to dwell.*

460. eatur: impersonal. — **gener:** as in 421.

461. nihil: cognate object — *I make no protest.*

462. paelicem: a favorite word in the speech of Seneca's heroines. Here and in 495 Medea applies it with pathetic irony to herself, but usually it is a term of reproach to a rival, as in 920.

464. saxo: *a prison of stone,* perhaps suggested to Seneca by the famous Tullianum. — **noctis aeternae:** gen. of quality, *of everlasting darkness.*

465. ingratum caput: voc. — *ungrateful man!*

469. hostis subiti: the *terrigenae,* warriors who sprang into life fully armed when Jason had sown the dragon's teeth (169 n.; Ovid, M. 7. 130).

470. miles: used collectively (cf. Vergil, A. 2. 20, *milite*).

471. For thought and form in the following passage cf. 130 n. — **spolia . . . arietis:** the golden fleece. It was Phrixus who was carried on the ram's back to Colchis, losing his sister Helle on the way — see these names in Classical Dictionary — **arietis:** a trisyllable, pronounced as if spelled *ar-ye-tis.*

473. monstrum: the sleepless dragon which guarded the fleece in Colchis. It was drugged by Medea (Ovid, M. 7. 149–156), who thus enabled her lover to secure the prize (see also 703). — **fratrem:** Absyrtus (see 130 n.).

474. *Crime done not once (but many times) in one act of crime* — not only was her brother slain, but his body was mutilated and cast unburied into the sea.

475. natas: sc. *Peliā* (or *Peliae*); see 133 n.

476. revicturi: from *revivo.*

479. monstra: the fire-breathing bulls, the *terrigenae* and the guardian serpent enumerated just above. — **manus:** *these hands of mine.*

481. coniugi: gen. of *coniugium*.

482. miserere: used absolutely, *have pity.* — **redde . . . vicem:** *reciprocate.*

483. Scythae: a name of rather vague application, here given by Medea to her own people, the Colchians (cf. 528).

485. quas: = *et eas — and, as the palace, filled with riches, could hardly contain this treasure, we decked the woods with gold.* The reference is to the golden fleece, which was hung upon a tree and there guarded by the dragon.

188. The first dipody may be treated as composed of anapest-anapest (*tibi pat | ria ces*), but better as proceleusmatic-iambus (*tibi patri | a ces*); cf. 670.

489. redde . . . sua: for the reference of *sua* cf. Vergil, A. 1. 461: *sunt hic sua praemia laudi.*   For the idea cf. Medea's demand from Creon in 197, 246, 272.

490. The truthfulness of this pitiful plea is confirmed by Creon's statement in 184.

492. poenam putabam: sc. *fugam — I thought exile a punishment.* Note the antithesis between *poenam* and *munus*, and the strong irony of the latter.   This is one of many places where Seneca has followed Ovid — cf. M 2. 99: *poenam pro munere poscis.*

494. Hoc . . . Creusae: *you urge this upon me and offer it (as a wedding gift) to Creusa.   Hoc* means Medea's departure, urged in 493.

496. obicit: *throw up to me* as a reproachful reminder.   *Caedem* and *dolos*, like *amores*, are objects of *obicit*.

500. tua . . . fecit: cf. 275–278.

501. arguant: subjunctive with concessive force — *though all should accuse.*

503. *You should hold him guiltless who for your sake is guilty.*

504. cuius acceptae pudet: *which one is ashamed of having received* (cf. 130 n. and the familiar *ab urbe condita* of Livy).

507. placare natis: *calm yourself for the children's sake* — middle voice. — **abdico:** *I reject, forswear, disown them.*

509. regina: sc. *fratres dabit.*

510. non: with the optative subjunctive we should expect *ne*, but *cf. non Teucros agat*, Vergil, A. 12. 78. — **miseris:** *for my unfortunate boys.*

512. Phoebi: see 28 n. — **Sisyphi:** the royal house of Corinth was descended from Sisyphus, whose ancestry ran back through Aeolus (105 n.), Hellen, Deucalion, Prometheus to Iapetus, one of the original Titans. Compared with the divine progeny of Phoebus, son of Jupiter, his offspring would be *foeda* (511).

514. supplicem: sc. *me.*

517. nos . . . sine: the reading here is corrupt and the sense obscure. Of *nos confligere* nothing can be made. The rest then will mean *let us (myself and the kings you fear) contend, and let Jason be the prize.*

521. Acastus . . . Creo: these are *the king on this side and on that* of 516.

522–524. *Medea does not require that you arm your hands against your father-in-law, nor that you stain yourself with a kinsman's blood.* — **caede cognata:** Jason and Acastus were cousins.

528. demersos dabo: *I will overwhelm them all.* The verb *do* often is used with a participle in the acc. in a causative sense.

529. ne cupias vide: sc. *sceptra.* To his statement that he feared the royal power she retorts, *See that you do not desire it,* i.e. *that your true motive be not ambition rather than fear.*

534. *Let not thy bolts be hurled with a hand that discriminates between us* (cf. 275: *cur sontes duos distinguis?*).

541. tantum: *only.*

545. pietas: see 438 n. — **ut possim:** *cogat* here has two objects, one *memet*, representing the person, and *ut possim*, the act required. Two accusatives, or acc. and infinitive, would be more usual.

547. perusti: *seared.* In 484 *perustis* had its more literal meaning, *sunburnt, swarthy.*

550. tenetur: *I have him!* The same expression, borrowed from the arena, occurs in Tro. 630. — **Sic . . . locus:** this idea of attacking him through his children has been hinted at repeatedly (26, 40), but has not perhaps even yet taken definite form in her mind. With *vulneri . . . locus* cf. 565, 1006.

551. abeuntem: in agreement here with the subject (*me*) of the infinitive. The most common construction after *licet* would have been *abeunti loqui.*

553. et: *even that,* i.e. *if I may not keep my children, even a last embrace will be grateful.*

555. melioris . . . nostri: *my better self.*

556. haec: sc. *verba.*

561. excidimus: sc. *memoria — have I been forgotten* (lit. *fallen from your recollection*)? The same expression occurs in H.O. 1332 (cf. *excidat Hector*, Tro. 714).

562. hoc age: *do this* to the exclusion of every other interest. She is addressing herself.

563. fructus . . . putare: *the fruit of sin is to deem no act a sin* (cf. *malorum fructum . . . nihil timere*, Tro. 422).

565. hac . . . timere: *attack on a side where none can dream of danger*, alluding again to the inhuman purpose now maturing in her mind (cf. *hac qua . . . doles*, 1006).

571. decus: appositive, like *munus* and *pignus*, to *palla — I have a robe, a gift from heaven, the glory of our house and kingdom*, etc. In 130 the golden fleece is referred to as *regni decus*. — pignus . . . generis: *as an earnest of his birth* (cf. the *pignora* demanded of the same god for the same purpose by Phaethon, Ovid, M. 2. 8).

573. quodque . . . comae: a third gift of *gold which the sparkle of jewels adorns, with which the hair is bound.*

575. nati. sc. *mei.* nubenti: *the bride*, who was said by the Romans to *veil* herself for her husband.

578. arae: in preparation for her invocation of the powers of darkness (740 ff.).

Scene 3 (vv. 579–669). — The chorus likens a woman's fury to the fiercest forces of nature, then recalls in detail the fate that has befallen many of the Argonauts, and prays that the gods may consider their punishment sufficient expiation and spare their leader, Jason. The meter is the lesser sapphic, with an adonic at the close of each stanza.

580. metuenda: not predicate, but attributive with *vis — no fearful force of hurtling spear is so great.*

585. iunctos . . . errat: *sweeps away the bridges (of boats) and wanders afield*, *i.e.* overflows its banks.

590. Haemus: a mountain range to the north of Thrace, believed by the ancients to be of amazing height (Pliny, N.H. 4. 18, says six miles, but may mean one must travel that distance to

reach the top). The disappearance of the white snow on its sum‑
mit in spring would produce for rustic onlookers at a distance much
the same effect as if the mountain itself were melting away.

591. ignis: the fire of passion (love) — *Love spurred on by wrath
is blind, cares not to be controlled,* etc.

595. parcite: used absolutely, *i.e.* without an object — *Show
mercy, O ye gods; we beseech your favor, that he may live in safety
who vanquished the sea.* Jason, of course, is meant.

597. vinci: the subject is *regna.* — **dominus profundi:** Neptune
(cf. *profundi . . . dominator maris,* 4).

598. regna secunda: the sea (for the meaning of *secunda* see
note on H.F. 53, and cf. *secunda maria sceptro regis,* H.F. 599;
secundum fluctibus regnum moves, Phaedra 904). Pluto's share,
the third (*tertia sors*), is mentioned in H.F. 609.

599. ausus . . . iuvenis: *the youth who dared to drive the ever‑
lasting chariot of the sun* was Phaethon, whose story is told at length
by Ovid (M. 2. 1–328).

600. metae: *course* (lit. *goal*). *Forgetful of his father's course
he caught himself the fire which he madly scattered in the sky.*

603. constitit . . . magno: *the beaten track has proved costly
to none. Constare* gives us the English word *cost,* and *magno* here
is abl. of price.

604. tutum: sc. *fuit.* — **populo priori:** *former generations.*

605. sacro . . . sancta: *sacrosancta,* divided by *tmesis;* the
sense is *inviolable, immutable.* — **violente:** voc., best translated by
an English adverb.

606. foedera mundi: *the laws of nature* (cf. 335, where the same
phrase occurs, in a different shade of meaning; see also *foedus
umbrarum,* H.F. 49 n.). For the sentiment cf. Ovid, M. 10. 353:
Neve . . . naturae pollue foedus — *Do not dishonor the law of nature.*
The particular law referred to was that by which the gods were
supposed to have confined man's sphere of conquest to the land
and forbidden him the sea (cf. 335 n.; Horace, C. 1. 3. 21 ff.).
In the following stanzas is detailed the punishment inflicted on the
various Argonauts for their part in this sin.

610. scopulos vagantes: the Symplegades (342 n.; 456).

612. funem: the cable with which the vessel was moored. —
barbara: anything not Greek was *barbarian* (Romans 1: 14: "I

am debtor both to the Greeks and to the barbarians "). *Barbara ora*, of course, here means Colchis.

613. externi . . . auri: the golden fleece.

614. exitu: abl. of means with *piavit* — *by a dreadful end.* — **temerata:** *outraged.*

617. in primis: this may be taken literally, among the first in time, or as the phrase *imprimis, especially.* Tiphys lost his life before the Argo reached Colchis, and was succeeded at the helm by Erginus (*indocto magistro*, 618), or, according to some accounts, by Ancaeus, a son of Neptune.

622. Aulis . . . retinet: this implies that the Greek fleet which was to sail against Troy had assembled at Aulis while Medea and Jason were still at Corinth. Tiphys was a Boeotian, and the Boeotian port of Aulis, here personified, is represented as detaining the ships from running into the same perils that had cost him his life. — **memor inde:** *mindful thenceforth.*

624. stare querentes: *lamenting that they must stand idle.*

625. Ille: Orpheus, who is said to have been the son of Apollo and the muse (*Camena*) Calliope. The instances given here of his power to charm inanimate objects with his lyre are familiar. Ovid (M. 10. 1–77) tells of his passionate love for Eurydice and his descent into Hades to rescue her from death. It is told further that the women of Thrace, incensed at the bard's devotion to his lost wife's memory and his consequent neglect of themselves, tore him in pieces (hence *sparsus . . . per agros*, 630). The head floated down the river Hebrus (631) and across the sea to the island Lesbos (Ovid, M. 11. 1–60), thus transporting the power of lyric song to that island, where Alcaeus and Sappho, the earliest of Greek lyric poets, afterward lived and sang.

628. *When the bird, leaving off its own song, stood near* to listen.

631. tristi: *saddened by the burden it bore.*

632. notam: because he had crossed it before, in his quest of Eurydice (cf. Ovid, M. 11. 61: *quae loca viderat ante*). — **Styga:** acc. sing.

634. Alcides: Hercules. — **Aquilone natos:** Calais and Zetes, the *Boreades*, called in 231 *sati Boreā.* They were among the numerous victims of Hercules' prowess.

635. Neptuno genitum: Periclymenus, who like Proteus had the power to change his form. His story is told by Ovid (M. 12. 556–572).

637. pacem: Hercules is pictured in these tragedies as the slayer of tyrants and defender of the feeble. He established peace by putting an end to oppression (cf. H.F. 882: *Pax est Herculea manu | Auroram inter et Hesperum — By Hercules' might there is peace from the sunrise to the evening star;* see also H.F. 250).

638. *After having opened up the kingdom of Pluto*, in his quest of the dog Cerberus. In H.F. 55 Juno complains that *Patefacta ab imis manibus retro via est — A way from the deepest abode of the dead has been opened.*

640–642. When the centaur Nessus attempted to carry off Hercules' wife, Dejanira, the hero shot him with one of his poisoned arrows. The dying centaur wiped away the blood as it flowed from his wound, mingled with the hydra poison (hence *gemini cruoris*, 641), with a garment which he then gave to Dejanira with the statement that it contained a powerful love charm, and if given to one she cared for would revive his waning affection. Some time later, when she thought her husband was forgetting her, she gave him the robe (*munere nuptae*, 642). When he had put it on the venom with which it was saturated ate into his flesh and caused such agony that to escape it he built a huge funeral pyre on Mt. Oeta and had himself burnt alive upon it (cf. 777). Ovid tells the story (M. 9. 141–272). Seneca's tragedy, *Hercules Oetaeus*, has this closing scene of Hercules' life for its theme.

644. saetiger: the Calydonian boar.

645. impius: *unnatural*, in slaying his kinsman. — **moreris**: from *morior*. — **dextra matris**: at Meleager's birth it had been foretold that his life would last only as long as a stick that then was burning on the hearth. It was removed from the fire and preserved, but when his mother learned that Meleager, grown to manhood, had killed her own brother, she threw the stick again into the fire and as it was consumed he slowly died (cf. 779; Ovid, M. 8. 445–525).

646. meruere . . . expiavit: a confusion of two thoughts: (1) all were guilty of the crime for which Hylas atoned with his death; and (2) all deserved the death by which he atoned for the crime.

In either case the idea is that in having ventured on the forbidden element all had deserved the fate that befell Hylas, *i.e.* drowning.

648. puer: Hylas, a handsome boy who was drawn by the nymphs into the spring to which he had gone for water, and drowned.

649. tutas: not the stormy ocean, but the quiet waters of a spring.

651. fonte timendo: abl. abs. of cause—*since it is the spring that is to be dreaded, go, plow the sea fearlessly (fortes).*

653. condidit: *killed* (lit. *laid away* in the tomb). The more common version of the story represents the seer Idmon as having lost his life in a boar hunt in Bithynia (Apollodorus, 1. 9). All accounts make him foretell his own fate.

657. Thetidis maritus: Peleus, father of Achilles, who after great vicissitudes died in wretchedness on the island of Cos, an exile.

661. It was Ajax, the son of Oileus, here called by his father's name, who perished *fulmine et ponto* on his way homeward from Troy (cf. Vergil, A. 1. 43 ff.). Our poet here intimates that the real reason for his destruction was his father's offense in joining the Argonautic expedition (*patrioque pendet*). To preserve the Sapphic measure a hemistich (half line) must be supplied. Leo suggests *occidet proles.* If instead we read *occidetque Aiax,* it will remove all difficulty about the name, for we shall have Aiax Oileus, as in Vergil, A. 1. 41.

659. Nauplius: there are three of this name in the old mythology. Seneca here identifies the Argonaut with another of the name, the father of Palamedes. Incensed at the treatment his son received from the Greek leaders (Vergil, A. 2. 82 ff.), in revenge he lured their returning fleet upon the rocks by means of a false beacon (*igne fallaci,* 658). He himself met a like fate later. In the story of the wreck, told by the courier Eurybates in Ag. 558–570, the expression *perfida face* is used.

662. coniugis . . . Pheraei: Admetus, king of Pherae, whose wife Alcestis voluntarily gave up her life to save his (*impendes animam marito*), and thus helped atone for the sin of her father, Pelias, who had caused the expedition of the Argo (664, 665). It is worthy of note that the tenses in 634–656 are perfect, implying that the heroes there named had already met their fate, while Peleus, Ajax, Nauplius and Alcestis are spoken of in the future as if still to meet their doom. The chorus then closes with a reference to Pelias' end and a prayer for Jason.

664. ipse . . . Pelias: see 133 n.

667. angustas . . . undas: not the mighty waves of ocean, but the bubblings of a caldron, a most unheroic fate (cf. 651 n.).

669. *Spare Jason . . . who merely obeyed his orders.* — **iusso:** Tro. 870: *Quid iussa cessas agere? ad auctorem redit sceleris coacti culpa* — *Why do you hesitate to do what is ordered? The guilt of a sin that is forced recoils upon its author.*

ACT IV

SCENE 1 (vv. 670–739). — The nurse describes Medea's gathering of deadly herbs and animal poisons from heaven and earth and hell, and her preparations for the magic rites that follow.

670. The first dipody may be read as tribrach-anapest (*pavét a | nimus hor*), but better as proceleusmatic-iambus (*pavet áni | mus hor*). It is questionable if Seneca ever admits the anapest in the second place of this measure (cf. 488).

671. immane . . . augescit: *'tis monstrous, how it swells* (cf. *immane quantum discrepat*, Horace, C. 1. 27. 6, and the frequent use of *mirum* in like connection).

673. furentem: sc. *Medeam;* so with *aggressam* and *trahentem*. — **aggressam deos:** cf. 271, 424.

674. caelum trahentem: invoking the gods with magic incantations (cf. *te quoque Luna traho*, Ovid, M. 7. 207).

676. penetrale funestum: *the unholy shrine*, the *arae* of 578 (cf. *triste sacrum*, 680).

677. totas . . . effundit: *is lavishing all her powers.* All the principal verbs in the sentence (*effundit, promit, explicat, vocat*) are present tense. The nurse is looking on and describing what she sees.

678. etiam ipsa: there were powers which even Medea had shrunk from invoking before, but now scruples and fears alike are forgotten.

680. laevā: touching the altar with the left hand instead of the right, which would have been used in lawful worship of the gods.

681–683. Libyae, Taurus: extremes of climate; Medea's power ranged over them all (cf. 373 n.).

685. squamifera . . . turba: *the serpent kind.*

687. exertat: for *exsertat.* — **quaerit . . . veniat:** *is searching for those at whom it may come dealing death.* — **quibus:** may be relative with antecedent omitted, or perhaps better interrogative. It is dat. after *mortifera.*

693. fraude vulgari: *such arts as the common herd can use.*

695. anguis: the constellation Draco. Cicero (N.D. 2. 106) quotes the Greek astronomical poet Aratus (translated) thus: *Has (arctos) inter, veluti rapido cum gurgite flumen, torvus Draco serpit — Between the great and little bears, like a river with rushing current, creeps the grim dragon.*

696. ferae: the Arctoe, Ursa Major and Ursa Minor. The former was known to the Greeks of Homer's time (Il. 18. 487; Od. 5. 275), while the latter, though long known to the Phoenicians, was not pointed out to the Greeks till the age of Thales, about 600 B.C.

698. solvat Ophiuchus: *let the serpent holder loose his tight grip,* and so release the serpent. Cicero (N.D. 2. 108) translates Ophiuchus into the Latin *Anguitenens, Quem claro perhibent Ophiuchum nomine Graii.| Hic pressu duplici palmarum continet Anguem — The serpent holder, whom the Greeks call by the splendid name Ophiuchus. He holds the Dragon with the twofold grip of his hands.*

699. virus: acc.; one of the few neuter *o*-stems in *-us*.

700. ausus: *which dared.* — **gemina . . . numina:** Apollo and Diana. It was the former who slew the python, and the oracle at Delphi, where the encounter occurred, was sacred to him alone, though here his twin sister is assigned a share in the exploit (cf. the inclusion of Juno in *tonantibus,* 59 n.).

702. serpens: *omnis serpens* may mean *every serpent that has fallen by Hercules' hand,* including the two that attacked him in his cradle (H.F. 214–222), the guardian of the garden of the Hesperides (H.F. 531), etc., but its position between *Hydra* and *reparans,* which certainly must be taken together, makes it more probable that the reference is to the many heads and lives of the

hydra itself, which in H.F. 241 is called *numerosum malum.* —
caede . . . sua: *re-creating itself by its own destruction;* whenever
one of its nine heads was lopped off, two sprang up in its place.

703. tu . . . serpens: the sleepless dragon (*insomne monstrum,*
473 n.) which guarded the golden fleece in Colchis.

706. frugis: to the venom of serpents she now adds the juices
of poisonous plants.

707. invius . . . Eryx: the famous mountain in western Sicily,
which in the first Punic war was the last stronghold of the Car-
thaginians in that island.

711. quis: abl. The antecedent is *mala* (706). — **divites:** an
epithet often applied to the inhabitants of Arabia Felix, which was
supposed to be exceedingly rich in its natural resources (cf. *the-
sauris Arabum,* Horace, C. 3. 24. 2). — **linunt:** *smear* with
poison.

713. Suebae: feminine, as if those who dealt in witchcraft and
poisons would naturally be women.

715. rigida: *stiff* with cold. — **decus nemorum:** the leaves.

720. pestes: *baneful herbs.* Athos, which was not really
Thessalian (*Haemonius*), but Macedonian; Pindus, on the western
boundary of Thessaly; and Pangaeus, near Philippi, all were
mountains well known to Seneca's readers. He next names four
rivers which roughly represent the points of the compass — Tigris
south, Danube north, Hydaspes east and Baetis west — to emphasize again the world-wide range Medea covered in her search
(cf. 373, 681 n.).

723. premens: the Tigris, noted for its swift current, is pictured
here as *checking its deep torrent* so as to water the plants that
grew in or near its bed (cf. *Hister . . . compressit undas,* 764).

725. gemmifer: the river Hydaspes, near the northwest border
of India, was supposed to be rich in diamonds; Claudian, a fourth-
century court poet, speaks of the *gemmae Hydaspeae* (III Cons.
Honorii, 4).

726. nomen . . . dedit: Seneca's native town, Corduba (modern
Cordova), was in the Provincia Baetica, which took its name from
the river Baetis.

727. Hesperia: a general term for *western, i.e.* in the direction
of Hesperus, the evening star. To the Greeks it commonly sug-

gested Italy (*e.g.* in Vergil, A. 1. 530); to the Romans it often meant Spanish, as here (cf. Horace, C. 1. 36. 4).

728–730. Some herbs must be gathered at dawn, others at midnight; some must be cut with a knife (*cruenta falce*, 722), others pinched off with the finger nail (*ungue*).

731 ff. Cf. the contents of the witches' caldron in Macbeth (4. 1. 4–38), "Fillet of a fenny snake," etc. — **serpentium:** the regular form of the gen. plu. In 705 it was written *serpentum* for metrical reasons.

734. vivae: the heart and other vital organs cut from a living screech owl. — **scelerum artifex:** Medea (see 121 n.).

735. discreta ponit: *separates, distinguishes.*

737. verba: incantations. — **illis:** abl. after the comparative.

739. mundus . . . tremit: *nature shudders.*

SCENE 2 (vv. 740–848). — Medea invokes the aid of the infernal gods, the shades of the wicked dead and Hecate, patron of magic arts, in a rhapsody of sustained intensity, and expresses her assurance and satisfaction that her prayer is answered. The meter is trochaic to 751, iambic trimeter to 770, alternately trimeter and dimeter to 786, anapestic to 842 and iambic trimeter to the end.

740–751. Medea begins her invocation with a passage in the long, swinging trochaic septenarius, which, making due allowance for the difference between quantitative and accentual meter, may be illustrated by referring to Tennyson's *Locksley Hall.*

742. ligatos: *bounded* (cf. *alligat*, Vergil, A. 6. 439) as well as *bound.*

743. supplicis: for *suppliciis*, abl. abs. with *remissis*. The lines that follow give details (cf. Theseus' account in H.F. 750 759, where the same stock examples are used). — **thalamos novos:** of Jason and Creusa; for the special meaning of *novos* in this connection see note on 894.

745. Pirenidas: acc. plu. of *Pirenis*, adjective from *Pirene*, the name of a famous fountain at Corinth. Tantalus is variously described by authorities as having been king of Lydia, of Phrygia, of Argos and of Corinth; evidently the last view is adopted here.

746. **sedeat:** *remain for,* i.e. *await.* — **socero:** dat. of in terest after *sedeat.* Creon is meant, his name suggested by mention of Tantalus, one of his predecessors on the Corinthian throne.

749. **vestras . . . manus:** the daughters of Danaus had slain their husbands, and the crime which Medea meditated was worthy of them.

750. **vocata . . . veni:** the participle agrees not with the neuter *sidus* but with *tu,* the subject of the imperative *veni,* with Hecate as antecedent; *induta* and *minax,* 751, have the same agreement. — **sidus:** appositive to *tu.*

751. **fronte non una:** cf. note on *triformis,* 7.

752. Having finished her solemn invocation, Medea recounts (in iambics) the wonders she has wrought by the aid of these powers. — **tibi:** *for thee,* Hecate. — **more gentis:** modifies *solvens — loosing my hair from its bonds in the manner of my people.*

753. **nudo . . . pede:** on a similar occasion Ovid (M. 7. 183) describes Medea as being *nuda pedem — bare of foot.*

755, 756. Two opposite movements of the sea are described: *I have driven the seas back to their deepest recesses, and (conversely) the ocean has sent its mighty waves farther inland, outdoing the tides.* With the examples of her power cited below cf. Ovid, M. 7. 199–209.

758. **et solem et astra:** at the same time. — **vetitum . . . tetigistis:** see 404 n.

759. **temporum . . . vices:** the seasons — *I have caused the flowers of spring to bloom in summer, grain to ripen in the winter, water to flow up hill.*

763. **Hister:** the Danube in its lower course. — **tot ora:** as the delta of the Nile had seven recognized branches, ancient writers seem to have taken it for granted that all great rivers had the same number. Thus Tacitus, writing of the Danube, says (Germ. 1. 1): *Danuvius . . . plures populos adit, donec in Ponticum mare sex meatibus erumpat; septimum os paludibus hauritur — The Danube . . . visits many nations, till it bursts forth into the Black Sea in six channels; the seventh mouth is swallowed up in the marshes.* Cf. Tro. 9, where the *seven mouths* of the Don (Tanais) are spoken of.

766. tacente vento: abl. abs. concessive — *though the wind is still.* — **nemoris . . . domus:** *the heart of the ancient wood.*

768. die reducto: that is, bright daylight enters the recesses of the dense forest. — **Phoebus:** the sun has stood still in mid heaven.

770. *It is time to attend thy sacred rites, O Phoebe.* Note the final *ē* in *Phoebe*, which distinguishes this feminine form from the masculine *Phoebe* in 874 (see note on 97). Phoebe here, as often, is identified with Hecate (7 n.). Other of her names used in this same passage are Trivia (787), Dictynna (795) and Perseis (814).

771–786. In alternating trimeters and dimeters she enumerates the horrid offerings she brings. — **tibi:** as in 752. — **cruentā:** abl.

772. novena . . . ligat: each bound with nine serpent coils. *Novena* agrees with *serpens*, while *quae* is acc. plu.

773. membra: the giants had feet like serpents. — **discors:** *rebellious.* — **Typhoeus:** one of the Giants who attacked the heavens in the attempt to dethrone Jupiter (see 410 n.).

775. vectoris: the centaur Nessus (640 n.), who served as ferryman on the river Evenus, and there tried to carry off Dejanira. one of his passengers.

777. Oetaeus . . . rogus: the pyre on Mt. Oeta, where Hercules ended his life (640 n.). This is the theme of the *Hercules Oetaeus* of Seneca.

779. impiae: cf. *impius*, 645. — **facem:** the firebrand on whose preservation Meleager's life depended (645 n.). With *ultricis Althaeae* cf. *matris iratae*, 646. It is natural for Medea, about to slay her own children, to think of Althaea, who had caused the death of her son.

782. Harpyia: a trisyllable, pronounced *Har-pyi-a.* — **dum fugit:** the harpies were driven by Calais and Zetes, sons of the north wind, from the house of the blind Phineus and pursued as far as the Strophades islands (Ovid, M. 7. 3; Vergil, A. 3. 211–213).

783. Stymphalidos: a Greek gen. sing., here modified by *passae* — *the wounded bird of the Stymphalian lake, which had felt* (lit. *suffered*) *the Lernaean arrow, i.e.* an arrow poisoned with the hydra's gall.

785. sonuistis: some phenomenon of sound or motion on the altar satisfies Medea that her invocation has been heard. — **tripodas:** acc. plu. of the Greek noun *tripus*. The words *I see my* *tripods have been shaken* involve an allusion to the oracle at Delphi, where the three-legged seat was an important part of the paraphernalia, and mean simply that the goddess (Hecate) has given some token of her presence and favor.

787-842. Here follows a rhapsody in anapests which fairly entitles Medea to the epithet *maenas* which is used by herself in 806 and is applied to her by the chorus in 849.

787. Triviae: Hecate, so called because her shrines were commonly placed where three roads met. In the following lines she is identified completely with the moon goddess: *I see the chariot of Trivia — not that which the clear, all-night moon with full round face is wont to drive, but that of the darkened luminary, with sorrowful countenance, when, assailed by the threats of Thessalian witches, she sweeps the sky with close-drawn rein.* She desires not the bright full moon, but one in eclipse. For some details see below.

790. Thessalicis minis: it seems that Thessaly was noted for the number and ability of its witches who like Medea had learned to control the forces of nature. Pliny (N.H. 30. 1) speaks of the "Thessalian matrons whose name this art long held in our part of the world." One feat much practiced, according to popular belief, was to darken the moon by magic. So we read in Seneca's Phaedra, 420, this prayer addressed to the moon: *Te . . . detrahere nunquam Thessali cantus queant — May Thessalian incantations never avail to draw thee down;* and again (Phaedra, 791): *Tractam Thessalicis carminibus rati — Thinking she had been drawn down by Thessalian charms. Thessalicis minis* then will mean the menaces, mingled with entreaties, with which the effort to *draw* the moon was made (cf. 674 n.). *Lurida* in 790 is nom. sing. and *maesta* abl., as is shown by the meter.

791. caelum . . . legit: for the meaning cf. *pontum legit* (V.A. 2. 207).

793. pallida: nom. sing. — **funde:** *shed.*

795, 796. An eclipse was the occasion of great terror, and efforts were made to counteract the magic which was supposed to cause it by beating on brazen vessels *in auxilium, for the assistance,* of the threatened luminary. Tacitus gives an instance from history (Ann. 1. 28. 3), when he says mutinous soldiers *aeris sono, tubarum cornuumque concentu strepere — made an uproar with the* *sound of brass and the concerted blare of fifes and trumpets,* in order to end an eclipse of the moon A.D. 14. Of course it is an anachronism for Medea to speak of *precious Corinthian bronze,* which was not known till B.C. 146, when Corinth was captured and burnt by the Romans.

797. caespite: an altar of turf.

799. A *torch caught from the midst of a funeral pyre* would be illomened and hence appropriate here (cf. H.F. 103: *Vastam rogo flagrante corripiat trabem* — Let her catch a great brand from the burning pyre; Ovid, M. 6. 430).

800. caput: acc. of specification with *mota,* or object of the same participle in a "middle" sense: *Having tossed my head, I offered thee with bended neck the words* of the magic ritual.

803. vitta: officiating as priestess Medea would wear a wreath, perhaps of cypress, which was associated with things funereal.

804. Stygia ramus ab unda: the *rapta sepulchro fax* of 799.

806. maenas: appositive to the subject of *feriam* (cf. 383 n.; 787 n.; 849). — **sacro:** with *cultro* — *accursed.*

807. manet: from *manare,* not *manere.* — **noster sanguis:** *my own blood.*

808. assuesce: a trisyllable, *as-sues-ce.* Tr. *accustom yourself, my hand, to draw the knife and be strong to shed blood that is dear to me.* The poet makes her gash her own arms (*bracchia*) that her hand may be the more ready to shed the same blood flowing in the veins of her children (*caros cruores*). In 810 (*sacrum laticem dedi*) she has accomplished this preliminary sacrifice. *Laticem* there, of course, means her own blood.

812. vocari: sc. *te.*

813. votis: *by my prayers.* — **ignosce:** sc. *mihi,* or take absolutely.

814. Persei: voc. of the patronymic *Perseis.* Hecate is so called as being daughter of Perses, a brother of Medea's father Aeetes, and granddaughter of Persa and Sol. Ovid (Rem. Am. 263) used the same word as an adjective, *Perseides herbae,* meaning plants used in magic. — **tuos arcus:** object of *vocandi.*

818. quas: equivalent to *ut eas, ut* introducing *urat* in a clause of purpose and *eas* object of *sumpserit* —*That when she has donned them the creeping flame may consume her very marrow.*

820. auro: the material of her gift to the bride (572–574). In 820–830 the effect of the poison she is concocting is described as if it were liquid fire, and this leads her to enumerate the mythical sources of 'fire — that stolen from heaven by Prometheus, the forge of Vulcan, the thunderbolt that killed her kinsman Phaethon, the breath of the Chimaera and of the fire-breathing bulls of Colchis, to all of which she adds " the gall of Medusa."

822. furta: the stealing of fire from heaven for man (cf. Horace, C. 1. 3. 27). — **viscere feto:** Prometheus' punishment was confinement on the barren rock of the Caucasus, where a vulture tore constantly at his liver, which grew as fast as it was consumed (cf. *fibris renatis*, Vergil, A. 6. 600).

823. condere: *store up*, here in the golden gift (cf. *condita*, 835).

825. Mulciber: Vulcan, god of fire. The name is derived from the verb *mulceo*, referring, of course, to the power of fire to soften (melt) metals.

827. cognato: Phaethon was son and Medea granddaughter of Phoebus (28 n.). His adventure with the sun's chariot ended with his being struck by lightning in order to prevent further disaster to the universe (Ovid, M. 2. 321).

831. tacitum: *latent*.

835 ff. visūs, tactūs: acc. — **artūs:** nom. plu. All the verbs are optative.

840. tenentur: *are heard* (lit. *received*). — **latratus:** Hecate was represented sometimes as having three heads (*triformis*, 7; *triceps*, Ovid, M. 7. 194), one of a horse, one of a lion, one of a dog; more often as merely attended by a pack of hounds, whose barking proclaimed her approach (*latravit Hecates turba*, Oed. 569; *visaeque canes ululare per umbram, adventante dea*, Vergil, A. 6. 257 – " Dogs seemed to howl through the darkness as the goddess drew near").

843 ff. The violence (*vis*) of her frenzy is gone, and only sullen determination remains. — **vocā:** to the nurse.

846. placate: *win to yourselves . . . your mistress — and stepmother.*

848. ultimo: to her hearers this would naturally mean the last before her own departure, but for herself it has another and deeper sense.

SCENE 3 (vv. 849–878). — The chorus describes the frenzy of Medea, expresses its dread of her power, and prays for the speedy coming of night. The meter is iambic dimeter catalectic, each stanza closing with a verse one syllable shorter.

849. cruenta: nom. The sense may be literally *blood-stained* (cf. 806–810, where she had gashed her own arms with the sacrificial knife), or it may refer to her past crimes.

850. amore saevo: her fierce passion for Jason (398 n.).

854. riget: *is set.*

856. Does not stand on the defensive, but dares attack.

857. Sc. *eam esse.*

858–865. The chorus observes Medea's intense emotion, evinced by change of color and uncertain gait (cf. 382–389).

866, 867. Cf. Medea's own expression, 397, 398.

874. Phoebe: note the short *e* final, and cf. Phoebe, 770 n. — **mitte . . . loro:** *drive the sun chariot swiftly.* Medea's reprieve was to end with the day (295, 297–299, 421, 1017), hence the prayer that night might come quickly.

876. alma: the epithet commonly applied to *dies, sol, lux* and words of kindred sense here is given to *nox* (cf. Tro. 438).

878. dux noctis: cf. *gemini praevia temporis,* 71.

ACT V

SCENE 1 (vv. 879–890). — A messenger narrates the destruction of Creon and his daughter by the unquenchable fire kindled by Medea's deadly gift, the chorus prompting him with questions.

884. quis cladis modus: *modus* may mean either manner or measure, probably the latter here (cf. *omnem, tota, urbi timetur*).

890. praesidia: the water. The fire is so fierce as to devour what ordinarily is a safeguard against it.

SCENE 2 (vv. 891–977). — The nurse urges her mistress to flee for her life, but Medea exults in the success of her plans thus far, recalls with satisfaction her past deeds, wavers in her purpose to destroy her sons but decides upon it, sees the apparition of her murdered brother, and finally ascends to the house top, there to finish her work.

891. **Pelopea:** Pelops was a son of Tantalus (745 n.), and be-came king of Pisa, in Elis. From his name the whole southern peninsula of Greece came to be called Pelops' Island, Peloponnesus. Here the adjective is applied to Corinth either as his father's home or in the general sense of Grecian (Vergil, A. 2. 193).

893. **Egone ut recedam:** *am I to retreat?* — an indignant ques-tion, implying that the proposed act is inconceivable (cf. 929).

894. **nuptias novas:** cf. *thalamos novos,* 743; *thalamis novis,* Tro. 900. It is a *new kind of marriage* in that it is to be a scene of mourning instead of rejoicing.

896. **quota:** *how small,* lit. *whath!* (cf. H.F. 383 n.).

897. *You love him still if you are content with simply depriving him of his new-made wife.* — **furiose:** masculine, with *anime;* so *violentus,* 904.

898. **caelebs:** both *caelebs* and *viduus* are used indifferently of persons widowed and those who never have been married.

899. **haut:** *haud.*

902. **incumbe:** *bend to, lend all your force and weight.* — **languen-tem:** *if you waver in your purpose.*

905. **pietas vocetur:** *i.e.* in comparison with what is contem-plated now. — **faxis:** *feceris,* perfect subjunctive used impera-tively — *Cause them to know how trivial and of what common stamp are the crimes I have done hitherto.*

907. **prolusit:** *took exercise* in preparation for greater deeds (cf. *proludens fatis,* Tro. 182).

910. **Medea nunc sum:** cf. 171 n. — **crevit:** from *cresco* — *my nature has developed through misfortune* (or *through evil deeds*).

912. **arcano . . . sacro:** the golden fleece, called in Thy. 226 *arcanus aries,* though referring there to another ram.

913. **senis:** Pelias (133 n.).

915. **non rudem:** *not inexperienced* (cf. *rudes,* 908; *non rude,* Tro. 67 n.).

916. **perfido hosti:** Jason, as in 920.

918. **nondum:** yet it is clear that the idea had occurred to her at least as far back as her interview with Jason (549), and hints of her growing purpose are given in 565, 848.

920. **paelice:** Creusa; for another use of the word see 462 n.

922. **Creusa peperit:** she first wishes that her rival had left children behind her, then exclaims that any children of Jason's, though her own as well, must now be thought of as Creusa's.

923. ultimum: *crowning.*

926 ff. With this wavering between right and wrong impulses cf. Ovid's account of Medea's reflections at first sight of Jason (M. 7. 9–99) and Dido's hesitation in yielding to her passion for Aeneas (Vergil, A. 4. 1–55).

928. The fury of the outraged wife gives place to the tender affection of a mother (cf. 443). — **tota:** probably nom.

931. incognitum: *unheard of.*

936. frater: sc. *meus.* Absyrtus had been innocent and yet was sacrificed, why not her sons as well?

938. variam: sc. *me;* so with *incertam,* 939.

950. osculis: the reading is doubtful and consequently the sense. We may translate *lamenting with their farewell kisses* as a makeshift. — **pereant:** *be lost to.*

953. antiqua Erinys: cf. 13–17 n. In 959–966 her frenzy leads her to imagine that she really sees the Furies and the ghost of her murdered brother.

954. turba Tantalidos: *the brood of Niobe, daughter of Tantalus,* who was the mother of seven sons and as many daughters (Ovid, M. 6. 182). **Tantalidos:** Greek gen. of *Tantalis.*

956. sterilis fui: my two are not enough. Another shade is given the thought in the next line, that in slaying her two sons she was sacrificing one each for the father and the brother she had wronged.

959. quo . . . parat: *against whom are they preparing their fiery blows?*

961. anguis: each of the Furies wielded a whip whose lashes were living serpents (cf. *viperea verbera,* H.F. 88). — **sonat:** *hisses.*

962. trabe: the torch with which the Fury tortured her victims (cf. *atram facem,* 15; *ramus,* 805).

964. incerta: *dimly seen* (cf. *incertam lunam,* Vergil, A. 6. 270).

965. omnes: best taken as acc. with *poenas,* supplied from preceding line as object of *dabimus — I'll grant it, but my atonement shall be complete, i.e.* it shall not be hasty, but shall include all that I can offer. — **fige faces:** *thrust firebrands into my eyes, tear, burn.*

The sudden apparition of her murdered brother throws her into a new paroxysm of fury and despair.

967. ultrices deas: the same phrase occurs in 13, where *ultrices*, there substantive, is followed by an objective genitive (cf. *ultrices Dirae*, Vergil, A. 4. 473).

970. victimā . . . istā: one of her sons, who is slain at this point.

972. petunt: the subject is general — they, the people.

974. tu: the living child; *tuum corpus*, 975, is addressed to the dead body of the other (cf. *hic, hic*, 1000, 1001).

976. hoc age: as in 562.

SCENE 3 (vv. 978–1027). — Jason enters, calling on all good subjects to assist in avenging the murder of their king. Medea from her house top taunts him with the loss of his bride and his helplessness to save his sons, and in his sight kills the second of them, then flies away in her winged chariot.

978. quicumque . . . doles: an exhortation more individual and personal than the plural would have been. Jason does not see Medea till 995, and is not recognized by her before 992. — **regum:** Creon and his daughter.

980. armiferi: voc. — **fortis cohors:** appositive to *armiferi*.

982–984. *I have recovered all I gave up for my lover, i.e.* this moment of vengeance is worth them all. In her interview with Jason she had reminded him of what she had lost for his sake, enumerating essentially the same details as are given here (477–489). — **germanum:** *brother*.

984. redit: contracted from *rediit*, as *peti* from *petii* in 248.

985. placida: *propitious.* — **tandem:** *at last*, after opposing me so long.

987. perage: sc. *vindictam*.

988. quid . . . potens: *having the power why do you hesitate ?*

989. A momentary feeling of regret, which gives way almost immediately (991) to a fierce joy as she sees her husband and thinks of his suffering.

991. invitam: *in spite of myself.*

992. derat: for *deerat* (cf. *derit*, 403 n.). — **hoc:** explained by its appositive *spectator iste*, Jason, whom she now sees approaching.

993. nil . . . reor: as he had not witnessed the death of the first child it counted for nothing in her vengeance (see next line and cf. 275–280, 500, 501).

994. perit: perfect, like *peti*, 248, and *redit*, 984 — *is lost, is wasted*.

995. ipsa: Medea; *lo, she herself is above us, on the house top.* — **parte praecipiti:** this means simply the street wall of Medea's house, from the top of which she looked down upon the gathering crowd.

997. suis: the fire was to be brought from the king's house, which had been destroyed by flames of Medea's devising.

998. funus: for *rogum*.

999. iusta . . . functis: *the services due the dead* (cf. *iusta Troiae*, Tro. 65). *Functis* is for *defunctis*. In sending her fiery gift to Creusa and by that means destroying the royal house and all it contained, Medea had provided for the cremation of Jason's bride and father-in-law (*a me sepulti*, 1000). She now tauntingly challenges him to do as he had threatened (996) — burn her house and so provide a funeral pyre for his sons.

1000, 1001. hic, hic: pointing to the dead and to the living boy (cf. 974 n.).

1003. fides: see 434–441 for the reasons he gave Medea for his desertion.

1006. hac: *here*, in the body of our son (cf. *vulneri . . . locus*, 550; and, for form of expression, *hac, qua*, 565).

1010. nullam: sc. *caedem.* — **ut perimam:** concessive, as shown by *tamen*.

1011. nimium angustus: *too small*, but cf. 957.

1015. moram: seeing it useless to plead with Medea for the child's life he begs for delay in the hope that " something may turn up " to save it. — **supplicis:** *suppliciis.* — **donā:** imperative.

1017. meus dies est: *i.e.* the day granted her by Creon (295); so *tempore accepto*. At this point she kills the second boy and so provokes Jason's despairing cry, *memet perime*, 1018.

1022. sic: in a chariot drawn by winged dragons (cf. 1023; Ovid, M. 7. 220).

1024. recipe . . . parens: *parent, take back your children now!*
With this parting taunt she throws the bodies down to Jason and
herself mounts the chariot and flies away.

1027. qua veheris: from its position this clause would most
naturally modify *esse* — *Bear witness that where'er you go there are
no gods.* Taking it with *testare* — *Where'er you go, bear witness that
there are no gods*, we have a stronger climax in the atheism into
which Jason is driven by the tragedy.

Printed in the United States of America

70
71
72
74
75
76
77
79
83
85